T0300628

Text Analytics for Corpus Linguistics and Digital Humanities

Language, Data Science and Digital Humanities

Series editors: Mikko Laitinen (University of Eastern Finland, Finland) and Jukka Tyrkkö (Linnaeus University, Sweden)

The growing availability of computer-readable language data, increasing computational power and rapidly evolving statistical methodologies have had a profound effect on how scholars study and analyse human language use. However, the fields of linguistics, computer science and digital humanities have largely developed their own separate approaches and paradigms, often failing to communicate across disciplines in an effective way.

Language, Data Science and Digital Humanities bridges these disciplinary gaps by publishing monographs and edited volumes that explore disciplinary synergies and introduce new theoretical principles. Written in clear and transparent language, these books offer cutting-edge digital methodologies and create new opportunities for understanding how problems and research questions can be approached from different perspectives.

The methodological range of the series covers empirical linguistics, natural language processing, machine learning, data visualization, text mining, mark-up and annotation, statistical tools in analysing language data, and multimodal analysis. The volumes explain methodological solutions in detail using worked examples, and are supported by companion websites, allowing authors to share primary data, scripts, sophisticated data visualizations and other digital content.

Haidee Kotze, Professor of Translation Studies (KU Leuven, Belgium)

Krister Linden, Adjunct Professor of Language Technology (University of Helsinki, Finland)

Dong Nguyen, Visiting Research of Text Mining Methods (Alan Turing Institute, UK)

Kari-Jouko Räihä, Professor of Computer Science (Tampere University, Finland)

Ute Römer, Assistant Professor of Applied Linguistics and English as a Second Language (Georgia State University, USA)

David Shepard, Professor of Germanic Languages, Comparative Literature, and Digital Humanities (University of California Los Angeles, USA)

Benedikt Szmrecsanyi, Associate Professor of Linguistics (KU Leuven, Belgium)

Text Analytics for Corpus Linguistics and Digital Humanities

Simple R Scripts and Tools

Gerold Schneider

BLOOMSBURY ACADEMIC
LONDON • NEW YORK • OXFORD • NEW DELHI • SYDNEY

BLOOMSBURY ACADEMIC
Bloomsbury Publishing Plc
50 Bedford Square, London, WC1B 3DP, UK
1385 Broadway, New York, NY 10018, USA
29 Earlsfort Terrace, Dublin 2, Ireland

BLOOMSBURY, BLOOMSBURY ACADEMIC and the Diana logo are trademarks of
Bloomsbury Publishing Plc

First published in Great Britain 2024

Cover design: Elena Durey
Cover image © Corey Ford / Stocktrek Images / Getty Images

A catalogue record for this book is available from the British Library.
Library of Congress Cataloging-in-Publication Data

Names: Schneider, Gerold, author.
Title: Text analytics for corpus linguistics and digital humanities : simple R scripts
and tools / Gerold Schneider.
Description: London; New York: Bloomsbury Academic, 2024. | Series: Language,
data science and digital humanities | Includes bibliographical references and index. |
Summary: "Helping to understand and apply state-of-the-art text analytics methods to
detect and visualize phenomena in text data, this book shows readers how to conduct
experiments with their own corpora and research questions, underpin their theories,
quantify the differences and pinpoint characteristics. It also demonstrates how to use
the programming language R, as well as simple alternatives and additions to R, to
conduct experiments and employ visualisations by example, with extensible R-code,
recipes, links to corpora, and a wide range of methods. The methods introduced can
be used across texts of all disciplines, from history or literature to party manifestos
and patient reports"– Provided by publisher.
Identifiers: LCCN 2023048287 (print) | LCCN 2023048288 (ebook) | ISBN 9781350370821
(hardback) | ISBN 9781350370869 (paperback) | ISBN 9781350370845 (epub) |
ISBN 9781350370838 (ebook)
Subjects: LCSH: Text data mining. | R (Computer program language) | Corpora (Linguistics)–
Data processing. | Digital humanities–Research–Methodology.
Classification: LCC QA76.9.D343 S33 2024 (print) | LCC QA76.9.D343
(ebook) | DDC 005.13/3–dc23/eng/20231229
LC record available at https://lccn.loc.gov/2023048287
LC ebook record available at https://lccn.loc.gov/2023048288

ISBN: HB: 978-1-3503-7082-1
ePDF: 978-1-3503-7083-8
eBook: 978-1-3503-7084-5

Series: Language, Data Science and Digital Humanities

Typeset by Deanta Global Publishing Services, Chennai, India

To find out more about our authors and books visit www.bloomsbury.com and sign up for
our newsletters.

Online resources to accompany this book are available at https://www.bloomsburyonlin
eresources.com/language-data-science-and-digital-humanities. If you experience any
problems, please contact Bloomsbury at: onlineresources@bloomsbury.com

Contents

Figures

Tables

Acknowledgements

I would like to express my gratitude to all the people who have contributed to this book, directly or indirectly, with linguistic and computational discussions, proof reading, comments on early manuscripts and their generous support, fun, coffee and friendliness!

First and foremost, I want to thank my partner Patricia Ronan for her huge support in all of these mentioned points. Then, the following list is certainly too short, and I sincerely apologize to all the colleagues and friends I did not include. My heartfelt thanks go to (in alphabetical order of first name) Ahmet Uluslu, André Ourednik, David McClure, Fabian Winiger, Giovanni Spitale, Hans Martin Lehmann, Irma Taavitsainen, Janis Goldzycher, Johannes Graën, Jukka Tyrkkö, Lawrence Anthony, Leo Vrana, Marianne Hundt, Martin Schweinberger, Martin Volk, Maud Reveilhac, Max Lauber, Michi Amsler, Miriam Butt, Noah Bubenhofer, Roland Lerch, Sarah Buschfeld, Silvio Liesch, Simon Clematide, Simon Peng-Keller, Stefanie Evert, Thomas Schlag, Tilia Ellendorff, Wouter van Atteveldt.

I am also grateful to the research project *URPP Digital Religions(s)* at the University of Zurich, which has partly supported the writing of this book.[1]

1

Introduction

1.1 Why should you read this book?

There are many motivations for reading this book: in a world where companies like Google and Facebook are exploiting our data, you may want to understand some of their techniques. Or you may want to find quantitative evidence for your literary theory (Moretti 2013, Gavin 2022), detect recent changes in the English language (Schneider 2022a) or investigate the differences in style and content between two different political parties (Card et al. 2022).

The book aims to give students of digital subjects, such as digital humanities, digital linguistics, corpus linguistics, but also of linguistics, history, political science or literature, an inroad into applications, enabling them to conduct projects and basic research themselves. The book will present practical examples, bridging the gap between theoretical or philosophical discussions (which are very frequent in digital humanities) and complex computational linguistic methods, which are often out of reach for students or too complex at the beginning of your studies. Corpus linguistic and computational linguistic methods, ranging from simple counting (e.g. Chapter 2) to language models (Chapters 5–9), will enable you to detect trends in your data and offer some automated understanding of its content, up to the latest models, so-called large language models (LLM) like BERT and ChatGPT. You do not need to have programming skills, and the basics of R programming are taught while we explore text collections, but you are encouraged to read a complete introduction to R, as we have to gloss over many details.

This chapter introduces the various disciplines in which text analytics are used, culturomics, stylometry, content analysis (CA), corpus linguistics (CL) and digital humanities (DH). Our aim is not to define or differentiate them but to show that the methods we are going to introduce and showcase are used in all of these disciplines.

We briefly introduce the corpora used in the book. Most of them are available in the public domain, such as novels from the Gutenberg archive, the historical corpus CLMET, a sampler from the classical British National Corpus (BNC), which is called BNC Baby, or the corpora of American political speeches. We give links to the corpora or, where possible, offer them for download on a companion website.

Culturomics is a new branch of research which has been established by Michel et al. (2010). They used a large sample of books collected by Google. Other related areas have been around for longer: corpus linguistics, stylometry, content analysis and digital humanities. In this book, we use methods from these fields and combine them. What these methods have in common is that although they operate on the surface, they allow us to gain insights into semantic domains.

We often refer to the current age as the information age or, most recently and more pessimistically, the age of fake news. What is clear is that to stay informed and to fight fake news equally require high-quality data and large amounts of it. In many areas, there is also a deluge of data, some of it misleading. Textual data is hard to process, as it is unstructured, as database specialists would say. The march of data has not yet reached its peak, but it is already fundamentally affecting our lives and a reason why you might be reading this book: to learn what is possible, what is difficult and how you can use textual data to investigate culture, history and language. Some motivations for reading and writing this book include the following.

- In a world where companies like Google and Facebook are exploiting our data, it is very useful to understand some of their techniques.
- In a society where some people are afraid that digitalization may affect low-skilled jobs, many see it as a chance to bring automated analysis of texts within the reach of dedicated students.
- In a scientific setting where intuitions and very plausible hypotheses need to be proven, linguistics is increasingly turning into an empirical discipline and an important approach of it is known as corpus linguistics. Also in literature, empirical analyses with methods from digital humanities add further independent support to one's interpretations.
- In our mind, where we verbalize concepts and thoughts into texts, there are mechanisms and patterns which can be measured at the surface. The correlations between frequency and importance can be exploited by keyword metrics and automated ways to detect topics.

- In a history which has shaped our beliefs, our democracy and our language, textual artefacts from many periods are waiting to be analysed. They are often too numerous to be systematically read by individual researchers that we need the support of automated distant reading methods.
- In a language in which the way that one expresses oneself reveals one's identity, attitude, style, stance and background, subtle methods that allow us to study each of them are in demand.
- In a text where we move from one idea to another, connected by arguments and associations, we can learn more from the text than the purpose for which it was originally written. In fact, given enough texts, we can learn which concepts are related, which political views favour which topics and frames and so on.
- In an economy in which data science has been touted as the job of the future with lucrative career prospects, we all want our piece of the cake (see, e.g., https://www.techinasia.com/data-scientist-salaries-singapore-revealed).
- In recent AI technology, where algorithms are beginning to reach human performance in more and more tasks, including open domain question answering and chatbot technology like ChatGPT, we are wondering where this leads to, what our role is and what understanding actually means.
- And perhaps most importantly, we want to know if data analysis really works. Not at the level of complex mathematical formula, not whether approach A works 0.3 per cent better than approach B, but what the gist of the algorithms is and in which way they need to be tuned, where they are susceptible to incorrectly set parameters.

1.2 Key concepts and ideas developed in this book

Which prerequisites do you need to read this book? **Basics of programming in R** are recommended. Basic programming skills are a sine qua non as soon as one wants to go one step beyond what the custom-made tools offer. In this book, we teach the basics of R by example and show that learning the basic skills is not difficult. Why not simply run the code, try if you can play with the parameters and later experiment with a data set from your own project. And try to interpret the errors that you may get or google for them.

After having read this book, readers may feel encouraged to tackle a programming book. If you have absolutely no experience in R, we recommend to first read the introductory chapters of Schneider and Lauber (2019) and play through all the steps that are new to you. After reading parts of that open-access book with fifty videos and exercises, you are perfectly prepared. Or you read it as additional reading where needed – or any other introduction to R.

Readers may also wonder what the learning outcomes and the concepts and ideas of this book are. In other words: What can you learn? What will we have to leave out?

The most central concepts will be empirical methods, concordancing, statistics, significance tests, data-driven methods, document classification, machine learning, distributional semantics, data pre-processing, suitable tools, basics of programming in R, big data and data science. These concepts are at the centre for the following reasons:

Empirical methods: In order to prove one's hypotheses, empirical methods are essential. Corpus linguistics is a branch of linguistics that has revolutionized linguistics and helped it to become an empirical science.

Concordancing: Concordancers allow one to search for words, phrases and patterns, and show all the matches, one per line, so-called hits, and all the contexts. The hit is always shown in the middle of the line to obtain a quick overview (KeyWord In Context = KWIC). Viewing keywords in the context and analysing frequencies was the starting point of corpus linguistics, and it still is the staple diet of every digital humanities or corpus linguistics project. This method is also quite simple.

Statistics: Differences between registers, speaker groups, topics, authors and so on are often very subtle. Without the help of statistics, our minds are unable to draw conclusions. **Significance tests**, for instance, tell us whether a difference is likely due to chance fluctuations in the data or big enough to be trustworthy. If you are new to statistics, we recommend first reading the relevant chapters of Schneider and Lauber (2019), an open-access book.

Data-driven: It is easy to test if given words are used particularly frequently by a certain author, a certain period, in a given variety or genre: we can compare its relative frequencies. But finding complete lists and more abstract patterns is considerably more challenging. Data-driven methods exploit the data to this level and come with a number of advantages, but also with new challenges.

Document classification: A widely used, well-known approach from information retrieval. Classification is the staple diet of automated media content analysis (Grimmer and Stewart 2013) and a very versatile method. Statistical approaches using reach features and state-of-the-art algorithms such as logistic regression are often referred to as **machine learning**.

Distributional semantics: The Firthian hypothesis, which is known as 'thou shalt know a word by its company', works surprisingly well if we can avail of large corpora. It is used in principal component analysis, vector space models and topic models. For our purposes, topic modelling will be most important.

Data pre-processing: Converting one's data to the right format is the key to using powerful tools. Usually, a few regular expressions or using Excel to prepare the data is sufficient, but sometimes encoding issues lead to problems. Practical hints like setting the locale, using the R package *readr* and *zap gremlins* as a last resort are given.

Suitable tools: Using suitable tools allows us to stand on the shoulders of giants. The tool *LightSide*, for example, brings state-of-the-art machine learning within the reach of non-programmers.

Big data and data science: What constitutes big data is a relative notion, and data sizes tend to grow ever bigger. From a statistical viewpoint, bigger is always better. To use ever larger data sets has also been called the Google trick. In fact, we have often reached a saturation point with corpora of billions of words, and your desktop computer will not be able to run algorithms such as GPT-3, which can fully exploit enormous data sets. We will rather use text collections in the area of several millions of words and profit for the so-called 80/20 rule: with 20 per cent of the effort and data, you can reach 80 per cent of the performance of what is currently cutting-edge research. But you can run it yourself, on your desktop or a powerful laptop computer.

The science of using as much data as we can lay our hands on has been around in various formats and names. In the following, we give a brief, tentative and necessarily incomplete overview.

1.3 Culturomics

Simply counting frequencies of words is easy to implement, but how much does it tell us about a given discourse, cultural differences and historical developments? An approach that places frequency counts centre stage, based on very large amounts of data, is *culturomics*.[1] While it may be seen as a niche in the field of computational lexicology, in its radical focus on lexical frequency and its broad application may serve as a good starting point.

The term *culturomics* was coined by Michel et al. (2010). They analyse social trends purely based on frequency using an extremely large collection of texts collected by Google, which comprises 4 per cent of all books ever printed. This sample is also known as the Google N-gram viewer,[2] which can be queried online. Michel et al. (2010) argue that the approach can be used not only to fill gaps in dictionaries or give frequency estimates for lexicographers to decide which words should be listed in which dictionary but also to trace historical, technical and social trends. As an example for technology, they discuss how new inventions have spread increasingly fast over the last two centuries.

> The inventions from the earliest cohort (1800–1840) took over 66 years from invention to widespread impact (frequency >25% of peak). Since then, the cultural adoption of technology has become more rapid. The 1840–1880 invention cohort was widely adopted within 50 years; the 1880–1920 cohort within 27. (Michel et al. 2010: 179–80)

We can all conduct culturomics experiments ourselves, either by using Google N-gram viewer or by calculating relative frequencies from very large corpora, as we will do in Sections 2.2 and 2.3.

Culturomics is neither the first nor a widely spread strain of quantitative investigation of word frequencies in text and their changes over time, but with its focus on big data simply counting frequencies and trust them if we have enough data, the belief that every correlation is meaningful, it is quite radical. In practice, it has been applied to conservationism, for instance the interest in species on Twitter and their danger of extinction are correlated (Ladle et al. 2016), but its theoretical claims go far beyond that, supporting the claim of Hey et al. (2009) that a new research paradigm is coming: after experimental science (empiricism), theoretical science (modelling), computational science (simulation), the fourth paradigm of exploratory science is introduced. These suggestions have created both enthusiasm and criticism (Kitchin 2014), enthusiasm because of the promise of finding patterns fully automatically and criticism because of the naïve assumption that frequency explains everything. The promise is succinctly summarized in Prensky (2009) as follows:

> scientists no longer have to make educated guesses, construct hypotheses and models, and test them with data-based experiments and examples. Instead, they can mine the complete set of data for patterns that reveal effects, producing scientific conclusions without further experimentation. (Prensky 2009: n.p.)

1.4 Stylometry

Stylometry deals with the quantitative analysis of style and typically focuses on authorship attribution. The pioneering research of Mosteller and Wallace (1964) looked at the distribution of the most frequent words in the Federalist papers to find out if they were written by James Madison, as historians suspected, or by two different likely candidates. The most frequent words are typically so-called 'function' words like *the, I, in, to* and *of*. They do not have any semantic content but control the functions that 'content words' (like *house, car, eat, sing*) have in the sentences. While writers consciously chose content words, and the topic of a text controls the content words, function words appear in almost any text, are largely chosen subconsciously and different people have subtly different preferences (see, e.g., Arun et al. 2009). In the authorship debate of the Federalist paper, the word *upon* played an important role. Often the combined distribution of many different function words is used (Burrows 2002).

Stylometry, like culturomics, started off as a small, well-defined subfield. It was one of the earliest approaches to the quantitative, automated analysis of text and therefore was a founding discipline of digital humanities. Its methods are now applied to related questions, for example what fingerprint different genres have and whether different styles lead to measurable differences in the use of single words, a path that we will explore in Section 3.3.

Unlike in culturomics, only the writings of selected authors or genres are compared to each other. While culturomics and the following content analysis focus on content words, stylometry often discards them. The study of stylistics has always been an important area of literature studies, so stylometry can be seen as one of the predecessors of, and base for, digital humanities.

After introducing the well-defined niches of culturomics and stylometry, let us now turn to the vast field of the big terms: 'digital humanities', 'content analysis' and 'corpus linguistics'.

1.5 Digital humanities

The quantitative revolution which has transformed linguistics is increasingly also reaching other fields in the humanities. In history, for example, particularly important events, questions, crises and wars left traces in the records and books of their period by being mentioned particularly often and by being discussed in particular ways. We can calculate automatically what was particularly salient at a given period and which associations writers had. Of course these calculations cannot tell us all the details that the text contains, but they can give us an overview and a bird's eye perspective, as we discuss in the context of the term *distant reading* in a moment.

Literature is a field of research in which it is central what the individual interpretation and which effect the text has on the reader. The personal impression cannot be automatically calculated, but an automatic analysis of stylistics can help scholars to support or question their interpretations or help them to find particularly important passages.

Moretti (2013) has revolutionized literature with its concept of *distant reading*. Particularly for literary studies, breaking up the unity of the text by means of statistical methods may be seen as a sacrilege, Moretti calls distant reading a pact with the devil. But the observation that whatever is important in a text appears repeatedly in it. Statistical observation may thus give us a broad, albeit reductionistic, overview, which equally applies to the literary genre. His conclusion of 'less is more' because 'distance is a condition of knowledge' reads like an introduction to statistics, which has the aim to allow us to focus on abstractions and central trends instead of getting bogged down in detail, and instead smoothing the creases which leads to data loss, is then also a virtue rather than just a vice.

> At bottom, it's a theological exercise – very solemn treatment of very few texts taken very seriously – whereas what we really need is a little pact with the devil: we know how to read texts, now let's learn how not to read them. Distant reading: where distance, let me repeat it, is a condition of knowledge: it allows you to focus on units that are much smaller or much larger than in the text: devices, themes, tropes – or genres and systems. And if, between the very small and the very large, the text itself disappears, well, it is one of those cases where one can justifiably say, Less is more. If we want to understand the system in its entirety, we must accept losing something. We always pay a price for theoretical knowledge: reality is infinitely rich; concepts are abstract, are poor. But it's precisely this 'poverty' that makes it possible to handle them, and therefore to know. This is why less is actually more. (Moretti 2000: n.p.)

While there may be a component of tongue-in-cheek, Moretti's pact with the devil, the assistance of a quantitative part to support one's literary interpretations and get an overview of key concepts, has left a lasting impression in the study of literature since. The demand for quantitative support for interpretations and also the increasing awareness that there is a strong correlation between psychological associations and textual co-occurrence (e.g. Schulte im Walde and Melinger 2008) are propelling the digital revolution also in literature. By contrast, the domain of automated media content analysis has used distant reading approaches for as long as the computing power has been available, as we discuss in the next section.

The field of DH also contains many aspects beyond content analysis and stylistics, aspects which we will not cover in this book. These are, for instance, optical character recognition (OCR), automated analysis of paintings, object recognition in pictures, geo-tagging of locations mentioned in texts, tracing the development of different editions of manuscripts, copied, hand-written and extended by different writers, the influence of digitalization on society and the humanities, and encouraging researchers to share their data in accordance with the FAIR principles (Wilkinson et al. 2016), if possible in open, inter-operable formats such as the text encoding initiative (TEI).[3] Attempts to define DH usually point out that its area is very large. For instance, Dubinsky and Nguyen (2012–23) define DH as follows:

> Digital Humanities is a diverse and still emerging field that encompasses the practice of humanities research in and through information technology, and the exploration of how the humanities may evolve through their engagement with technology, media, and computational methods.
>
> Dubinsky and Nguyen (2012–23: n.p.)

1.6 Content analysis

Content analysis is the quantitative, systematic analysis of textual or spoken utterances and has a long tradition in political science, where it was used long before computers were able to process large amounts of text and here without any tongue-in-cheek element as in digital humanities – but of course it has been used with criticisms and caveats. Webster's *Dictionary of the English Language* (1961) defines *content analysis* as 'analysis of the manifest and latent content of a body of communicated material . . . through classification, tabulation, and evaluation of its key symbols and themes in order to ascertain its meaning and probably effects'.

With the advent of ever faster computers, the approach is now used at a large scale in political and communication science and other fields. Krippendorff (2004, 2019) is and has been an excellent and comprehensive introduction to content analysis across many editions (currently the fourth edition is out). The book cover of its second edition underlines the versatility of the approach as follows:

> Two decades ago [i.e. in the 1980s], content analysis was largely known in journalism and communication research, and, to a lesser extent, in the social and psychological sciences. Today, content analysis has become an efficient alternative to public opinion research – a method of tracking markets, political leanings, and emerging ideas, a way to settle legal disputes, and an approach to explore individual human minds. (Krippendorff 2004: book cover)

While it is acknowledged that accuracy of automated content analysis usually lags behind the fine-grained taxonomies of manual annotation projects, its obvious advantage is speed and ability to treat unlimited amounts of text. From the perspective of political science, '[it] can make possible the previously impossible in political science: the systematic analysis of large-scale text collections without massive funding support' (Grimmer and Stewart 2013: 268). The dominant approach used is document classification, which we will introduce in Chapter 5.

Authors like Grimmer and Stewart (2013) also often use the term *text-as-data* for automated content analysis to stress the fact that text is not just unstructured data but highly structured data. First and foremost that word frequency strongly correlates and thus bridges to saliency and cognitive importance (Ghanem 1997: 12). Second, word sequences and contexts allow us to obtain fine-grained semantics, be it by means of collocations or distributional semantics (Chapter 8).

Unlike in culturomics, texts on a specific topic by a specific political party or author are used, and metadata is central. Texts are often compared to a large general reference text collection, though.

1.7 Corpus linguistics and computational linguistics (CL)

After a long period of dominance of rule-based approaches, linguists increasingly realized that linguistic change and also linguistic categories are partly gradient that there is a strong interaction between words and structures (e.g. Sinclair 1991, Goldberg 2003, Goldberg 2006, Bybee 2007) and that these interactions need to be considered by carefully constructed grammaticality judgement studies, by psycholinguistic research or by the quantitative analysis of large text collections, so-called corpora. Analysing corpora is, as it is done in content analysis, by far the simplest, fastest and cheapest approach. If we agree that there are strong correlations between frequency of a given phenomenon in corpora and the cognitive effort to process the information (e.g. Smith and Levy (2013) have proven this for word frequency), corpora can provide a good stopgap to psycholinguistic studies and allow one to study gradience in all its shades.

Corpus linguistics shares with stylometry the approach that the content of the documents in the corpora is typically ignored. The interest of the application is not prototypically the description of content or style but rather linguistic changes across time (we will see an example of this in Section 2.3) or between different dialects or regions (e.g. British, American, Australian or Indian English).

Having said that, the borders between the outlined disciplines are fuzzy: there are, for example, corpus linguistic studies that are interested in the cultural background or content analyses that largely use the culturomics approach of counting frequencies across time. Just as the approaches are related and partly overlap, it is useful to combine forces and mix and match methods.

One practical consequence of the fuzzy discipline boundaries is that in our introduction starting from small, well-defined areas like stylometry and culturomics and then stepping to the vast fields of, for example, corpus linguistics, the term *computational linguistics* has remained undefined. As the abbreviation CL can stand for both, the ambiguity is sometimes intended, as the fields are related. On the one hand, you could consider computational linguistics as the cover discipline for all our activities here, as we compute linguistic dimensions. At the other extreme view, computational linguistics uses cutting-edge research methods such as BERT models, GPT-3 and other LLMs, and places a central focus on quantitative evaluation and less on interpretation, society, history and explainability as we do here. This is why, after careful consideration, the slightly better-fitting term *corpus linguistics* is in the title of this book, while computational linguistics is also implied.

1.8 How are these subjects related?

Before we combine the forces of these subject areas and mix and match and blur, we would like to draw possible boundaries and differences. Observe that the boundaries between the related disciplines are most likely contested, and constantly in flux, and each researchers' home disciplines are typically foregrounded in their approaches. If you want to get a feel for this, ask a corpus linguist and a digital humanist which of the discipline is a subset of the other. Alternatively, ask a computational linguist like myself, who might tell you that both may be seen as subsets of computational linguistics, but that corpus linguistics is more interested in language change and digital humanities more in the social changes and challenges that digitalization brings. The aim of corpus linguistics studies is typically to find differences in language form, while the prototypical aim of a digital humanities study is to find differences in content. Areas involving both form and content, for example stylistics and stylometry (Section 1.4), are of interest to both areas of research.

Despite largely disparate areas of application, a considerable part of the methods are shared. In digital humanities, many of the methods that are used are well-known in corpus linguistics, for example concordancing, wordlists, collocations, overuse metrics, linear regression. Particularly the tradition of the data-driven approaches (Tognini-Bonelli 2001) has been using such approaches for a long time. Other popular approaches, for example document classification, topic modelling and text mining, have a long tradition in computational linguistic approaches.

Table 1.1 A Simple Overview of Methods and Research Topics Which Are Shared or More Prominent in Corpus Linguistics and Digital Humanities, Respectively

Corpus linguistics	Shared	Digital humanities
METHODS		
Significance testing	Concordancing	Topic modelling
Logistic regression to predict alternations	Wordlists	Kernel density estimates
	Collocations	Document classification
Zipf's law	Vocabulary richness	Keyword detection,
Idiom and syntax principle	Clustering	TFIDF
Lexical chains	OCR	Word clouds
N-gram models	Spelling normalization	Text mining
Surprisal	XML and data reuse	Sentiment detection
Readability, TTR	Feature engineering	Visualization
Information theory	Programming	Geo-tagging
Syntactic parsing	Machine learning	NER
Phylogeny	POS tagging	Network analysis
RESEARCH TOPICS		
Differences in form	Stylometry	Differences in content
Regional variation	Distributional Semantics	Distant reading
Register studies	Multimodality	History
Sociolinguistic variation	Discourse	Literature
Learner language, CALL	Argumentation	Political science
Language acquisition		Library studies
Parallel corpora		Digitalization and society
L2 English		
EFL, Language and identity		Open sources and standards
Cognitive linguistics		
Ambiguity and disambiguation		Human–computer interaction
Diachronic linguistics		

Table 1.1 gives a tentative, non-complete and possibly debatable overview of popular methods used in corpus linguistics (on the left) by both domains (in the middle column) and in digital humanities (on the right). The bottom of the table also compares typical topics of interest.[4]

The following chapters will not elaborate further on possible distinctions between digital humanities and corpus linguistics but focus on methods and case studies that are interesting for both fields of study. A major motivation for writing this book is the recognition that many of the methods are shared across the subjects.

Recommendations for further reading: A very short, minimal introduction is given in Baker (2010a), a book-length introduction is Lindquist (2009), and Baker (2010b). McEnery and Wilson 2001) is classic introduction to corpus linguistics. Krippendorff (2004, 2019) are standard introductions to comntent analysis. Moretti (2013) introduces the concept of distant reading. Schreibman, Siemens and Unsworth (2004) is a good introduction to digital humanities.

1.9 Our case studies and corpora

In the following chapters, we will first discuss the theoretical background, which will be very simple in Chapter 2 and then increasingly more difficult, in a moderately steep learning curve. You will probably need to consult further reading in the later chapter, as the methods get exponentially more difficult. The explanation will not focus on technical details but explain the gist, particularly in the advanced chapters. Our aim is to offer a book which travels the whole journey from concordancing to BERT models and pointing out many excellent methods in between and real applications and case studies.

The second component will be case studies to showcase successful applications and inspire your own ideas. We show applications from an intentionally broad, interdisciplinary range: literature, history, politics, psychology and medicine.

Third, you can do experiments yourself: with corpora that you can download, code that we offer and tools that you can install following our instructions.

Linguistic corpora are often smaller than those used for culturomics, and ideally they are carefully balanced to represent genres or regional varieties to an equal degree. Many of the smaller linguistic corpora could not serve as a base for content analysis, as they would just reflect the topics of the few selected texts. Some of the earliest corpora, for example the Brown Corpus of American English or the LOB Corpus of British English, contained just 500 documents. By contrast, many of the more recently compiled, very large corpora, though, even if they have been collected for linguistic purposes, can be used for culturomics, content analysis, detection of trends, political agendas and so on. Each case study in this book is based on a large text collection. We will centrally use the following corpora or text collections. Our list is roughly sorted diachronically.

1.9.1 EMEMT and LMEMT

The EMEMT (Early Modern English Medical Texts, Taavitsainen and Pahta 2010) and LMEMT (Late Modern English Medical Texts, Taavitsainen and Hiltunen 2019) are carefully compiled corpora from one specific domain, namely medical writing. They are two of the three parts of the CEEM corpus.[5]

1.9.2 EEBO

Early Books Online (EEBO) is not a balanced corpus but a collection of available books printed between 1470 and 1710. It covers about 135,000 books. Over 30,000 of them can be downloaded for free.[6]

As there is far more material in the later than in the early periods and also in order to create a corpus of manageable size, we have created a more balanced random selection, containing forty million words.

1.9.3 OBC

The Old Bailey Corpus (OBC, Huber et al. 2016) is a corpus of the protocols of the decisions and trials at the criminal court of justice in London. The proceedings of the Old Bailey (Huber 2007), London's central criminal court, were published from 1674 to 1834 and offer a large body of texts, about fifty-two million words, from the beginning of Late Modern English. A corpus of a large subset made available for linguistic research, it contains fourteen million words and documents spoken English from 1720 to 1913.[7] Originally recorded for purely legal purposes, it is now a unique mirror of society and the history of crimes and court procedures, used equally by historians and linguists. As OBC consists of transcriptions of spoken court interactions, it is also a unique resource for studying spoken language in the period of Modern English.

1.9.4 CLMET (Corpus of Late Modern English Texts)

The CLMET3.0 corpus (De Smet 2005) was compiled by Hendrik de Smet and Jukka Tyrkkö. It is distributed for free from the University of Leuven.[8] CLMET contains over thirty-four million words from six coarse genres. It is composed of three periods of seventy years each and covers material from 1710 to 1920. It is a clean and carefully POS-tagged corpus. It is distributed via the companion website especially for this book.

1.9.5 ARCHER

The ARCHER corpus (Biber et al. 1994) is a corpus compiled for linguistic purposes. It comprises 3.2 million words and texts from 1600 to 2000. It is balanced in several ways: it contains a similar number of texts from British and from American English, similar number of texts from each century and nine carefully selected genres.[9]

1.9.6 Literature: Brontë, Dickens, Woolf

For literary analysis, you can download several pieces of literature, particularly from the Victorian period: the Brontë sisters, Charles Dickens, Virginia Woolf. The used texts can be downloaded for free from the Oxford text archive[10] or from the Project Gutenberg.[11]

1.9.7 COHA

The corpus of historical American English (COHA) is the largest historical corpus of American English. It contains texts from 1800 to 2000 in four coarse genres (the genre news is available from 1860 on). The corpus can be queried for free,[12] and a downloadable version can be purchased.

1.9.8 BNC and BNC Baby

The British National Corpus (BNC) is one of the most widely used corpora. It contains ninety million words of written texts and ten million words of transcribed conversation, and has been carefully sampled and annotated. It is described in detail in Aston and Burnard (1998). For our hands-on experiments we will use the BNC Baby (BNC Consortium 2007), a four-million word sampler that can be downloaded directly for the Oxford Text Archive.

1.9.9 CORPS-II

CORPS-II is a collection of over 3,000 political speeches, mostly by American and also by British politicians, up to the year 2006. It has been compiled by Guerini et al. (2013). Its main aim is political studies and because it has been annotated for applause and laughter, it can also be used to study audience reactions. We use all US American politicians with at least ten speeches in the corpus. The relevant part for our studies has been made available for download on the companion website for this book.

1.9.10 NYT Corpus

The New York Times (NYT) Corpus contains all articles from *The New York Times* from 1987 to 2007. It is distributed by the Linguistic Data Consortium (LDC) and a perfect source for political and media science studies.[13]

1.9.11 Collected US presidential speeches

Some of our hands-on experiment use the corpus of American speeches compiled by Karl Fogel, available at https://code.librehq.com/kfogel/presidential -speeches.

We will use the sections of Barack Obama and Donald Trump. As these texts are in the public domain, the relevant part for our studies has been made available for download on the companion website for this book, as the file *TrumpVSObama2.csv*.

Spikes of Frequencies

Let us delve into our first method. Like all chapters, we first explain the method and then we provide several illustrative case studies. These are then followed by step-by-step descriptions of how the reader can carry out similar research themselves.

2.1 Theoretical background

In this chapter, we introduce the first, simple method of data analysis, namely frequency. We discuss how to measure relative frequencies and their increases or decreases over time, following the culturomics approach which has been introduced in Section 1.1. Discovering peaks and sudden local rises followed by falls (so-called spikes) allows us to confirm and quantify well-known diachronic linguistic changes and historical trends in several case studies.

2.2 Case studies from content analysis (CA)

In order to showcase content analysis approaches, we investigate two social trends in this section: the role that religion played in society and how wars are reflected in any type of writing.

2.2.1 Religion and society

Our first case study investigates the role of religion in medieval society, based on EEBO. As Figure 2.1 shows, the frequencies of attestation (per 10,000 words) of *God* are higher and rise until about 1550 and then decrease. The frequency of the

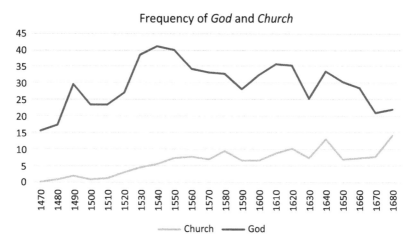

Figure 2.1 Frequencies of the words *God* and *church* in the EEBO corpus, relative per 10,000 words.

word *church* increases strongly during the entire period, marking a shift towards institution and administration.

2.2.2 War and society

Wars affect society like no other events, their adverse effects are sorely felt in each of the social strata and their impact is reflected in all types and genres of writing. A second case study shows the frequency of the word *war* and related concepts in the COHA corpus, summarized in the top half of Figure 2.2, an Excel screenshot that can be produced within seconds. We can observe peaks in the periods of the First World War (in the 1910s) and the Second World War (in the 1940s). In addition, and perhaps less well known to all readers, in this American corpus we can see a peak in the 1860s due to the American Civil War. There is no peak in the 1930s, indicating that the effects of the Second World War arrived later in the United States than in Europe.

Excel figures are very easy to produce, and many people already know how to create them. If you are new to Excel, there are thousands of tutorials, and you will need Excel skills almost irrespective of which job you work in. Do not hand in screenshots in your term papers. The top half of Figure 2.2 illustrates how easily they are produced: select the data range and then 'Recommended Charts' from the Insert tab.

Alternatively, simple plots can be created almost equally easily in R. The bottom half of Figure 2.2 shows the corresponding screenshot. After assigning

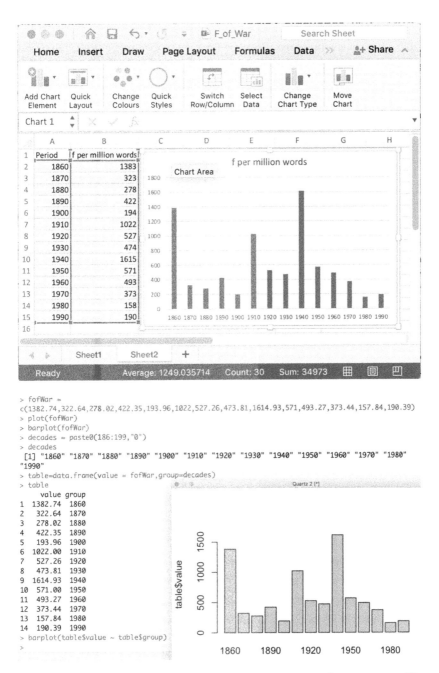

Figure 2.2 Frequency of the word *war* in the COHA corpus, relative to one million words, in *Excel* at the top and in *R* at the bottom.

the data to the variable *fofWar*, we can create a plot directly with *plot(fofWar)* or better a bar chart with *barplot(fofWar)*. This chart does not yet show the decades on the vertical axis. We create the labels with the command *paste0*, giving it the range from 186 to 199 and adding a '0'. Then we create a table (variable name *table*) which we can finally display with a syntactic variant of the *barplot* function.

There are many types of visualizations, ranging from the two 'quick and dirty' examples shown in Figure 2.2 to elaborate works of art. One obvious way to improve the R version of the bar chart is to add meaningful labels with the arguments *xlab* and *ylab*, for example.

barplot(table$value ~ table$group, ylab="Frequency",xlab="Decade"). Happy experimenting!

2.3 Case study from historical linguistics: Language change in the Old Bailey Corpus

Here, we present a third case study whose orientation is mainly of diachronic linguistic nature. It will be more technical and a bit more detailed, and offers an insight into current historical linguistic research. We use the Old Bailey Corpus (OBC, Huber et al. 2016, Section 1.9.3) to trace a number of developments that have been described in diachronic linguistics.

López-Couso et al. (2012) state that in Late Modern English (LME), which is the period represented by the OBC, the following changes have taken place:

1. rise of the progressive passive
2. the grammaticalization of the *get*-passive
3. increased use of progressives
4. decrease of *be* as perfect auxiliary
5. decrease of periphrastic *do* in affirmative sentences
6. tendency to replace finite complements by non-finite clauses
7. tendency to replace *to*-infinites by *-ing* forms
8. relativizers

As you will see in the following, we can confirm changes 1 to 4 and partly 6 to 7 using the OBC. We do not investigate changes 5 and 8. Additionally, we also describe changes in noun style and complexity. We will come back to this research topic in Section 4.3, where we investigate stylistic differences by social class. As the entire court protocols in the OBC contain valuable background information beyond the utterances of the witnesses, lawyers and judges, and as utterances are sparse in the early protocols, we are using not only the utterances but the entire protocols, including descriptive passages, and important meta-information, for example verdicts (*guilty, not guilty*) and punishment type (*fine, prison, transportation, whipping,* etc.).

2.3.1 The progressive passive

The progressive passive combines the continuous form with the passive form. Continuous forms, also known as progressive or as *-ing* forms, are, for example,

(1)   Peter is eating a fish.

In passive forms, the object of the active sentence is moving forward into the subject position. The former subject can facultatively be added to a phrase with the preposition *by*.

(2)   The fish is eaten by Peter.

In present-day English (PDE), the two forms can be combined, resulting in:

(3)   The fish is being eaten by Peter.

Passive verb forms are rarer than active verb forms, and continuous verb forms are rarer than simple verb forms, therefore the combination of the two, the progressive passive, is quite infrequent in present-day English, but a sentence like (3) seems perfectly acceptable to today's native speakers of English.

In order to search for passive forms, we rely on sequences of word classes, so-called part-of-speech (POS) tags. An overview of part-of-speech tags, which follows the PENN Treebank scheme, is given in Box 2.1.

Many tags, such as CC for co-ordinating conjunction, are intuitive, and we can recognize certain patterns – for example nouns all start with an NN, verbs with a VB, all prepositions seem to be IN. But the regularities also have limitations: while all tags starting with VB are verbs, not all verbs start with VB: modal verbs (*can, must,* etc.) have the tag MD. While most prepositions have the tag IN, the word *to*, irrespective of whether it is a preposition or an infinitive particle (e.g. 'She likes *to* run'), always has the tag TO. Not all words tagged as IN are prepositions: subordinating conjunction such as *if* and *that* also have the tag IN.

The tag JJ for adjective is not intuitive, and the various question words and pronouns (all starting with W) take some getting used to. As tagsets annotate real language in use, entities that are not necessarily thought of as words need to be included, for instance LS for list item markers such as bullet points, SYM for symbols, *'s* as the possessive ending and – alas! – interjections such as *alas* or *uh* which gave the tags its iconic form.

We can also see that the tags are a mixture between word classes and surface morphological features, leading to iconic tag endings. NNS mimics plural noun endings, and VBZ, VBD and VBN mimic verb endings.

While we all think that we know what word classes are and that we can distinguish verbs from nouns, some classes are more difficult: for instance, *give up a plan* in which *up* is a particle versus *walk up the road*, in which it is a preposition. There is also some gradience: in *the reader is interested* the word *interested* is typically seen as adjective (JJ), but it is close to a verb participle (VBN). For a thorough discussion on word classes and gradiences, Aarts (2019) gives a good introduction.

We will see later in the hands-on Section 2.4 that you can assign POS tags automatically using suitable tools.

Box 2.1 Part-of-speech tags of the Penn Treebank tagset

Part-of-speech (POS) tags

If you are a linguist, you probably know part-of-speech tags and word classes in the given context. Each word in the text is assigned to its word class, such as noun, verb or adjective. This word class information allows us to formulate grammatical patterns abstracting away from individual words to word classes.

#	Tag	Description	Example
1.	CC	Co-ordinating conjunction	*and*
2.	CD	Cardinal number	*12*
3.	DT	Determiner	*the*
4.	EX	Existential *there*	*there*
5.	FW	Foreign word	*cogito*
6.	IN	Preposition or subordinating conjunction	*of*
7.	JJ	Adjective	*great*
8.	JJR	Adjective, comparative	*better*
9.	JJS	Adjective, superlative	*simplest*
10.	LS	List item marker	*(1)*
11.	MD	Modal	*can*
12.	NN	Noun, singular or mass	*house*
13.	NNS	Noun, plural	*cars*

14.	NNP	Proper noun, singular	*Peter*
15.	NNPS	Proper noun, plural	*General_NNP Electrics_ NNPS*
16.	PDT	Predeterminer	*many*
17.	POS	Possessive ending	*Peter_NNP 's_POS house_NN*
18.	PRP	Personal pronoun	*you*
19.	PRP$	Possessive pronoun	*my*
20.	RB	Adverb	*frankly*
21.	RBR	Adverb, comparative	*worse*
22.	RBS	Adverb, superlative	*least*
23.	RP	Particle	*give_VB up_RP*
24.	SYM	Symbol	*&*
25.	TO	*to*	*to*
26.	UH	Interjection	*gee!*
27.	VB	Verb, base form	*go*
28.	VBD	Verb, past tense	*wrote*
29.	VBG	Verb, gerund or present participle	*written*
30.	VBN	Verb, past participle	*eating*
31.	VBP	Verb, non-third person singular present	*say*
32.	VBZ	Verb, third-person singular present	*eats*
33.	WDT	Wh-determiner	*which_WDT car_NN*
34.	WP	Wh-pronoun	*who*
35.	WP$	Possessive wh-pronoun	*mine*
36.	WRB	Wh-adverb	*why*

The development of the progressive passive is shown in Figure 2.3. We count all sequences of a verb in the progressive (tag VBG) followed by a participle (tag VBN). As we can see, the frequency of the progressive passive form increases, particularly after about 1860.

The progressive passive was stigmatized and generally stays rare. An early example, from the 1740s, is:

(4)   it_PRP is_VBZ being_VBG armed_VBN and_CC assembled_VBN
        to_TO such_PDT a_DT number_NN (1740X)

The progressive passive form here is, *is being armed and assembled*.

2.3.2 The *get*-passive

In present-day English, the *get*-passive is quite frequent, and the perceived difference is that the action and the process form the focus of attention, and the

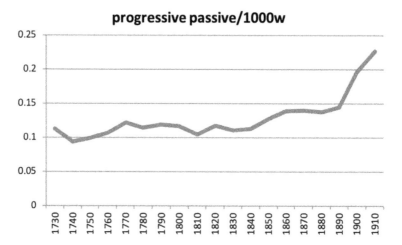

Figure 2.3 Frequency of the progressive passive in OBC, per 1,000 words.

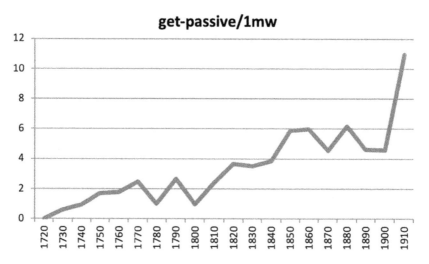

Figure 2.4 Development of the *get*-passive in OBC, per one million words.

get-passive may also be seen as less formal. The use of the *get*-passive was mainly viewed negatively by prescriptive grammarians (Anderwald 2017), nevertheless, its use increased (Hundt 2001, Anderwald 2017).

The development of the *get*-passive in OBC is given in Figure 2.4. We count all instances of *get* followed by a participle (tag VBN), per 1,000 words. We can see that the form is almost absent in 1720, then its frequency rises steadily and soars after 1900. The earliest instances are from the 1730s, for example:

(5) I_PRP wanted_VBD a_DT Guinea_NNP to_TO be_VB changed_VBN
    for_IN a_DT Stranger_NNP ,_, who_WP had_VBD drank_VBD a_DT
    Pint_NNP of_IN Beer_NNP at_IN our_PRP$ House_NNP ,_, gave_VBD
    the_DT Guinea_NNP to_TO this_DT Bed-ford_NNP to_TO get_VB
    changed_VBN for_IN me_PRP ,_, and_CC he_PRP ran_VBD away_RB
    with_IN it_PRP ._SENT (173X)

2.3.3 Increased use of progressive forms

The progressive form can be seen increasing in Figure 2.5, showing the relative
frequency of the -*ing* form (tag VBG) per 1,000 words. We can see that the
frequency indeed increases, but it was already a frequent form in 1730.

2.3.4 Decrease of *be* as perfect auxiliary

It is difficult to automatically assess the frequency of this feature as most
instances of BE + participle are passive or adjectival forms. We thus focus on
verbs that cannot be passivized, such as verbs of motion. The most frequent verb
of motion, *go*, is shown in Figure 2.6.

2.3.5 From finite complements to -*ing* clauses

The change from complementation by full clause to non-finite and finally -*ing*
form has been described as most typical for verbs of retrospection such as
remember, for example in Mair (2006).

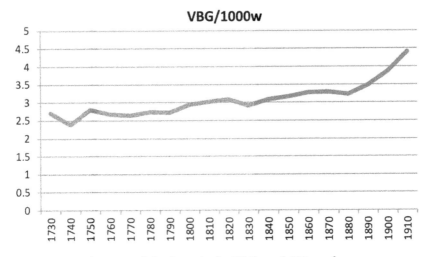

Figure 2.5 Development of -*ing* forms in the OBC, per 1,000 words.

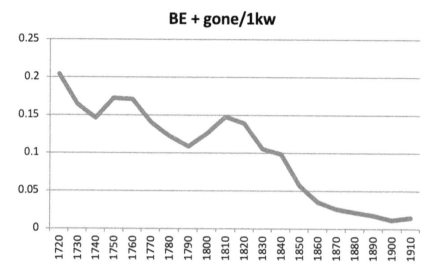

Figure 2.6 Development of BE + *gone* in the OBC, per 1,000 words.

Examples with full subordinate clauses are:

(6) I don't *remember that* I heard any more than one (OBC 1730X).

(7) I *remembered what* had hapned over Night, and asked the Porter if there was any Quarrel between the Gentlemen? (OBC 1730X)

Examples with non-finite subordinate clauses are:

(8) I *remember to* have seen her before in my house three times, but do not recollect the days (OBC 180X).

(9) I do not *remember to* have sold him any wood within the last twelve months – I have sold him some at different times (OBC 183X).

Examples with -ing forms are:

(10) I do not think there were any remaining at that time; this identical bag I can *remember being* started by the number; I only know that from my book (OBC 180X).

(11) Do you *remember going* with Hill to buy a gown? (OBC 180X)

The verb *remember* is interesting as it is frequent in court proceedings. Particularly in cases where the (potentially implicit) subject in the subordinate and the matrix clause are identical, that is, co-referenced (as in example (6) and (11)), so-called subject-control structures, a full clause is redundant.

The development from full clause via *to*-infinitive to -*ing*-form can be seen as a two-step process, an argument that has been made in Schneider

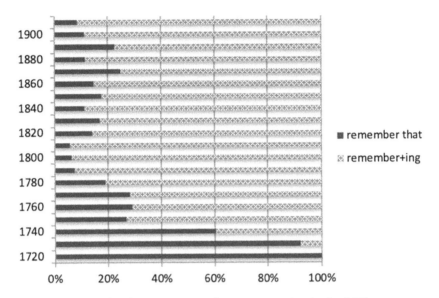

Figure 2.7 *Remember that* versus *remember -ing* across time in the OBC.

(2022). The intermediate form with *to* (Los 2005) is relatively rare in the OBC, however, probably because it prototypically has a more prospective rather than retrospective function. We report the full clause realization in comparison to the *-ing* form in Figure 2.7. Full clause realizations use a fully inflected subordinate clause, while *-ing* clauses only use a participle form in the subordinate clause.

Figure 2.7 shows a dramatic change. While the *-ing* form is absent in the 1720s, it becomes the dominant form from the 1750s on. The strong change observed with the verb *remember*, although it is also apparent in other corpora such as ARCHER or COHA, cannot be generally observed with other subordinating verbs. Schneider (2022) concludes that the process observed with *remember* is rather an isolated lexical change than a structural change.

2.3.6 Increase in nominal style and noun complexity

Noun complexity has increased over time in many corpora (e.g. Schneider 2022). A movement from a verbal style towards a more nominal style can be observed. The change to *-ing* forms can be seen as part of this movement, as *-ing* forms share nominal characteristics.

We can also observe a general small increase in the frequency of nouns and particularly in compound nouns (Leech et al. 2009). Figure 2.8 shows noun frequency, and Figure 2.9 shows compound nouns.

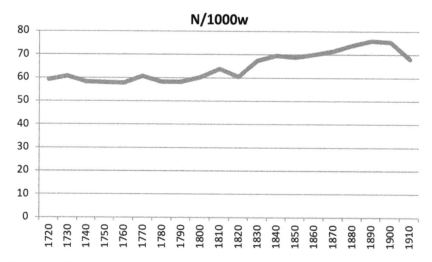

Figure 2.8 Noun frequency across time in the OBC, per 1,000 words.

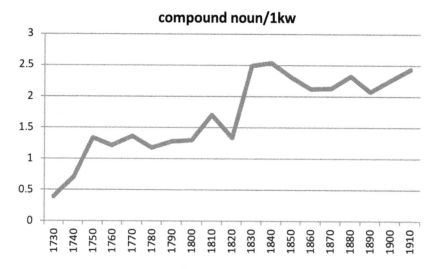

Figure 2.9 Frequency of compound nouns on the OBC, per 1,000 words.

2.4 Hands-on experiment from DH: Virginia Woolf's *To the Lighthouse*

Virginia Woolf's novel *To the Lighthouse* can be freely downloaded from the Oxford Text Archive.[1] To work with this data set, select the version in plain text, save it as raw text and remember where you have saved it.

We will compare the Virginia Woolf text to Charles Dickens' novel *Great Expectations*, which can also be downloaded from the Oxford Text Archive.[2]

2.4.1 Lexical search

The novel uses introspection and retrospection as the narrator's perspective and also as one of its main themes. The complex perceptions can be investigated by searching for events of reflection such as *had happened*. This application is based on Adolphs (2006: 73). We can search for this string in the downloaded text. While every text editor, and even MS Word, has a search function, the nice thing about using a concordancing program such as *AntConc* (Anthony 2004) is that one gets an overview of all the results, the hits of a query, very quickly.

The majority of the results of the query *had happened* in *To the Lighthouse*, displayed in Figure 2.10, are questions, attempts to recover the past. If we contrast this finding with the reference corpora, we find that the frequency of *had happened* in *To the Lighthouse* is very high. In other corpora, for example BNC Baby and Charles Dickens' *Great Expectations*, the context of *had happened* also typically expresses negative connotation, but the wondering, hesitating tone which is a striking feature and predominates in *To the Lighthouse* is absent.

Figure 2.10 Query for 'had happened' in *AntConc* V3.4 on *To the Lighthouse*.

Also, note the difference between *happen* and *happen to*. The latter, which is very frequent in *To the Lighthouse*, indicates an unexpected event, typically one which negatively affects a person, such as an accident.

2.4.2 Differences in the use of word classes

We have investigated diachronic changes in Section 2.2 using word classes based on part-of-speech (POS) tagging. A slight shift in the use of part-of-speech tags can also be observed in different literary styles. Let us compare the frequency of selected POS tags in *To the Lighthouse*, with its introverted focus, to a strongly extroverted style. A novel that concentrates on internal and external processes and developments could, for instance, be expected to contain more verbs and fewer nouns.

In order to do these experiments yourself, you will need to install a tool that assigns POS tags. You can download the user-friendly GUI tool *TagAnt*,[3] or you can install the tool *Tree-Tagger*,[4] which is started from the command line (also known as *shell*, see below). Both are available for many operating systems and many languages besides English. *TagAnt* is sufficient for small corpora like *To the Lighthouse*, while *Tree-Tagger* scales up to corpora of almost unlimited size.

The installation of *TagAnt* is straightforward. So is the installation of *Tree-Tagger* if you have some experience with using command-line tools. The installation on Mac systems is described in Box 2.2.

In the following description, we assume that you use *TagAnt* to tag *To the Lighthouse* and our comparison base, *Great Expectations*. When starting up *TagAnt*, a window opens in which you can either tag a text that you paste in to the top field or select an entire file to be tagged at the bottom. We illustrate the option of tagging the files (probably 3041.txt for Great Expectations and wooligh -1656.txt for To the Lighthouse). The files are automatically tagged and saved once you hit 'Start'. The output file contains '_tagged' in its name, otherwise the filename is taken over from one of the input file.

We can now inspect the tagged file, for instance, by opening it in a text editor or by using the terminal, which is often also called 'shell'. We will show how to use the terminal. The terminal is a text-based command-line tool, which is present in all Mac or UNIX computers, and Windows also has its own version called powershell. Powershell uses different commands from Mac or UNIX, but there is also a program called Cygwin which allows one to use the same commands.

What follows in the rest of this section is an example of how the shell can be used. Some people do everything in R, and I have seen colleagues who were surprised to discover only later how powerful the shell is, that for many pre-processing and analysis steps just a few lines of shell code can do a job for which considerably more R code is needed. Further, the shell is much faster and can deal with almost unlimited file sizes, also with files that are much larger than your computer's RAM memory, because it reads files line by line, and complex tasks are done by piping the outputs of one command to the next.

The following example is too short to be an introduction to the UNIX shell. You can execute it and continue with R, or you may well come back to it and use the UNIX shell with your own data later. As a more structured introduction I can recommend Rouberol (2020).

On Mac computers, open Terminal from the Applications/Utilities folder. A window pops up, showing a prompt (the $ sign) and a blinking cursor. You have an entire programming language at your disposal now, which is super fast and very close to the system, closer than your usual graphical user interface (GUI). There are many good introductions to the UNIX shell, for instance, https://swcarpentry.github.io/shell-novice/01-intro/index.html . Here, we will just focus on what is important for our own purposes.

First, we need to go to the directory where you have saved your files. The UNIX command 'cd' allows us to do so. If you have saved both novels in the Downloads folder, you will need to type

```
$ cd ~/Downloads
```

The dollar sign ('$') at beginning of the line is not part of the command but the prompt of the UNIX shell. Do not enter it. The reason why we typically leave it is to signal that this is shell command. In a brief moment we will also see the R prompt ('>') to signal that the line contains R code.

There are several ways to get to the correct directory. On Mac, you can also drag and drop the folder directly from the finder, after you have typed 'cd' and a space. If you are unsure where you are, the command 'pwd' (present working directory) shows you where you currently are. You can also look at the contents of your current directory with the command 'ls'. It should contain the files '3041.t xt', '3041_tagged.txt', 'wooligh-1656.txt', 'wooligh-1656_tagged.txt' and probably many others.

You can inspect a file, that is, look at it, by using the commands 'cat', 'more' and 'less'. 'cat' displays the entire, possibly very long, file, while 'more' and 'less' display one page after the other. Move to the next page with the SPACE bar, and press 'q' to stop.

```
$ more 3041_tagged.txt

Great_JJ Expectations_NNS
by_IN
Charles_NP Dickens_NP
1861_LS
Chapter_NP One_NP ._SENT
My_PP$ father_NN 's_POS family_NN name_NN being_VBG Pirrip_NN
,_, and_CC my_PP$ Christian_JJ name_NN Philip_NP ,_, my_PP$
infant_JJ tongue_NN could_MD make_VV of_IN both_DT names_NNS
nothing_NN longer_RBR or_CC more_RBR explicit_JJ than_IN Pip_NP
._SENT So_RB ,_, I_PP called_VVD myself_PP Pip_NP ,_, and_CC
came_VVD to_TO be_VB called_VVN Pip_NP ._SENT
```

What differences do we expect to find between an introspective novel and Dickens' style? Dickens describes scenes, machines and social settings in meticulous detail in a style that has been called literary realism (Kailash 2012, Mahlberg 2013, 2015). We hypothesize that on the one hand, complex technical terms will be more frequent in Dickens, and on the other hand, that modal verbs (e.g. *could, should*) will be frequent in *To the Lighthouse*'s quest to reconstruct the uncertain past and its dim memories.

To find modal verbs, we can search for the POS tag MD (see Box 2.1), and complex technical terms often consist of a sequence of several nouns. In Dickens' time we would expect complex nouns like *steam engine* or *factory worker* .

The output of *TagAnt* is in a format in which every word is given a POS tag, separated by an underscore symbol ('_'). In order to filter lines containing nouns, we can thus search for the corresponding POS tag '_NN', for verbs we search for '_VB', and so on, following the set of tags presented in Box 2.1. Compound nouns can be found by looking for a sequence of nouns and modal verbs by looking for '_MD'.

Let us start with the modal verbs. The command 'egrep' allows us to filter the output by lines containing a specific pattern. The commands used for these patterns are so-called regular expressions, which are literal character sequences in the simplest case. In more complex cases we can use so-called wild cards, which use placeholders and a powerful combination for extracting information. The tag 'MD' is a simple case: we just filter all lines in the novels by the 'MD' tag, which returns all sentences containing a modal verb.

```
$ cat wooligh-1656_tagged.txt | egrep '_MD' | more
```

The output will be:

```
Ramsay_NP ._SENT "_`` But_CC you_PP 'll_MD have_VH to_TO be_VB
up_RB with_IN the_DT lark_NN ,_, "_''
```

```
age_NN of_IN six_CD ,_, to_TO that_DT great_JJ clan_NN which_WDT
cannot_MD keep_VV
this_DT feeling_NN separate_JJ from_IN that_DT ,_, but_CC must_
MD let_VV future_NN
drawing-room_NN window_NN ,_, "_'' it_PP wo_MD n't_RB be_VB
fine_JJ ._SENT "_''
weapon_NN that_WDT would_MD have_VH gashed_VVN a_DT hole_NN
in_IN his_PP$ father_NN 's_POS
breast_NN and_CC killed_VVD him_PP ,_, there_RB and_CC then_RB
,_, James_NP would_MD
should_MD be_VB aware_JJ from_IN childhood_NN that_IN/that
life_NN is_VBZ
```

...

The 'egrep _MD' command filters all the lines containing '_MD' and displays all the hits, page by page. In order to assess the relative frequency of modals, we could now compare all lines containing '_MD' to all lines in each novel to determine the relation of lines with modal verbs to all the lines of the novel.

To do so manually would be very cumbersome. Fortunately, UNIX can count words and lines for us, using the command 'wc'. 'wc -l' returns the number of lines to us and 'wc –w' the number of words. If we take the (slightly bold) assumption that every sentence contains maximally one modal verb, or at least that this simplification does not matter for our purposes, we count the number of hits as follows:

```
$ cat wooligh-1656_tagged.txt | egrep '_MD' | wc -l
   1084

$ cat 3041_tagged.txt | egrep '_MD' | wc -l
   1569
```

This operation tells us that *Great Expectations* contains more modal verbs than *To the Lighthouse*, but it also is considerably longer. So let us compare the length in words:

In words:

```
$ cat wooligh-1656_tagged.txt | wc -w
   90638

$ cat 3041_tagged.txt | wc -w
   225929
```

So, the relative number of hits is 1084/90638 = 1.2 per cent in *To the Lighthouse* and 1569/225929 = 0.7 per cent for *Great Expectations*, which seems to confirm our hypothesis that modal verbs are more frequent in *To the Lighthouse*.

You may think that our assumption of maximally one hit per line is bold. We can convert our novels to a one-word-per-line format to check, using the command 'tr' which converts letters, in this case spaces (' ') into new lines, which are expressed as '\n' in regular expressions.

```
$ cat wo_ligh-1656_tagged.txt | tr ' ' '\n' | egrep '_MD' | wc -w
   1181

$ cat 3041_tagged.txt | tr ' ' '\n' | egrep '_MD' | wc -w
   2873
```

According to this, more precise relative count we have is 1.301 per cent modal verbs in *To the Lighthouse* and 1.272 per cent in *Great expectations*. This difference is smaller and statistically no longer significant. In order to test significance levels, we can use the following dialogue in R to perform a chi-square test. If you do not yet know what significance tests are and how they can be made very easily in R, refer to Schneider and Lauber (2019) to catch up.

```
> rbind(c(1181,90638),c(2873,225929))
      [,1]  [,2]
[1,]  1181  90638
[2,]  2873  225929
> chisq.test(rbind(c(1181,90638),c(2873,225929)))

      Pearson's Chi-squared test with Yates' continuity correction

data: rbind(c(1181, 90638), c(2873, 225929))
X-squared = 0.46584, df = 1, p-value = 0.4949
```

At first sight, our hypothesis seems to have failed, as the p-value (0.49) is much higher than any acceptable significance level. On second thoughts, *will* is included in the list of modal verbs. If we search for prototypical modals expressing uncertainty, for example *could*, we obtain robust differences: 0.318 per cent in *To the Lighthouse*, compared to 0.229 per cent in *Great Expectations*, a significant difference:

```
> chisq.test(rbind(c(288,90638),c(517,225929)))

      Pearson's Chi-squared test with Yates' continuity correction

data: rbind(c(288, 90638), c(517, 225929))
X-squared = 19.704, df = 1, p-value = 9.04e-06
```

Now we can turn to compound nouns, which were generally much less frequent in the times of Dickens and Woolf than nowadays (Leech et al. 2009). The regular expression needed to find sequences of nouns is more involved. We find a compound noun by looking for a noun tag followed by a word (which is a sequence of anything but an underscore) followed by the underscore and the second noun tag. In regular expression syntax, this is:

```
egrep '[^_]+_NNP?S? [^_]+_NN'
```

The command to look for compound nouns in *To the Lighthouse* is then:

```
$ cat wooligh-1656_tagged.txt | egrep '[^_]+_NNP?S? [^_]+_NN' | more
```

The beginning of the output looks as follows:

```
<_SYM Text_NN id_NN =_SYM WooLigh_NP >_SYM
<_SYM div0_JJ type_NN =_SYM part_NN n_NN =_SYM I_NN >_SYM
<_SYM div1_JJ type_NN =_SYM chapter_NN n_NN =_SYM 1_CD >_SYM
<_SYM milestone_NN n_NN =_SYM 9_CD >_SYM
the_DT sound_NN of_IN poplar_NN trees_NNS ,_, leaves_VVZ whitening_NN
```

Only the last line in this excerpt contains raw text, before that we can see XML tags which were erroneously tagged. The XML at the beginning is <Text id = WooLigh>.

Our results will also be affected by the presence of such metadata in XML tags, as it is considerably richer in the case of *To the Lighthouse* than in *Great Expectations*. A simple workaround is to exclude lines containing XML tags, with the egrep -v option. As XML tags always start with the diamond bracket '<', we exclude each line containing one.

```
$ cat wooligh-1656_tagged.txt | egrep -v '<' | egrep '[^_]+_NNP?S?
[^_]+_NN' | wc -l
      316
$ cat 3041_tagged.txt | egrep -v '<' | egrep '[^_]+_NNP?S? [^_]+_NN'
| wc -l
     1043
```

As the total wordcount is also affected by our filtering of XML tags (in fact we filter all lines containing XML tags), we also need to redo the wordcount of the novels, because the filtered text are considerably smaller:

```
$ cat wooligh-1656_tagged.txt | egrep -v '<' | wc -w
    75650
(base) gerold-schneiders-macbook-pro:Bloomsbury_Book gschneid$ cat
3041_tagged.txt | egrep -v '<' | wc -w
   225929
```

This gives us 0.417 per cent compound nouns in *To the Lighthouse*, compared to 0.462 per cent in *Great Expectations*. While this shows an encouraging trend, we had to take a number of dangerous assumptions (e.g. maximally one hit per line) and we actually do not reach significance levels – it is thus too early to draw conclusions on the differences between the two novels. The calculation of the significance, again using chi-square, is:

```
> chisq.test(rbind(c(316,75650),c(1043,225929)))
```

```
            Pearson's Chi-squared test with Yates' continuity correction
data: rbind(c(316, 75650), c(1043, 225929))
X-squared = 2.3209, df = 1, p-value = 0.1276
```

Box 2.2 Installation of the *Tree-Tagger*

Tree-Tagger Installation (Mac OS)

The installation of the *Tree-Tagger* typically involves the following steps.

1. Download and install the *Tree-Tagger* application.
2. Download and copy the scripts files.
3. Download and copy the parameter files of your desired languages.
4. Test the tagger.

The procedure is described on the website from which the tool can be downloaded:

http://www.cis.uni-muenchen.de/~schmid/tools/TreeTagger/

We give additional hints on the installation as it is needed on a Macintosh system.

Step 1. Download and install the *Tree-Tagger* application.
Download the tagger package for Mac OS-X. A file called *tree-tagger-MacOSX-3 .2.tar* is created in your Downloads folder. The file-ending *.tar* stands for tape-archive, a traditional backup format. If you double-click the file, a folder named *tree-tagger-MacOSX-3.2* should appear. If double-clicking results in an error message, you may not have a suitable decompression tool. Check if you have such a tool, for example *Archive Utility, Stuffit Expander* or *The Unarchiver*.

The *Tree-Tagger* application is located in the bin/directory inside the folder. As it is a command-line program, double-clicking it will not have a useful effect. We will see in step 4 how to use it.

While it is theoretically possible to use the *Tree-Tagger* from the Downloads folder directly, we recommend to copy it somewhere else, because the Downloads folder gets cluttered sooner or later and usually deleted after a while. We copy the entire folder *tree-tagger-MacOSX-3.2* to *Applications*.

Step 2. Download and copy the scripts files.
The *Tree-Tagger* website tells you to download the linked tagging scripts. The downloaded file *tagger-scripts.tar* should again create a folder on double-clicking. This folder, *tagger-scripts*, contains a file (README.script), a folder *lib* and a folder *cmd*. Copy all of these into the folder *tree-tagger-MacOSX-3.2*. As the folder cmd already exists there (it contains an older version of *lookup.perl*), you will be asked if you want to overwrite it. Say yes.

Step 3. Download and copy the parameter files of your desired languages.
We will assume that you minimally download the file *English parameter file (PENN tagset)*. It creates a file *english.par.gz*. Depending on your settings, it may automatically be decompressed into *english.par* or you may need to use one of the above decompression tools. Copy the file to the folder *tree-tagger-MacOSX-3.2/lib*.

Step 4. Test the tagger.
We are now ready to test. As the *Tree-Tagger* is a command-line application, we need to start it from the command line, which is often also called *shell* or *terminal*. You need to start the application called Terminal, which is in the subfolder *Utilities* inside *Applications*.

After double-clicking, a text window appears which will display your computer name, probably your user name, a dollar sign and a cursor. You can enter UNIX commands now. A simple command, the first one that we need, will bring us to the directory containing the *Tree-Tagger* application. The command is called *cd* (which stands for *change directory*), it needs the directory as its argument, that is, you need to add the name of the directory to the cd-command. Assuming that you have copied the *Tree-Tagger* folder to Applications, you can enter

cd /Applications/tree-tagger-MacOSX-3.2/

We can now test the installation by entering the following:

echo 'Hello world!' | cmd/tree-tagger-english

A screenshot of this small UNIX Terminal session is given here.

Screenshot of a UNIX Terminal session testing the Tree-Tagger.

The output of the *Tree-Tagger* is a format in which every word appears on a separate line and the columns are separated by a tabulator character. Accordingly, we can count how many lines contain whichever pattern we are interested in. Good text editors such as BBEdit for Mac allow you to search for special characters such as the tabulator by using regular expressions. The tabulator is \t as regular expression. In order to count nouns, we can thus search for '\tNN', for verbs for '\tVB', and so on, following the set of tags presented in Box 2.1.

The commands used in UNIX are a bit different now, and the *Tree-Tagger* also provides scripts using the exactly same output that we have seen with *TagAnt*. Happy experimenting!

Further Reading

Aarts (2019): A thought-provoking discussion of word classes and cases where definitions and the number of classes are contested.

Adolphs (2006): The source of the search for 'had happened'. A good introduction.

Anthony (2004): The paper introducing *AntConc*.

Hoffmann et al. (2008): An article showcasing the use of complex regular expressions, a good exercise.

Schneider (2013). A practical guide to investigating characteristics of Irish English, using the ICE Corpora and *AntConc*.

Sinclair (2003): An entire book showing what can be done with concordancing.

Rouberol (2020). A good introduction to UNIX for text processing. Highly recommended if you want to use UNIX for pre-processing, format conversion and so on. Their online resource is a book project that has not been finished yet.

Wikibooks: A quick introduction to UNIX: https://en.wikibooks.org/wiki/A_Quick _Introduction_to_Unix Highly recommended if you have nor used UNIX (or Windows Cygwin) before. A free book with exercises.

Frequency Lists

While we can test given hypotheses by looking at frequencies of specific words (Sections 2.1 and 2.2) or linguistic phenomena (such as POS tags, see Section 2.4), it is hard to assess which diachronic changes or which differences between classes we miss. In many areas, for example in lexicology, where there are tens of thousands of possible changes (each lexeme), it is hard to get an overview. A more systematic, data-driven approach is thus desirable. In this chapter, we present a more advanced method of determining changes, which is able to take not only pre-specified words but all words into account.

3.1 Theoretical background

Our second method, which we present now, allows us to not only evaluate specifically predetermined changes of words or structures but also compare structural differences between two or more corpora. This method is also quite simple: we just count words. In Section 2.1, we counted and compared individual selected words. A more systematic approach can be achieved by counting all words. The advantage of such systematicity comes at the price of an apparent loss of overview: we cannot go through lists of thousands of words, so what can we do? There are several answers: one is to restrict ourselves to only the most frequent words, as we do in this subsection. Another one is to compare the frequency of each word to a reference and to look only at those which are particularly frequent relative to this reference. We will do so in Chapter 4.

3.1.1 A glimpse of the content

Word lists have many applications. The most obvious one is that it allows us to see the most frequent and thus probably most important words of a text, of a topic (if we collect similar texts) or of a genre (if we collect, for example, many scientific texts or many newspaper articles). However, only some of the words that we will see in the wordlists in Section 3.2 tell us about the content of the documents, because the most frequent words, in any type of document, are words like 'the', 'in', 'that', words that do not denote anything in the real world but that relate words to each other and specify their function – that is why they are also called function words. Function words come from the word classes determiner (POS tag DT, see Chapter 2), prepositions (IN and TO) and so forth.

3.1.2 Zipf's law

The fact that the most frequent words are function words and not content words may be surprising. There are several reasons for this. First, the roles that hold between the words need to be established – these are, for instance, quantification with determiners, simple verbs (e.g. *have, be*) and local or temporal prepositions expressing the relations between nouns. Second, a successful communication strikes a balance between too boring and uninformative (too many frequent words) and too dense and hard to understand (too many rare and highly informative words). The forces of informativity and fluidity (or simplicity) are in a constant tug of war. Shannon (1951) uses the metaphor of a noisy channel which breaks down if the information is too dense. Shannon was mainly thinking in terms of an analogous telephone line which distorts the signal and adds clicking noise in many places. But the metaphor also holds under perfect acoustic conditions or with written text. We can only understand what we hear due to the fact that many words in the sequence to which we are exposed are not surprising but we expect them. The correlation between expectedness and our ease of understanding, or alternatively the risk of failing to understand, is very strong (Smith and Levy 2013).

So, while dealing with word frequencies, we will also playfully answer the question of how frequent frequent words are and how infrequent infrequent words, and whether, due to Shannon's noisy channel, there are expectations concerning these frequencies. Zipf's law (Zipf 1965) explains the type of distribution that we get when counting word tokens from a large corpus. The Harvard linguistic professor George Kingsley Zipf (1902–50) has formulated a number of linguistic laws. The most well-known of them, also called Zipf's law, says that in a sorted frequency list of words (i.e. for each word type: How many tokens does it have?):

rank * frequency is nearly constant.

We will see that Zipf's law indeed calculates these expectations, and the law holds quite well. We will compare four different registers, where we can see that vocabulary richness in spoken language is much smaller than in the written genres, and different written genres also behave differently.

3.1.3 Spoken and written genre

While there seems to be a balance between frequent and infrequent words, we all know that scientific texts are denser than fiction texts or that spoken language is simpler: speakers do not always remember the best-fitting rare words, so they say what comes to their mind, and listeners cannot always ask for a sentence to be repeated, so they also appreciate simple language. Accordingly, as also pointed out by, for example, Biber (1988: 36), we expect to see differences. To check if it really is the case that word frequencies are constant, we will test this as a hypothesis in the hands-on Section 3.2.3 and see that the four genres of BNC Baby differ considerably.

3.1.4 Vocabulary richness

In addition to genre differences, we know gifted speakers whose spontaneous speech is as complex as written texts with a rich vocabulary that is always to the point, ready to be printed, while others hardly manage to utter or also write a few coherent sentences. Pupils with a small vocabulary need special tuition or even speech therapy (e.g. Yang et al. 2022), language learners' levels can be measured through their vocabulary richness and finally a reduction in vocabulary richness in elderly speakers may be a first symptom of a neurodegenerative disease such as Alzheimer's dementia. Vocabulary richness is typically measured by the so-called type-token ratio (TTR), the ratio of the total vocabulary of a text divided by the total of the words appearing in the text. Its use can be summarized as follows.

> The type-token ratio (TTR) is a measure of vocabulary variation within a written text or a person's speech. The type-token ratios of two real world examples are calculated and interpreted. The type-token ratio is shown to be a helpful measure of lexical variety within a text. It can be used to monitor changes in children and adults with vocabulary difficulties. (http://www.speech-therapy-information -and-resources.com/type-token-ratio.html. Last accessed 7 January 2023)

Accordingly, we will also explore individual differences: some speakers have a considerably richer vocabulary than others. The results that we obtain in this simple research project have many cognitive applications and consequences.

3.2 Hands-on: Spoken versus written language in BNC Baby

As a case study, we consider spoken versus written language. It is shown how to import text collections consisting of several files into the statistics language R and how to create wordlists.

We will use the BNC Baby corpus for our investigation.[1] BNC Baby consists of four genres: news, spontaneous speech, academic texts and fiction. All texts were collected (and recorded and transcribed in the case of the spoken part) in the year 1994. BNC Baby is a sampler of the British National Corpus (BNC, Aston and Burnard 1998), one of the most popular corpora worldwide.

Read the licence agreement, download the corpus and unzip it. You will see four folders in the 'Text' directory, called 'news' (newspapers), 'fic' (fiction), 'dem' (demographically sampled spontaneous speech) and 'aca' (academic texts). Each of these folders contains 25 to 100 XML files, about a million words for each of the four genres.

3.2.1 Creating a word list is simple

Creating a word list is really simple: R has a command which counts how often which element in a vector occurs, this is the *table* command. A typical use of a table command is to count if you have categorial data, how often many categories occur. For instance, if you have a table (a data frame in R) with 1,000 data points and thus 1,000 rows, 400 from female and 600 from male participants, then the table command will tell you how many male and female participants you have. Box 3.1 shows how to create a table from a vector. The term *vector* is used in R for a list in which all elements have the same variable type.[2]

Box 3.1 Creating a table from a vector

How can we create a frequency table?

```
> afewnumbers <- c(11,13,13,13,14,16,16,17,17,17,17,18,11)
> table(afewnumbers)
```

11	13	14	16	17	18
2	3	1	2	3	1

In Box 3.1, we see that the number 11 occurred twice, the number 13 even three times in the variable 'afewnumbers', 14 just once and so on.

Creating a wordlist can be done in exactly the same way: we first read a text into a vector and then create a table. The pre-processing code preceding the table command is basically more difficult. We first load in just one file, for example *news/A1E.xml*.

```
afile    <-    scan(file="/Downloads/Texts/news/A1E.xml",sep="\n",
what="raw", quote="\"") ## adapt your path
```

You need to adapt your file path unless you happen to have unzipped or moved the file to exactly the location/Downloads/Texts/news/A1E.xml. Make sure that you have the quotation marks around the file path and that you copied the complete file path, including the full document name. Windows users should observe that R uses forward slashes for directories. Further potential failure modes here are umlauts and other symbols beyond the twenty-six letters and ten numbers. Paths can also be copied from the UNIX command line, or Windows Explorer has a bottom which exports the file path (though with backward slashes, which you need to correct). If you get completely lost, you can set the default path in which R searches, most simply to your home directory, with setwd('~'), then use the Filebrowser (*Finder, Windows Explorer,* ...) to copy the file(s) there.

The end of the line of the above code, ## *adapt your path*, is a comment. The end of a line after a hashtag symbol is not executed. There is no need for you to enter it, but it is a good idea to leave ample comments explaining what the code is doing and where users may need to adapt something, as here. Henceforth, there will be many comments.

You can inspect the beginning of the file with

```
head(afile)
```

and you will see, line by line, that it contains a lot of XML information, first the file-level metadata and then for each word the part-of-speech tag. A quick-and-dirty method to delete all XML information is to use a regular expression that deletes all XML tags. Its logic is that an XML tag starts with an opening diamond bracket (<) and is followed by several characters – they can be anything except for a closing diamond bracket (>). Finally, we do get the closing diamond bracket. We want to replace what we found by nothing. We simply overwrite our variable *afile*.

```
afile = gsub("<[^>]+>","",afile)   ### get rid of XML tags
```

Similarly, we delete punctuation marks.

```
afile = gsub("[,.!?'']","",afile) ### get rid of punctuation
```

If you now inspect the file again with the head command, you see text without annotation:

```
head(afile)  ## just for inspection, let us see
[1] " Independent electronic edition of ..."
[2] ""
[3] "Latest  corporate  unbundler  reveals  laid-back  approach:
Roland Franklin who is leading a 697m pound break-up bid for DRG
talks to Frank Kane"
...
```

In order to obtain a vector of words we first concatenate all lines into one very long string and then separate it at each space:

```
longstring = paste(afile,collapse="\n") ## all lines into one
longstring = gsub("\n"," ",longstring)
words = strsplit(longstring," ")[[1]]  ## split text into words
```

The word at position 200, for example, is DRG:

```
words[200]
[1] "DRG"
```

Now we can create the table:

```
wtable = table(words)                        ## create the table
```

You can inspect this table, again with head(wtable), but as the table is sorted alphabetically by default, we do not see anything easy to interpret when we look at the output of the command. Instead, it makes more sense to sort the table in a way that the most frequent words appear at the top, in other words by descending frequency, for which we can use the *sort* command:

```
sortwtable = sort(wtable, decreasing=T)
```

Let us inspect this sorted table of the highest-frequency words in BNC Baby:

```
head(sortwtable, n=50)
words
   the      of      to       a      in     and      is     for    that
   562     315     260     205     191     179     146      99      89
    by      on     has      it      be     The     its     was      at
    74      65      59      59      57      57      53      52      51
  from    have     not      as     per   which    cent    with     are
```

50	50	50	48	48	47	46	44	40
he	market	US	business	last	Mr	this	will	year
35	34	34	33	33	31	31	31	31
—	UK	more	one	an	would	been	company	British
30	29	28	28	26	26	25	23	22
But	tea	about	could	their				
22	22	21	21	21				

You have been warned (Section 3.1) that the list will be dominated by function words (*the, of, to*), and we also see generally uninformative words (*is, have, not*). We can glean from the data that this text is probably about business between US and UK companies. When we use a larger corpus of several texts, these content words will move even further down.

3.2.2 Word lists of entire corpora

To investigate differences between genres of course requires to load in more than just one text, but in fact all the texts of the genre that we want to investigate – for example all the texts in the *news/* directory. Let us now do so.

In the UNIX shell, accessing all texts in a folder is trivial, and we just need to specify an appropriate pattern. For example, *news/*.xml* refers to all the appropriate texts in the *news/* folder. One simple way to load all texts would thus simply be to concatenate them all into one file:

```
$ cat news/*.xml > ALL_news.xml
```

While this would be a reasonable option, we now want to do everything in R. This requires that we first read the contents of the directory (with the function *list.files*), and then read in each file, one after the other (hence the *for* loop), and append the current file to what we have read in before (with *paste*).[3]

The rest of the code is analogous to when we read in just one single file. It contains one further improvement – all words are lowercased with the function *tolower*.

The code is given in Box 3.2 and the output in Box 3.3.

If you want to know for a given word which rank it has, you can query the table heading: for example, assuming that you have loaded the news genre, the frequency for the word *war* is 279.

```
wtable[["war"]]
[1] 279
```

Box 3.2 Code for the 100 most frequent words in BNC Baby news genre

```
path <-"/Downloads/ota_20.500.12024_2553/download/Texts/news/" ## adapt!

files <- list.files(path=path, pattern="*.xml")
myfiles=""; ## create / empty / reset
for(file in files) {
 fullpath = paste(path,file,sep="")
 print(fullpath) ## let us see what we read in
 myfile = lapply(fullpath, scan, sep=NULL, what="raw", quote="\"")
 myfiles = paste(myfiles,myfile) ## append to what we already have
}

myfiles = gsub("<[^>]+>","",myfiles)        ### get rid of XML tags
myfiles = gsub("[,.!?'']","",myfiles)       ### get rid of punctuation
myfiles = gsub("\n","",myfiles)             ### get rid of linebreaks
myfiles = tolower(myfiles)                  ### lowercase

words = strsplit(myfiles," ")[[1]]
words = noquote(words)                       ## remove quotes
words = gsub("[ [:punct:]]", "" , words)     ## remove punctuation

length(words) ## inspect size
head(words)   ## look at the beginning

wtable = table(words)
sortwtable = sort(wtable, decreasing=T)
head(sortwtable, n=100)
```

Box 3.3 The 100 most frequent words of the genre news in BNC Baby

```
> head(sortwtable, n=100)
words
    the     to     of      a    and     in    for     is     on
  58786  26103  25612  23260  22864  18854  10438   9889   7928
    was   that     at   with     it     by     he     be     as
   7308   7306   6696   6611   6560   6353   6147   5950   5346
    but   from   have    his    are    has          will   said
   5051   4916   4677   4623   4596   4339   3934   3620   3600
      i    not   this     an   they    had  their   been  which
   3596   3583   3354   3350   3283   3077   3039   2897   2865
    who   were    its     we    one    all     up  would  after
   2815   2751   2555   2389   2228   2212   2191   2123   2103
    out  there   when     or   more   last     mr  about    two
   2089   2080   2068   2053   2051   1991   1877   1803   1755
    new     if  first    you   than    she    her   into     no
   1737   1707   1575   1566   1555   1527   1519   1505   1498
```

over	can	also	years	now	only	people	year	time
1483	1418	1384	1382	1369	1363	1360	1359	1340
so	could	them	yesterday	him	some	just	what	back
1286	1277	1220	1219	1180	1159	1155	1126	1032
other	should	being	any	before	may	like	against	my
1026	999	996	950	950	939	934	925	918
off	down	way	do	three	world	most	because	made
908	903	899	887	884	884	875	864	848
home								
834								

Finally, while we have seen that creating wordlists in R is easy, I would like to use the opportunity to briefly mention that, as always, many paths lead to Rome – a quick, easy, fast and dirty way to create wordlists all in the UNIX shell. Try the following, you can also look at the intervening steps by only executing the initial parts of the pipeline.

```
$ cat ALL_news.xml | tr " " "\n" | sort | egrep "hw=" | uniq -c
| sort -rn | more
```

3.2.3 Type-token ratio

In order to determine how varied the vocabulary is that is used in a corpus of text, we calculate the type-token ratio. The lower the ratio is, the more varied the language. The calculation of TTR is now trivial. The length of the corpus is the token count, and the length of the wordlist is the type count. In the news genre of BNC Baby, TTR is 0.059. Some people find the token-per-type ratio easier to interpret, which tells us the average frequency of occurrence of all the types. For the news genre, it is 19.2.

```
> length(wtable) ## types
[1] 50452
> length(words)  ## tokens
[1] 967338
> length(wtable) / length(words) ## type-token ratio (TTR)
[1] 0.0521555
> length(words) / length(wtable) ## tokens per type
[1] 19.17343
```

We have hypothesized that spoken language will be less dense than written language. If we want to see whether our hypothesis that spoken language has a lower vocabulary richness is correct, we just need to compare different genres. In order to do so, we adopt the path used above: we will change *news* to *dem*, the BNC code for spoken language, and rerun the code in Box 3.2.

You will see, for instance, that the personal pronoun *I* is far more frequent in spoken than in written language, as are other personal pronouns, although to a lesser degree.

Complex noun phrases (NPs) (containing, for example, the preposition *of*) are less frequent in spoken language. Blogs, chats and other forms of computer-mediated communication share some characteristics of both spoken and written language (Jonsson 2015).

For the TTR, we get the following results from *dem*, that is, spoken language:

```
> length(wtable) ## types
[1] 18975
> length(words)  ## tokens
[1] 998249
> length(wtable) / length(words) ## type-token ratio (TTR)
[1] 0.019000828
> length(words) / length(wtable) ## tokens per type
[1] 52.60864
```

The difference is indeed very strong. The token-per-type ratio, for instance, tells us that a word type is used 19.2 times on average in one million words of news texts, but 52.6 times in one million words of spontaneous spoken language. You may wonder about the other genres now, fiction and academic writing, and where they are placed in this comparison. What are your expectations? You can then test your hypotheses.

At the end of this subsection, an important remark is due. TTR strongly depends on the size of the corpus (Malvern et al. 2004). We could directly compare TTR values only if the four genres in BNC Baby are nearly identical in size. If you want to compare corpora of different sizes, you either need to cut them all to the same size of the shortest corpus or even better, you can compare the means of TTRs of segments of given length. This metric is also known as mean segmental TTR, or short MSTTR (Lu 2014: 82), which stands for mean segmental type-token ratio.

3.2.4 Zipf's law

While you may find the results of our comparison of genres expected, you will see that Zipf's law (Zipf 1965) is unexpected – unless such distributions (Zipf's law is a subclass of Pareto distributions) are your daily business.

Let us start by comparing frequent words to infrequent words by using a visualization, namely a histogram.

```
hist(sortwtable[1:5000], n=1000)
```

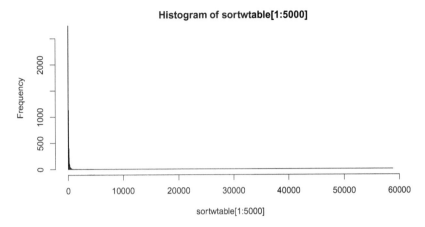

Figure 3.1 Word frequency by word rank in BNC Baby news.

The histogram is shown in Figure 3.1. The vertical axis expresses the frequency of a word, the horizontal axis its rank in the frequency list. It is hard to believe that the small smudge in the bottom left corner expresses all the beauty of language of common well-formed texts. Very few words are very frequent, and most words are very rare. What regularity may hold in this extreme distribution?

Zipf's law says that in a sorted frequency list of words (i.e. for each word type: how many tokens does it have?):

rank * frequency is nearly constant.

Let us first look at two random ranks, 3 and 30, from the news genre:

```
> myrow = 3; freq = sortwtable[[myrow]] ; zipfconstant = freq *
myrow ; zipfconstant
[1] 76836
> myrow = 30; freq = sortwtable[[myrow]] ; zipfconstant = freq
* myrow ; zipfconstant
[1] 100620
```

The result is not too bad, the value for zipfconstant is similar. In order to test this systematically, we again need a loop. The following code uses the top 5000 types.

```
for (i in 1:5000) { freq = sortwtable[[i]] ; zipfconstant[i] = freq * i}
plot(zipfconstant)
```

The resulting plot is shown in Figure 3.2. We can see that Zipf's law holds fairly well. The constant fluctuates in the beginning, then it has a 'belly' between about

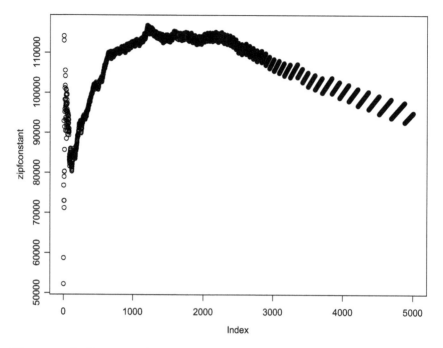

Figure 3.2 Zipf's constant for the *news* genre in BNC Baby.

ranks 1200 and 3000 and then slowly falls off. The funny pattern at the right is due to the fact that many low frequencies occupy quite a long range of ranks.

3.3 Hands-on: *To the Lighthouse*

As the next hands-on exercise, we could test how Zipf's law applies by taking a look at the most frequent words in *To the Lighthouse*. We can use the same code as the one for reading in one file from the BNC Baby corpus (Section 3.2.1). Results are given in Box 3.4.

Box 3.4 The eighty most frequent words in *To the Lighthouse*

```
> head(sortwtable, n=80)
words
     the            and    to      of     she     was      her           a
    3203    2206   2184   1535    1522    1470    1302    1298         1293
      he      in    that    had      it     his    with            at         not
```

1019	1006	936	898	848	727	543	521	487
on	for	as	they	would	all	said	one	him
478	469	464	439	429	417	411	400	389
She	--	be	He	Ramsay	them	so	which	thought
369	367	359	322	307	305	291	289	284
were	could	there	this	if	up	Mrs	what	like
284	282	267	265	263	255	252	240	231
But	about	but	from	did	out	Mr	or	It
229	226	226	212	211	211	210	209	204
some	now	by	have	And	then	their	been	something
204	201	187	187	168	168	163	160	160
when	little	felt	The	over	down	into	looked	must
159	156	152	145	143	142	138	137	135
is	how	They	Lily	again	seemed	an	herself	
134	132	129	128	127	127	126	115	

Box 3.4 shows that frequent words in *To the Lighthouse* are *Ramsay* (which is simply the name of a character), *thought* (which points to the introspective theme), *could* (weighing possibilities), *felt* (feelings), *must* (in either epistemic or deontic modality) and *something* (unspecific, indeterminate threat). Also *felt*, *seemed* and *again* already give us a sense of the content of the novel.

In contrast to spoken dialogue and egocentric blogs, the pronoun *I* is almost absent in *To the Lighthouse*. *I* is the most frequent word in the spoken part of BNC Baby, the tenth most frequent word in fiction and still the twenty-sixth most frequent word in its news genre. However, in *To the Lighthouse* it only appears at position 93. About 3 per cent of all tokens in BNC Baby spoken are *I*, while in *To the Lighthouse* its frequency is below 0.2 per cent. This is not only due to the narrator's perspective but also because dialogues, which typically use *I*, are rare and inner events take centre stage in this novel. The effect of remoteness, solitude and absence of a central actor culminates in the famous Chapter 2, 'Time Passes', where the empty house decays – it only contains a single instance of *I*.

3.4 Case study from CA – Political science: Donald Trump's words and vocabulary

When Donald Trump assumed office in the beginning of 2017, it was immediately clear that his style would be different from the one of his predecessor, Barack Obama. Not only his political style of 'America first' marked a strong difference but also his language was perceived as simple and populist if not deficient.

Referring to an answer that Trump had given at a press conference, Begley (2017) commented:

> [w]hen President Trump offered that response to a question at a press conference last week, it was the latest example of his tortured syntax, mid-thought changes of subject, and apparent trouble formulating complete sentences, let alone a coherent paragraph, in unscripted speech. (Begley 2017)

Simple, informal style is typically closer to spoken language and thus has a lower TTR. The TTR of all US presidential candidates used during the presidential debates from 2000 to 2016 is computed in Vrana and Schneider (2017). These TTRs are compared to the Santa Barbara corpus of Spoken American English (SBC).[4] The SBC is a carefully sampled corpus of spontaneous American speech. The result is given in Figure 3.3. We can see that Trump's vocabulary richness is considerably lower than that of any other presidential candidate and even lower than in SBC.

Also looking at simple word frequency lists can already be revealing. The first person pronoun *I* is used more frequently by Trump than by any other candidate, as Figure 3.4 shows. Also *they* is most frequently used by Trump, as Figure 3.5 reveals. Increased use of *I* may indicate egocentricity (Tausczik and Pennebaker 2010), while *they* often contains accusations against unclear targets (the famous 'us versus them', see Tajfel and Turner (1986)).

If you want to do these or similar experiments yourselves, the pre-processed files used in Vrana and Schneider (2017) can be downloaded from github.[5] They are derived from the collection of presidential debates (Peters and Wooley 2023).

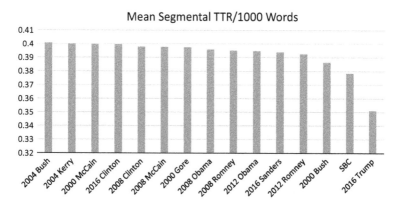

Figure 3.3 Mean segmental TTR of US presidency candidates during the presidential debates, sorted by decreasing MSTTR value.

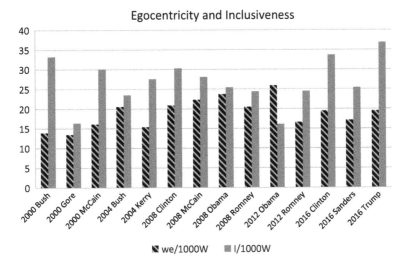

Figure 3.4 Frequency of *I* and *we* in US presidential debates, per 1,000 words, sorted by year.

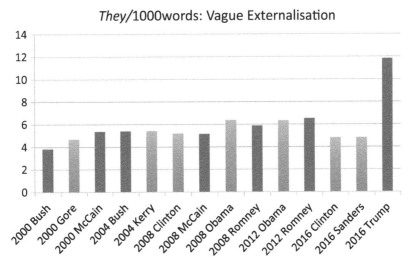

Figure 3.5 Frequency of *they* in US presidential debates, per 1,000 words.

The fact that Donald Trump's linguistic style is an outlier, for instance, in terms of vocabulary richness and frequency of vague pronouns also gave rise to the debate on whether he suffers from early stages of dementia. Although the results are ultimately inconclusive, Tyrkkö (2016), Sclafani (2018) and Ronan and Schneider (2020) give an analysis of his vagueness and incoherence.

Further Reading

Jockers (2014): An introduction to using R in digital humanities. It has a literature perspective, goes less far than this book, but also introduces further aspects. Recommended if you are not yet a programmer.

Schneider and Lauber (2019). A step-by-step introduction to R. A free book which will give you the first steps in R. Highly recommended if you are not yet a programmer and which will bring you to the required level of statistics. (https://dlf.uzh.ch/openbooks/statisticsforlinguists/)

Baker, Paul, 2010. *Sociolinguistics and Corpus Linguistics*. EUP.

Lindquist, Hans. 2009. *Corpus Linguistics and the Description of English*. EUP.

McEnery, Tony and Andrew Hardie, 2012. *Corpus Linguistics*. CUP

These three coursebooks are general, accessible introductions to corpus linguistics and its concepts. They have no intention of introducing the students to programming or using advanced tools. They are recommended background reading to this book for students who are new to corpus linguistics.

4

Overuse and Keywords

In Chapter 3, we have seen that frequency lists are dominated by function words. In order to find out which words are most typical, most important for a document (genre, topic, period, politician or political party), we need to compare it to a reference. This is what we are going to do in this chapter and also partly in Chapter 5. Again, we are setting out by presenting some theoretical background and then case studies with guidelines for hands-on application of the methodologies. This is followed by a case study on the Old Bailey Corpus.

4.1 Theoretical background

Keywords are the most important words in a text. Scanning frequency lists in order to find keywords is quite tedious. It would be desirable to be able to compare words directly between different texts. This can be achieved by automatically comparing frequencies of each word in relation to a reference corpus. This allows us to calculate how much more a given term is used in one corpus than in the reference corpus and to obtain a ranked list of overuse of all terms in that specific corpus. The simplest measure which delivers such values is the so-called O/E measure. O is the observed value from our target corpus and E is the expected value, based on a well-informed model or more likely from a large reference corpus. A simple formula, one which gives equal weight to the reference corpus $C_{reference}$ and the target Corpus C_{target}, is:

$$\frac{O}{E} = \frac{p(C_{target})}{p(C_{target}) + p(C_{reference})/2}$$

There are several other variants and related measures. One famous related measure is *TFIDF*. We now introduce the *TFIDF* algorithm and its motivation. *TFIDF* is important for topic classification and automatic index generation.

TFIDF stands for term frequency inverse document frequency, or *TF/DF*:

- If a term occurs many times in a given document (*TF*), it probably refers to a concept which is important for the semantics of this document.
- But if this term is generally a frequent word, that is, if it occurs in most documents, it is less important, not semantically discriminant and low in semantic content.

$$TFIDF = \frac{f(term, doc)}{f(docs \ where \ term \in doc)}$$

Often the *DF* is calculated with a logarithmic version, as it leads to better results if the number of documents is very large.

Despite its simplicity, *TFIDF* is still one of the best keyword detection algorithms (see Firoozeh (2020 for a comparison), or in other words, those few algorithms that have the potential to perform better are considerably more complicated.

4.2 Hands-on: Fairy tales and presidential debates

For this approach, we first use a collection of fairy tales from the Gutenberg archive to extract keywords. For the second activity, we use the US presidential debates from 2000 to 2016 (Vrana and Schneider 2017). Those data sets were selected because many of us remember at least some of Grimms' fairy tales from our childhood and because most of us remember some aspects of recent US politics. Further, the collections are also very different, one from literature and cultural history, the other from politics and recent history.

We first show how we could program all necessary code ourselves, step by step, but then we will introduce a powerful library which can do the job for us.

4.2.1 Keywords from fairy tales

Many of us know and love at least some of the fairy tales which the Grimm brothers collected, or in short Grimms' fairy tales. Let us see if the keywords that come up are what we expected or perhaps support us in our partial recollection of what really happened.

We first show how we could program the necessary code ourselves and give a recipe in Box 4.1. After the usual pre-processing (step 0) we need to read in each file, for example, with the *scan* function. We give the example of a text called *haensel.txt*, which probably contains the tale of Haensel and Gretel. The calculation of the *TF* part of *TFIDF* is easy – we have done it in Chapter 3. We would probably have to do these separately for each fairy tale, though, as each plot is different.

The calculation of *IDF* is a bit less obvious. For each word type, we want to know if it occurs at all in each tale. We can create a vocabulary list, a list of types, by just looking at the table headers of the wordlist for each tale, irrespective of the count of the individual item. We do so in step 3, which we need to do separately for each tale.

In step 4, we need to combine the vocabularies of all the tales. We can again use the *table* function. We can now access the *TF* and *IDF* values for any word in the current fairy tale. The example in step 5 looks up the counts for the word *in*.

Finally (step 6), we need to go through all the words, we 'loop over' all the words in coding lingo or at least all the relatively frequent words in the tale of interest. In programming terms, we apply a loop from the most frequent word down to a reasonable threshold, for instance, a frequency of 5. As mentioned, you need to do the calculations for each fairy tale, so either you need to write another loop or you need to load many individual files.

Box 4.1 summarizes the recipe in R.

STEP 0. Clean up: remove XML tags etc.

STEP 1. We read in (for each file)
```
> haensel <- scan(file="~/Downloads/haensel.txt",sep=" ",what="raw")
```

STEP 2. We calculate a token-frequency table → TF (**term frequency**).
```
> table_haensel = table(haensel)
```

STEP 3. For the calculation of → DF (**document frequency**) we only need to know if a document contains a term or not, to create a vocabulary
```
> voc_haensel = rownames(table_haensel)
```

STEP 4. We need to calculate how many fairy tales contain which word. This is our DF (**document frequency**) list.
```
> alltales = c(voc_aschen,voc_haensel, …)
> table_alltales=table(alltales)
```

STEP 5. We can now calculate TFIDF. E.g. for the word "in":
```
> table_haensel[["in"]] / table_alltales[["in"]]
```
STEP 6: Now loop over all the words of the tale of interest

4.2.2 *Fairy* tales with the library *quanteda*

While calculating the *TFIDF* values manually as outlined in Box 4.1 would be a good exercise, it also gets fairly tedious. We are now reaching the point where we can start to profit from the fact that many R libraries exist, which can take over part of this routine work for us.

The *quanteda* library calculates *TFIDF* values for us. We will see that this is also an important step for document classification (Chapter 5). Libraries are very powerful tools, and we will use many of them from now on. In order to use them, you need to install them once, then they will be ready on your hard disk until you do a major R upgrade. The function that is used is *install. packages*, for the case of *quanteda install.packages* ('*quanteda*'). In R Studio, you can also install libraries with a GUI using 'Install Packages . . .' from the Tools menu.

Most libraries that we will use are available at CRAN, the comprehensive R Archive Network. You can check which libraries are available:

https://cran.r-project.org/web/packages/index.html

Some packages that we will need later may not be available there but, for example, on github. We will see an example in Chapter 7.

A further very useful library for anyone interested in literature is the *gutenbergr* library. It allows us to directly load any of the texts that are offered at the Gutenberg project – an impressive collection of popular works and literature classics, currently over 60,000 books.

https://www.gutenberg.org

Needless to say, Grimms' fairy tales are also available. As the Grimm brothers are not authors, they only collected popular fairy tales, and finding them is not so easy on the Gutenberg archive. We are searching for the string "Grimms'" in all the titles using the function *str_detect* of the library *stringr*. Execute all the commands in Box 4.2 to load the fairy tales into the variable *grimmcorpus*.[1,2]

Box 4.2 Loading the necessary libraries and the Grimm corpus

```
library(gutenbergr)
library(tidyverse)
library(stringr)
library(quanteda)

grimm <- gutenberg_works(str_detect(title, "Grimms' "))
grimm
## this will tell you that the ID is 2591

grimmcorpus <- gutenberg_download(2591, meta_fields = c("title","author"))

grimmcorpus

# A tibble: 9,230 x 4
   gutenberg_id text                                      title               author
   <int> <chr> <chr>                                                         <chr>
1    2591 "Grimms' Fairy Tales"                           Grimms' Fairy Tales NA
2    2591 ""                                              Grimms' Fairy Tales NA
3    2591 "By Jacob Grimm and Wilhelm Grimm"              Grimms' Fairy Tales NA
4    2591 ""                                              Grimms' Fairy Tales NA
5    2591 ""                                              Grimms' Fairy Tales NA
6    2591 ""                                              Grimms' Fairy Tales NA
7    2591 "PREPARER'S NOTE"                               Grimms' Fairy Tales NA
8    2591 ""                                              Grimms' Fairy Tales NA
9    2591 "     The text is based on translations from"   Grimms' Fairy Tales NA
10   2591 "     the Grimms' Kinder und Hausmärchen by"    Grimms' Fairy Tales NA
grimmcorpus[90:100,]
# A tibble: 11 x 4
   gutenberg_id text                                                  title       author
   <int> <chr> <chr>                                                              <chr>
1    2591 ""                                                          Grimms' Fairy … NA
2    2591 ""                                                          Grimms' Fairy … NA
3    2591 ""                                                          Grimms' Fairy … NA
4    2591 ""                                                          Grimms' Fairy … NA
5    2591 "THE GOLDEN BIRD"                                           Grimms' Fairy … NA
6    2591 ""                                                          Grimms' Fairy … NA
7    2591 ""                                                          Grimms' Fairy … NA
8    2591 "A certain king had a beautiful garden, and in the gard…   Grimms' Fairy … NA
9    2591 "which bore golden apples. These apples were always cou…   Grimms' Fairy … NA
10   2591 "the time when they began to grow ripe it was found tha…   Grimms' Fairy … NA
11   2591 "of them was gone. The king became very angry at this, …   Grimms' Fairy … NA
```

As we can see in the column 'title', we are given only the title of the whole book but unfortunately not the individual fairy tales. In fact, this meta-information is not provided, so we need to gather it ourselves – pre-processing is often complex, unexpected, different in each case and requires flexibility and imagination.

The titles are provided in the text, as we can see, for instance, by inspecting lines 90 to 110, where the fairy tale *The Golden Bird* is starting. The titles are given in all caps; this is a feature that we can use to extract the titles: each time that we see a sequence of at least three characters in upper case at the beginning of a line, it is a title, which we want to remember in the variable *tale*. We also mark the beginning of a new tale with the pseudo-XML marker <NEW>, which will allow us later to split the book into its tales. We initially give the dummy value 'HEADER' to the variable *tale* and then loop through the entire book, line by line. To each line, we add the new meta-information into the column *tale*. The notation with the dollar sign (*grimmcorpus$tale*) is a standard way to refer to or assign columns in table-like R structures such as data frames.

Box 4.3 Adding the metadata *tale* to the corpus

```
grimlines = 1:(length(grimmcorpus$text))

tale="HEADER"

for(i in grimlines) {
  # print(grimmcorpus$text[i]);
  currline = grimmcorpus$text[i]
  if   (grepl("^[A-Z]{3,}",currline))   {print(currline);   tale   =
     currline; grimmcorpus$text[i] = paste("<NEW>",currline) }
  grimmcorpus$tale[i] = tale
}
```

If you now inspect the corpus (e.g. with *grimmcorpus[90:100,]*), you should see the new column. Our corpus still reflects the lines in the printed book. This is not the format which the *quanteda* library can use. It needs an object that is split into documents, that is, the tales. We first join all the lines of the printed book into one large string with the *paste* command and then split at the pseudo-XML element <NEW> (which we inserted for this purpose, see Box 4.3). We should get seventy tales.

For the purpose of calculating TFIDF, but also for text classification (Chapter 5), most methods need a so-called document-term (or document-feature) matrix, a table which shows for each document how many times the found words (terms) are present. Box 4.4 shows how to collapse and then split the corpus, and then creates a document-feature matrix using the *quanteda* function *dfm* (we give the variable name *dtm* to this object). The *dfm* function comes with useful argument options, here we lowercase the corpus and delete English stopwords (i.e. function words, which typically have nothing to do with the content of the document). In the result we can see, for example, that *golden* appears 22 times in document 5 (this is the tale *The Golden Bird*, which we have seen before) or that document 7 contains *luck* 6 times (probably the tale *Hans in Luck*).

The calculation of the *TFIDF* values is done by means of the *quanteda* function *dfm_tfidf*. When inspecting the table with the *TFIDF* weights, we can see that the *TFIDF* value of *golden* is lower than its raw count (as this word occurs in many tales), while, for instance, the proper names *Jorinda* and *Jorindel* have *TFIDF* values that are higher than their raw counts (as they do not occur in many tales).

Box 4.4 Building a document-term matrix and calculating the *TFIDF* values

```
longstring = paste(grimmcorpus$text,collapse=" ")
length(longstring) # should be 1 -> whole corpus in 1 line
documents=strsplit(longstring,"<NEW>")[[1]]
length(documents)   ### 70 tales
documents[5] ## an example

dtm <- dfm(documents, tolower=T, remove = stopwords("english"))

dtm[4:8,20:30]   ### documents 4 to 8, features 20 to 30

Document-feature matrix of: 5 documents, 11 features (63.6% sparse).
         features
docs     . contents  : golden bird hans luck jorinda jorindel travelling
  text4  0           0 0      0    0    0    0    0       0          0
  text5  73          0 15     22   25   0    1    0       0          0
  text6  80          0 16     1    0    25   6    0       0          1
  text7  35          0 7      0    1    0    0    11       11         0
  text8  33          0 2      0    0    0    0    0       0          1

dtm_tfidf = dfm_tfidf(dtm)
dtm_tfidf[4:8,20:30] ## cf. e.g. jorindel vs. golden

Document-feature matrix of: 5 documents, 11 features (63.6% sparse).
        features
docs        . contents    :   golden    bird      hans     luck    jorinda jorindel
  text4 0           0 0       0         0         0       0        0        0
  text5 1.3886963   0 0.68636236 11.0588579 13.601701 0     0.6690068 0      0
  text6 1.5218590   0 0.73211985 0.5026754 0       28.6532 4.0140407 0      0
  text7 0.6658133   0 0.32030243 0        0.544068 0       0        16.98475 16.98475
  text8 0.6277668   0 0.09151498 0        0       0        0        0        0
```

So far so good. In order to know which words are the top keywords for a given tale, we sort them by decreasing *TFIDF* values, similar to when we sorted the words by frequency in Chapter 3. Our hope is of course that this time we will not mainly see high-frequency content words (remember we have already removed the function words with the *dfm* function) but distinctive content words at the top. In early versions of *quanteda*, this sorting could also be done with the standard *sort* function, but *quanteda* now provides a dedicated function called *dfm_sort*.

For document 5 (*The Golden Bird*) or 6 (*Hans in Luck*), we get, for instance,

```
dfm_sort(dtm_tfidf[5,],decreasing=T, margin="features")
Document-feature matrix of: 1 document, 4,862 features (91.1% sparse).
       features
docs        fox     bird   golden princess    horse      cage  son counsel  saddle
  text5 21.97255 13.6017 11.05886 10.70411 9.366095 8.022896 7.843181 7.468628 7.380392

dfm_sort(dtm_tfidf[6,],decreasing=T, margin="features")
Document-feature matrix of: 1 document, 4,862 features (89.1% sparse).
       features
docs       hans      cow      pig     milk butcher grinder    goose fat countryman  silver
  text6 28.6532 25.99156 24.70509 10.94381 9.22549 9.22549 7.536064  7  6.839884 6.760784
```

If you want to do this systematically for each fairy tale, here is a loop running through all the tales and giving us the top twenty keywords for each tale and its title.

```
for (i in(2:length(documents))) {
  mytfidf = dfm_sort(dtm_tfidf[i,],decreasing=T, margin="features")
  mytfidf20 = as.data.frame(mytfidf)[1:20]
  mytitle = substr(documents[i],1,100)
  print(i); print(mytitle); print(mytfidf20)
}
```

The loop runs through all the documents (the first one is empty, thus the loop starts at 2). The curly bracket delimits the so-called block, the part of the code that is iterated in the loop. The indentation in the layout makes the structure obvious – also programs should be accessible to distant reading to help the reader. You can also enter the entire block in one line and separate the commands by a semicolon but that would be harder to read.

4.2.3 Keywords of American presidential candidates

If recent US politics is more your thing than old fairy tales, you can extract keywords in just the same way from the presidential debates corpus (Vrana and Schneider 2017).

Download the files from github at https://github.com/LeoVrana/PresidentialDebates.[3]

The documents in the distributed corpus are files ordered by candidate and campaign. In other words, the relevant metadata is provided, but we need to get it into R. We saw in Chapter 2 that the standard R methods to load all files in a directory are a bit cumbersome. Fortunately, the library *readtext*, which also comes from the developers of *quanteda*, offers a simple method to load an entire folder and keep the filenames as metadata.

The commands in Box 4.5 first set the current directory – you will need to adapt this depending on where you save the corpus. Instead of entering long paths we can change the working directory with the *setwd* function. Then all the files ending in *.txt* are read in to the variable debates, and the document variables are kept by means of the *docvarsfrom* argument.

Now we are almost ready to calculate the *TFIDF* values. The variable type of the debates variable is an object of the type *readtext*. As in every object-oriented language, objects have complex internal structure. One can always inspect the type of a variable with the function *str*, which is often handy if one gets lost in the variable-type jungle. The easiest way to create a document-term matrix is to convert the *readtext* object into a *quanteda corpus* object, using the *corpus* function (we will explain the different object types in Section 5.4.1). Then we can proceed with the fairy tales from Section 4.2.2. The method to create a keyword list for each document from presidential debate data in R is shown in Box 4.5.[4] We adapt the code from Box 4.4, first loading the data, then converting to a corpus object and then to a document-term matrix with the *dfm* function. We obtain a version with *TFIDF* values instead of raw frequencies by means of the function *dfm_tfidf*.

Box 4.5 *TFIDF* keywords from the US presidential debates, 2000–2016

```
setwd("/Media_Content/DebateProjectVrana/Corpora/Debates") # adapt!
library(readtext)

debates = readtext("*.txt", docvarsfrom = "filenames")
cdebates = corpus(debates)

dtm <- dfm(cdebates, tolower=T, remove = stopwords("english"))

dtm_tfidf = dfm_tfidf(dtm)

for (i in 1:length(cdebates)) {
   mytfidf = dfm_sort(dtm_tfidf[i,],decreasing=T, margin="features")
   mytfidf20 = as.data.frame(mytfidf)[1:20]
   print(i); print(mytfidf20)
}
```

For space reasons, we cannot discuss the results in detail; let us perhaps look at two examples: George W. Bush in 2000 and Barack Obama in 2012. The top twenty keywords of Bush's 2000 campaign are:

```
          document  texas     % accountability guidelines hemisphere booth
1 2000BushMasteruntagged.txt 32.42865 16.85768    13.98312 12.60741 11.83137 11.46128
 abortions consequence  morale   opec  crude exploration  scores value-added  steve
1 11.42543  10.30335 10.14118 10.14118 10.14118  9.366095 9.296078  9.169024 8.705089
    swear  uphold humble    d.c
1 8.697088  8.496003 8.45098 8.442963
```

As George W. Bush was the governor of Texas, the top hit *Texas* is expected. He argues with many detailed percentage figures (%) and presents his plan to establish a system of *accountability* in education; as a conservative Republican he wants to reduce the number of *abortions*; he wants to boost the *morale* in the army; he plans to reduce dependence from *OPEC* and its *crude* oil, including gas *exploration* in Alaska and nature reserves. There is considerable pathos in his contribution (*humble, swear, morale*). *Steve* is the moderator.

Finally, his use of the word *hemisphere* is a bit surprising – he refers to the area of US interests.

```
Having a hemisphere that is free for trade and peaceful is in our
nation`s interests.
But there`s got to be priorities, and Middle East is a priority for
a lot of reasons, as is Europe and the Far East, our own hemisphere.
Our own hemisphere is in our national strategic interests.
```

Let us briefly turn to Obama's campaign of 2012. He addresses the moderator (*Candy*) and his opponent (*Romney*), who he accuses of offering tax *deductions* that aggravate the *deficit*. He proposes his own *recipe* of *nation-building* and *Obamacare* and clean energy *production*. The Libyan dictator *Qaddafi* had just been deposed, which Obama presents as a success.

```
          document  romney  candy deductions  decade consequence qaddafi
1 2012ObamaMasteruntagged.txt 41.94935 15.21176  7.616953 4.918738  4.783698 4.584512
 obamacare nation-building shipping production  repeal indicated administrative 800,000
1 4.352544    4.22549 4.014041  3.61236 3.577264 3.577264    3.438384 3.380392
    skilled deficit  lands  recipe    4
1 3.380392 3.351531 3.345034 3.345034 3.068689
```

4.2.4 Overused words in the spoken register

We saw that there is a large stylistic difference between spoken and written genres in terms of vocabulary richness. But probably the words that are used are also different. According to Biber (1988), the spoken genre is typically more involved, more personal and less abstract. We can use *O/E* to systematically check overuse. For simplicity, we restrict ourselves to comparing spoken genres to news. With very few classes (here: two), *TFIDF* makes less sense. Because most words are present in both classes, the *TFIDF* value would thus only be a variant of *TF*, unable to reflect the frequency in the other class. In such a setting an overuse measure, *O/E* (Section 4.1), is more meaningful. The expected (*E*) value is the frequency from both corpora, divided by 2.

The table heading allows us to query the raw frequencies, that is, the observed (*O*) value: for example, assuming that you have loaded the news genre, the frequency for the word *war* is 279.

```
wtable[["war"]]
[1] 279
```

If we load the spoken register to check the corresponding frequency of the word *war* (actually 20), we would overwrite the variable containing the values for the written register. Let us save the sorted word frequency table for the news genre, for instance, by copying it to a variable called *news_sortwtable*. We can now run through the most frequent words in a loop: look up the frequency from spoken at the current rank and check what this word is, for which we have stored the column heads into a variable *colhead = rownames(sortwtable)*, in which we can retrieve the word at its current rank in the loop (*colhead[i]*).

Before checking the solution in Box 4.6,[5] try to program it yourself, developing step by step in the R command line and pasting each command that works into the script.

Box 4.6 Overused words in the spoken register with *O/E*

```
## load news, then:
news_sortwtable = sortwtable
## then load spoken

oetable=0;
colhead = rownames(sortwtable);    ## the column heads = words
for (i in 2:500) {
  spof = sortwtable[i];            ## f of the word at rank i
  spow = colhead[i];               ## which word is it?
  newsf = news_sortwtable[[spow]]; ## f of this word in the news
  oe = (2*spof) / (spof + newsf);  ## overuse with O/E
  print(oe);
  oetable[[spow]] = oe;            ## save it into a table
}

head(sort(oetable, decreasing=T), n=100)
```

```
       mm        cos       yeah       ooh   alright        ha        er     gonna       erm
 1.999646  1.999284  1.998878  1.998172  1.997647  1.996983  1.996840  1.995027 1.994747
       oh      gotta      fifty     wanna        ah     mummy      okay       yes       mum
 1.993647  1.993266  1.992970  1.992322  1.986957  1.980254  1.980241  1.975414 1.973643
   twenty     thirty       shes     youve  thousand     whats       dad    theyre     thats
 1.969008  1.968689  1.955526  1.955112  1.954861  1.951033  1.942549  1.940106 1.937500
  hundred     bloody      youre     youll      dear      mean    theyve    havent       ill
 1.936534  1.933635  1.931034  1.930490  1.928994  1.918091  1.918009  1.914625 1.906977
   anyway       isnt        you      nice      know    theres    please       got     arent
 1.904878  1.904762  1.899670  1.895954  1.891053  1.879963  1.877221  1.877164 1.876636
    thank       dont       well   wouldnt       ive      cant     didnt       bit     think
 1.859477  1.857286  1.852111  1.838780  1.832676  1.829328  1.827237  1.821467 1.815997
       im       sort       weve     wasnt    really         i     right      wont        do
 1.812896  1.795918  1.794175  1.792651  1.790446  1.787797  1.786920  1.785592 1.782465
      hes       ones   remember        id  actually   couldnt        go    doesnt      what
 1.781628  1.781122  1.778125  1.777240  1.775255  1.774955  1.774344  1.772770 1.757118
     your       look        god       get      tell        no     doing      want     thing
 1.756695  1.750104  1.746789  1.735176  1.734078  1.733642  1.725347  1.724328 1.718845
      see       here         me       ten       did      then      nine  probably      done
 1.712105  1.709641  1.700638  1.696629  1.694234  1.685698  1.685125  1.683190 1.682909
something      quite        why      like        so   thought     going      come     eight
 1.680223  1.674201  1.671397  1.670314  1.653323  1.648366  1.633774  1.633371 1.622857
      say
 1.622833
```

The results show us hesitation markers (*er, erm*), backchannels and short answers (*yeah, alright, yes*), contractions (*gonna, youre*), interjections (*oh, ah*), discourse markers and downtoners (*really, sort* (of), *actually, anyway*), swearwords (*bloody, god*), vague expressions (*something*), indirect speech (*say, like*). Family conversations (*mummy, dad*) are particularly frequent.

The program in Box 4.6 actually stops at i=253 with an error message (subscript out of bounds). The word at this rank is *mhm* and the problem is that it does not exist in BNC Baby news genre. Instead of returning zero, as we might have expected, we get an error message, as we are referring to a column of the table *news_sortwtable* which does not exist. We can correct this by checking if a column, in this case *mhm*, is defined.

```
"mhm" %in% rownames(news_sortwtable)
FALSE
```

The improved code and results are given in Box 4.7. If a word is not found in the news genre, it is assigned a smoothing count of 0.5. Adding such a low number has the practical advantage that we never get an error (as we never have to divide by zero) and the theoretical advantage that we are less affected by sparse data. The argument is simple: if we have not seen a word in a corpus of finite size, it either means that the corpus is too small and it was a coincidence that we did not encounter it. Then a count of 1 would be appropriate. Or, alternatively, the word never appears and a count of zero would be appropriate. To take a count of 0.5 is a compromise between these two options. In mathematical terms, this method is a simple way to use Laplace smoothing. Statistical systems usually perform better with modest smoothing.

We see in the smoothed results in Box 4.7 that on the one hand new convincing entries such as further swearwords (*fucking*, *shit*), topics of conversation (*quid*) and interjections (*doo*, *urgh*) appear among the most frequent words, on the other hand corpus coincidences, i.e. coincidental biases, are increasingly reflected the further we go down the list (1000 here). *Unspecifiedsurrey* is probably an error in the corpus, and *upstairs* looks like a corpus coincidence. With only one million words, a sparse data problem is showing: even proper names (*Charlotte*) are starting to appear in the list. By convention, numbers (e.g. *ninety*) seem to be transcribed as words, while they are printed as numbers in the news genre.

Box 4.7 Improved code and further lexical differences from the spoken register

```
for (i in 2:1000) {
  spof = sortwtable[i];          ## f of the word at rank i
  spow = colhead[i];             ## which word ist it?
  if (spow %in% rownames(news_sortwtable)) {
   newsf = news_sortwtable[[spow]] }
  else {newsf = 0.5};  ## f of this word in the news
  oe = (2*spof) / (spof + newsf);   ## overuse with O/E
  print(oe);
  oetable[[spow]] = oe;          ## save it into a table
}

head(sort(oetable, decreasing=T), n=100)
```

mm	cos	yeah	ooh	mhm
1.999646	1.999284	1.998878	1.998172	1.997870
alright	innit	ha	er	fucking
1.997647	1.997564	1.996983	1.996840	1.996779
dunno	th	eighty	gonna	erm
1.996604	1.996219	1.995062	1.995027	1.994747
oh	hmm	unspecifiedsurrey	gotta	fifty
1.993647	1.993528	1.993311	1.993266	1.992970
aha	wanna	doo	eighteen	yep
1.992883	1.992322	1.992278	1.991561	1.991453
int	eh	aye	ya	cor
1.991342	1.990741	1.990588	1.990338	1.989529
fourteen	daddy	ho	mummys	yo
1.989418	1.988889	1.988439	1.988439	1.988304
dya	urgh	ee	da	ah
1.988304	1.988166	1.987421	1.987261	1.986957
sh	sixty	shit	wheres	quid
1.986755	1.985765	1.984252	1.982857	1.982456

thatll	grandma	nought	mummy	okay
1.982379	1.981308	1.980583	1.980254	1.980241
biscuit	hows	pardon	ninety	yes
1.978947	1.977011	1.976285	1.975610	1.975414
itll	redditch	mum	huh	seventy
1.975385	1.974684	1.973643	1.972603	1.969231
twenty	thirty	fifteen	hello	oclock
1.969008	1.968689	1.967742	1.966019	1.964602
abbot	aint	hi	ma	ta
1.964497	1.962466	1.960396	1.958904	1.958333
shes	youve	thousand	bye	whats
1.955526	1.955112	1.954861	1.953488	1.951033
minus	forty	tha	twelve	dad
1.950530	1.950000	1.948718	1.947368	1.942549
theyre	thats	hundred	till	nineteen
1.940106	1.937500	1.936534	1.935714	1.934959
bloody	youre	charlotte	bloke	youll
1.933635	1.931034	1.931034	1.931034	1.930490
sa	dear	darling	u	whos
1.929204	1.928994	1.927126	1.924242	1.919192
sixteen	upstairs	mean	theyve	y
1.918367	1.918129	1.918091	1.918009	1.917526

To alleviate the sparse data problem, we could use the other BNC Baby genres, and frequent words can be given a boost, for instance, by using O^2/E, or $O*\log(O)/E$. This will probably lower the position of the proper name *Charlotte* in our example. Boosting frequent words this way also eases interpretation: the meaning of relatively frequent words is often clearer. You are free to experiment.

4.3 Case study: Overuse of POS tags by social class in the Old Bailey Corpus

While comparing keywords, as we have done in Section 4.2, delivers insights into the content of documents or speakers' utterances, stylistic differences are harder to see in keyword comparisons. Fortunately, in order to observe such stylistic differences, we can apply overuse metrics at any level. In our next case study, we want to explore stylistic differences between the social classes in the Old Bailey Corpus (Huber 2007, Huber et al. 2016, Section 1.9.3). We have seen in Section 2.3 how the OBC can be used to trace linguistic changes over time. Now we will give an insight into how sociolinguistic research can be done by using digital humanities approaches.

In the metadata of the OBC, only two social classes are annotated, higher and lower. To compare the language of members of different social classes, we could compare the differences in their language use with *TFIDF*, with two pseudo-documents, higher and lower social class. *DF* would then indicate if the word is ever used by the corresponding class. However, as only two different classes are annotated in the OBC, using *TFIDF* does not make so much sense. This is because most words are present in both classes, and the *TFIDF* value would thus only be a variant of *TF* (as *DF* would be 2 for almost all words), unable to reflect the frequency in the other class. In such a setting, an overuse measure such as *O/E* (Section 4.1) typically leads to better results.

A particular merit of the OBC is that it represents the spoken genre/register. We have seen in Chapter 2 that genre differences are very strong. While there are relatively many textual sources from Early Modern English, there are very few spoken ones. Obviously, audio recordings of this time do not exist, and spoken language was, if anything, simply considered a corrupt and sub-standard form of the written register, and the OBC is a transcription of such spoken utterances. Of course, we cannot expect the transcription to offer meticulous detail, such as false starts or hesitation markers. But some characteristics, such as swearwords to illustrate the vile character of accused subjects or their limited vocabulary to reflect low education, are likely to be present, and we will partly search for them. If we find them, a certain circularity of the argument cannot be avoided: whether we measure language use or the degree to which non-standard forms are recorded has to remain unknown.

We hypothesize that lower class speakers have a smaller vocabulary, more self-centred egocentric language features (such as the pronoun *I*), less complex noun phrases and fewer subordinate clauses (which would reflect a less argumentative and less abstract style). These are also characteristics that are unlikely to be changed by a transcriber. In this section, we want to focus on spoken language because the class differences are recorded only for spoken utterances.

To gain a high-level overview of stylistic differences, we report the distribution of POS tags in Table 4.1.

First, let us observe a few differences where lower class speakers use considerably more or fewer words of a given word class. This difference can be observed well by considering the second last column (Lower/Higher); we have highlighted noticeable differences in **boldprint**. Lower class speakers use slightly fewer nouns (NN, NNS) indicating less complex NPs, but more personal pronouns (PP) indicating a more involved, less abstract, more narrative and possibly more emotive style. They use more past tense forms (VBD) further indicating narrative style, but fewer participles (VBN), indicating fewer passive forms and present perfects (such as the resultative, which explains consequences).

Lower classes use more verbal particles (RP, a typical spoken-language feature). As the frequency of phrasal verbs increases diachronically, we see indications for what is called a change from below, that is, language change that is effected by ordinary people. The lower class speakers use more modal verbs (MD) than the higher class speakers, which indicates a more emotional style (Culpepper and Kytö 2000). Third-person singular verbs are less frequently used in the lower class data, as the lower class speakers use the first person more often, indicating a more egocentric perspective. Indeed, the pronoun *I* covers 4.9 per cent of all tokens in the lower classes, compared to 3.8 per cent in the higher classes. However, to assume that these observations are genuine differences between the social classes in early modern England falls too short. We must also take into account that in the Old Bailey Corpus data, many defendants, and also some of the victims, belong to the lower classes, and their speech contributions entail a more egocentric perspective than the language of witness or lawyers or judges.

The biggest difference indicated in Table 4.1 is that the lower class speakers use 58 per cent more interjections (UH), indicating a more involved, emotive style. The higher class speakers use more attributive WH-words (WP$, e.g. *whose*) and more adverb superlatives (RBS). There seems to be a fashion to use the elative *most* instead of the intensifier *very*, which is more widespread in the data from the higher social classes. Unsurprisingly, the higher classes use more foreign words (FW).

The data in Table 4.1 is sorted by decreasing frequency in the lower social classes. We have marked those cases in *italics* where the ranking is noticeably different in the higher than in the lower social classes. Past tense verb forms, VBD, indicating narrative style, and DT (determiner), indicating nominal style, have swapped places. CC (co-ordinating conjunctions), indicating narrative, paratactic style, and JJ (adjectives), indicating nominal styles, have equally swapped ranks. Interjections (UH), some of which are also swearwords, are several ranks lower in the higher classes.

The higher frequency of narrative, paratactic style indicated by co-ordination (CC) begs the question if argumentative, hypotactic style is less frequent in lower social class data. The complementizer *that* (i.e. the word-tag sequence *that_IN*) in lower classes only reaches 71 per cent of the frequency of higher classes.

If we consider the distribution of POS tags (cumulative tag frequencies, columns 4 and 8), we notice that the lower class speakers reach a higher percentage of how many of all the tags present are used, that is, a higher coverage and a slightly less Zipfian distribution a bit earlier, as summarized in the last column. This indicates that the rarer, more complex word classes are slightly

Table 4.1 Differences of POS Tag Frequencies between Lower and Higher Social Class

Lower tag (%)	Lower class (f)	POS tag	Cumulative lower (%)	Higher tag (%)	Higher class (f)	POS tag	Cumulative higher (%)	Lower/ Higher (%)	Cumulative lower/higher (%)
12.71	745978	NN	12.71	13.09	1664619	NN	13.09	97.12	97.12
11.86	695853	PP	24.57	11.07	1407871	PP	24.16	107.12	101.70
9.30	545932	IN	33.88	9.60	1221474	IN	33.77	96.86	100.33
9.13	535675	VBD	43.01	8.59	1093341	VBD	42.37	106.18	101.52
8.61	504932	DT	51.61	9.03	1148825	DT	51.40	95.26	100.41
5.35	313927	,	56.96	5.02	639180	,	56.43	106.44	100.95
4.62	271279	NP	61.59	4.94	628391	NP	61.37	93.56	100.36
4.35	254971	.	65.93	4.03	512732	.	65.40	107.77	100.81
4.25	249244	RB	70.18	3.86	491718	RB	69.27	109.85	101.32
3.38	198586	CC	73.56	2.99	381161	CC	72.26	112.91	101.80
3.17	186261	JJ	76.74	3.46	439980	JJ	75.72	91.75	101.34
2.84	166359	SENT	79.57	3.08	391915	SENT	78.81	92.00	100.97
2.64	154882	VB	82.21	2.60	330891	VB	81.41	101.44	100.99
2.11	123939	TO	84.33	2.13	271622	TO	83.54	98.89	100.94
2.07	121745	NNS	86.40	2.24	285074	NNS	85.79	92.56	100.72
1.92	112849	VBN	88.32	2.32	295526	VBN	88.11	82.76	100.24
1.80	105435	VBP	90.12	1.94	247101	VBP	90.05	92.47	100.08
1.67	97944	CD	91.79	1.55	197358	CD	91.60	107.56	100.20
1.66	97196	PP$	93.45	1.42	181740	PP$	93.03	115.91	100.44
0.91	53443	VBG	94.36	0.92	118171	VBG	93.96	98.01	100.42
0.90	52776	RP	95.26	0.63	80915	RP	94.60	141.36	100.70
0.86	50486	MD	96.12	0.63	108489	MD	95.24	135.22	100.93
0.70	41139	VBZ	96.82	0.87	110924	VBZ	96.11	80.38	100.74

(*Continued*)

Table 4.1 (Continued)

Lower tag (%)	Lower class (f)	POS tag	Cumulative lower (%)	Higher tag (%)	Higher class (f)	POS tag	Cumulative higher (%)	Lower/ Higher (%)	Cumulative lower/higher (%)
0.53	31146	WRB	97.35	0.61	78479	WRB	96.73	86.01	100.65
0.42	24392	POS	97.77	0.41	52644	POS	97.14	100.42	100.64
0.37	21813	WDT	98.14	0.44	56204	WDT	97.58	84.11	100.57
0.33	19644	WP	98.47	0.47	60312	WP	98.06	70.59	100.42
0.33	19257	``	98.80	0.46	59087	``	98.52	70.63	100.28
0.26	15056	UH	99.06	0.16	20589	UH	98.68	**158.48**	100.38
0.24	14026	EX	99.30	0.24	31024	EX	98.93	97.98	100.37
0.19	10944	"	99.48	0.26	34060	"	99.19	69.64	100.29
0.10	5620	JJR	99.58	0.09	11556	JJR	99.28	105.40	100.30
0.09	5084	PDT	99.66	0.08	10560	PDT	99.37	104.34	100.30
0.06	3702	(	99.73	0.08	10503	(	99.45	76.39	100.28
0.06	3700	)	99.79	0.08	10456	)	99.53	76.69	100.26
0.05	2927	RBR	99.84	0.04	6120	RBR	99.58	103.65	100.26
0.03	1944	NPS	99.87	0.04	5400	NPS	99.62	78.02	100.25
0.03	1843	JJS	99.91	0.03	4097	JJS	99.66	97.49	100.25
0.03	1762	xml	99.94	0.04	5426	xml	99.70	70.38	100.24
0.03	1762	/xml	99.97	0.04	5426	/xml	99.74	70.38	100.23
0.02	895	SYM	99.98	0.01	1359	SYM	99.75	142.73	100.23
0.01	338	**WP$**	99.99	0.01	1337	**WP$**	99.76	**54.79**	100.22
0.00	277	**RBS**	99.99	0.00	985	**RBS**	99.77	**60.95**	100.22
0.00	277	LS	100.00	0.00	930	LS	99.78	64.55	100.22
0.00	257	**FW**	100.00	0.00	788	**FW**	99.78	70.68	100.22
100.00	5867497	Σ		100.000	12716360	Σ		100.00	

underused in the lower class speech. However, if we compare the TTR of the data from the two classes, no difference is reported. Thus, on the evidence of the data, the total vocabulary of the two classes is equally large. Here, again, the question arises whether this is due to the fact that participants of higher and lower classes often have different roles in the court cases. Higher class participants in the court proceedings might contribute less varied data: lawyers, for example, might tend to ask similar questions again and again, whereas we would expect the defendants' narratives to differ.

Table 4.1 has shown us many sociolinguistic differences and confirms our hypothesis: the language of the lower social classes in the Old Bailey Corpus shows more involved, emotional, narrative, paratactic style, fewer nouns, but more pronouns, modal and phrasal verbs. While some of these differences may be due to the roles that the participants play in the court proceedings (esp. members of the lower classes often being defendants), others may point to lower education.

If you feel inspired, the OBC can be downloaded from CLARIN at http://fedora.clarin-d.uni-saarland.de/oldbailey/.

Various formats are offered, ready to be used in Python or in CQP. For most purposes, you will probably need to do further pre-processing, for instance extract a comma-separated format to use the data in R and the shell as I did. However, the OBC offers a varied and interesting source of historically, socially and linguistically highly interesting material.

Further Reading

Schneider and Lauber (2019) Chapter 8: n-grams. The natural extension of the current chapter of this book. It repeats *O/E* and then introduces collocations, another very popular content analysis method (https://dlf.uzh.ch/openbooks/statisticsforlinguists/chapter/n-grams/).

Lu (2014): An excellent introduction to corpus linguistics and text processing. The book has a strong application-oriented perspective with a focus on different methods.

Document Classification

5.1 Theoretical background

Data-driven approaches like document classification have the advantage that they can show patterns that have hitherto gone unnoticed. However, their use is not yet widespread in many areas of application, for example historical linguistics, as Hilpert and Gries (2016) summarize:

> An attractive potential of quantitative corpus-based methods that has yet to be fully realized in diachronic studies lies in exploratory, bottom-up approaches. . . . Whereas for instance a logistic regression analysis requires a fundament of qualitative analysis which is subsequently scrutinized statistically, bottom-up approaches may start with the statistical processing of raw data, which then yields results that function as a stepping stone for a qualitative analysis. Starting with automated computational procedures has the benefit of a 'fresh start' that may serve to eliminate preconceptions and to reveal previously overlooked aspects of a given phenomenon. (Hilpert and Gries 2016 44–5)

We will introduce a data-driven case study from historical linguistics in Section 5.2. Before we do so, a few explanation are due of what document classification is.

5.1.1 Bag-of-words language models

Document classification is used widely in computational linguistics and in media content analysis. In Grimmer and Stewart (2013), it is given a dominant position. Document classification is used for many tasks, including:

- creating binary classes of relevant or irrelevant documents for an information retrieval task which is carried out, for example, in a Google search (see Jurafsky and Martin 2009: chapter 23.1)
- authorship identification tasks in forensic linguistics (see Oakes 2014)

- positive or negative assessment of a political issue in automated content analysis (see Grimmer and Stewart 2013).

Document classification works on the principle that the word tokens in the documents are used as discriminators between the classes without respecting their sequence or syntactic context. Every word type (above a certain minimal token frequency, e.g. $f > 4$) is a feature that helps us to classify the document. This entails that document classification typically uses thousands of features. These models are thus called *bag-of-words*. Each feature in isolation is usually not a good discriminator, but many "weak" discriminators together achieve high classification accuracy. Some of the algorithms used are well known in quantitative linguistics, for example logistic regression. While quantitative linguists use multivariate analysis with perhaps a dozen of features, thousands of features are standard in document classification.

The simplest approach, Naïve Bayes, simply gives equal weight to each feature (e.g. Lee et al. 2011). The probability of a text to belong to the binary class A is thus calculated as the product of the probability of each word to come from a document belonging to class A. In Bayesian statistics, the mathematical definition is thus:

$$P(A \mid text) \cong P(A) * \prod_{word \in text} P(word \mid A) \qquad \text{(Equation 5.1)}$$

If *P(A)* is bigger than 50 per cent (or another threshold), class *A* is chosen. More advanced algorithms, for example logistic regression, which we use in the present study, give optimal weight to each feature. Logistic regression is based on linear regression, which is easier to understand. Linear regression does not predict class membership but a linear value *y* (the *dependent* or *response* variable) based on its correlation to *n independent* variables or *predictors* $x_1 \ldots x_n$. Linear regression learns a regression line in such a way that the predicted y is as close to the *x*'s provided in the data as possible, as illustrated in Figure 5.1. The distance from five fictive data points (large dots) to the regression line (solid line) is minimized to make the distances (dotted lines) as short as possible. The solid line is adjusted in such a way that the sum of the squared distances is minimal. The method is thus also called ordinary least regression (OLS). In logistic regression, the prediction of a linear value y is replaced by a logit function which predicts the probability of a class membership.

In the simple representation of Figure 5.1, we have only one predictor, *x*. In text classification, we typically have thousands of features, one for each word

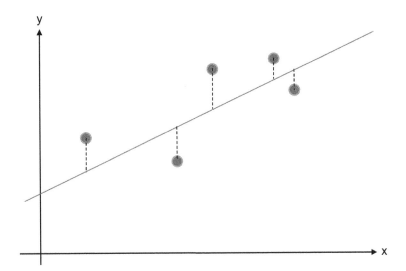

Figure 5.1 Illustration of linear regression. The distance from the data (dots) to the regression line (solid line) is minimized so that the squares of the distances (dotted lines) are minimal.

type, leading to not two but thousands of dimensions, but the principle stays the same – with one important addition. Unlike in Naïve Bayes, every feature is given an optimal weight to allow the most accurate values for the predictor variable. In other words, those features which do not discriminate well between the classes are given low weights, while those which discriminate well because they are typical for the class are given high weights. The formulation in Bayesian statistics of the linear regression function is thus:

$$y = \sum_{i=0}^{N} w_i * f_i \qquad \text{(Equation 5.2)}$$

where w_i is the weight of feature i, and f_i is the feature $i = x_i \ldots x_{N}$. If linear regression were used for document classification, the formulation would be:

$$P(A) = \sum_{i=0}^{N} w_i * P(A \mid word_i) \qquad \text{(Equation 5.3)}$$

Logistic regression maps the linear value for the predictor to a probability. For further details on linear and logistic regression for document classification, see Jurafsky and Martin (2009, Section 6.6).

The advantage of a multinomial model instead of looking at individual features is that it gives us statistical evidence of the impact of each feature. The results that we will inspect are thus given sorted by decreasing feature weight. This has the advantage that the impact of each feature is considered in collaboration with all other features, while reporting the best individual features would not take the interaction of features into account – this is precisely the added value of using a model. Additionally, algorithms in which the features are weighted fit the data better, and allow us to list the features that are most discriminant, and thus most typical. The features, that is, words which have the highest weights, can be interpreted as keywords, because document classification is also one possible keyword extraction algorithm.

We have just discussed that some classification algorithms, for example linear and logistic regression, learn which words are particularly strong disambiguators by giving each feature the best-fitting weight. Those features (e.g. words) that have the highest weights are the best discriminators between the classes and are thus one of the meaningful patterns that we want to detect as keywords.

Computational linguists, statisticians and the machine learning community are often more interested in choice of algorithm, accuracy of the model and feature engineering than in actually interpreting the features, but this is what we want to do here. In technical terms, here we are performing keyword extraction using document classification. We are interested in the interpretation of strong features. We use feature weights as keyness measure. This is used, for example, by Yang, Zhu and Tang (2013) to detect keywords, or Schneider (2018) interprets dialect features for comparing Swiss German to German German.

You may wonder now what the difference is between overuse measures such as *O/E* and feature weights via document classification. Partly, they indeed deliver similar answers and partly different, complementary ones. There are two major advantages of using document classification compared to *O/E*.

First, we can evaluate the performance of document classification and assess how well words allow us to distinguish between the classes. If the accuracy that we reach is reasonably high, then we can trust the discriminatory power of our language model. We know that we do not just report fluctuations in the general noise.

Second, the problem with overuse measures is that we do not know if differences are statistically significant (see Schneider and Lauber (2020) if you are new to significance testing). To remedy this, we can add a significance test to test if the differences are significant. For example, if the frequency of a word (or any feature) in corpus A is *f(A)* and in corpus B *f(B)*, and *N(A)* is the size of corpus A and *N(B)* the size of corpus B, we can use the chi-square test on the data shown in Table 5.1. The problem that still remains, though, is that each feature is tested in isolation. For this reason, significance testing is a so-called monofactorial approach. The

Table 5.1 Template for Chi-Square Significance Testing

	A	B
f	$f(A)$	$F(B)$
N	$N(A) - f(A)$	$N(B) - f(B)$

consequence is that we cannot know if a significant difference is just a side effect of another, stronger difference. A good example is the use of the passive form, which has been claimed to decrease in the last few decades, mainly due to prescriptive pressure. Significance tests generally confirm the decrease between the period from the 1960s and the 1990s, but such comparisons miss the influence of a factor that is much stronger than period, namely genre. For example, in spoken language, only 2–5 per cent of all verbs are in the passive, while in scientific writing, it can be 20 per cent and more, a difference that is much stronger than any diachronic change in the use of passive forms. This is shown, for example, by Hundt et al. (2016), who tease apart the different factors and show that there is still a significant diachronic decrease in scientific writing, albeit smaller than what significance tests would predict.

In general terms, we need language models that respect all the factors in their interaction in order to deal with the second point – whether differences are statistically significant. Multifactorial language models such as regression rank the various factors by their importance and discern significant factors and factor interactions, thus making it possible to distinguish significant factors from side effects of other factors (see, e.g., Evert 2006, Gries 2006, Gries 2010, Bresnan et al. 2007). Gries (2010) discusses an example where the application of monofactorial analysis, and multifactorial analysis without considering all interactions, can lead to incorrect results. He concludes that 'multifactorial data must be analyzed multifactorially: . . . the complexities of linguistic data do not reveal themselves easily either to the naked or to the monofactorial eye' (Gries 2010: 143).

5.1.2 Vector space models

We have argued that multifactorial models with thousands of bag-of-words features are necessary. Keeping count of thousands of word features and thousands of documents obviously leads to complex objects and complex calculations. A text representation which allows computers to efficiently calculate which documents are similar to each other is the document-feature-matrix representation.

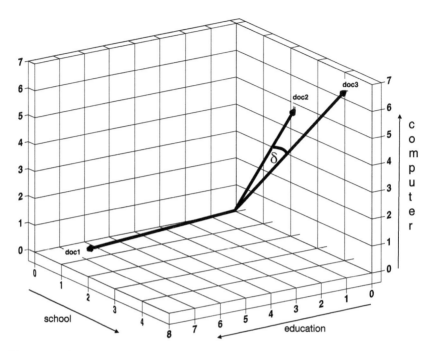

Figure 5.2 Document-term representation, its corresponding vector space and the angle δ between *doc2* and *doc3*.

One frequently used method is document similarity in vector space models. To understand how vector space models work, we will illustrate a radically simplified example, in which we only consider three terms and three documents. Every term needs a dimension in the vector space. Although we are typically dealing with thousands of terms and thus dimensions, a space that humans cannot imagine, the logic will be identical.

In our example, we consider the terms *school*, *education* and *computer* across three documents (*doc1*, *doc2*, *doc3*). The document-term matrix is given at the top of Figure 5.2 and the corresponding vector space at the bottom. We can see that the angle δ between *doc2* and *doc3* is much smaller than between *doc1* and *doc2*, indicating that *doc2* and *doc3* are much more similar. The document similarity can be expressed as a number between 0 and 1 by using the cosine function: cosine of 0 degrees is 1 (maximum similarity) and cosine of 90 degrees is 0 (maximum dissimilarity).

	school	education	computer
doc1	2	8	1
doc2	4	2	6
doc3	5	1	7

Intuitively, documents that are very similar probably belong to the same class. In an unsupervised approach (see Section 6), they should end up in the same cluster. In a supervised approach, such as document classification which we do here, we would calculate the mean of all the documents in a given class, the so-called centroid, and then, for new documents that need to be classified, find which class centroid is closest.

5.2 Case study: Lexical changes in the Old Bailey Corpus

As a case study, we continue our investigation of the Old Bailey Corpus.

While testing the hypotheses expected from López-Couso et al. (2012) in Section 2.3 revealed diachronic developments, we could first confirm that diachronic developments also exist in OBC. Second, looking at the data also prompted us to look for changes in nominal complexity, which revealed a very strong change. What other strong changes have we missed? Corpus-based approaches are unable to detect them. A more systematic approach is needed, one which allows us to discover all quantitatively salient additional changes. We thus use a systematic, corpus-driven approach at the level of lexis, based on machine learning: document classification with logistic regression on a bag-of-words representation in order to classify each trial to a century of origin. If our classification model works well, most texts will be assigned to the correct century.

In order to do so, we use settings that are standard in machine learning: monograms, $f>4$, $L2$ regularization, 10-fold cross-validation.

Let us briefly explain these settings:

- *Monogram*: We use only individual words as features, a so-called bag-of-words model, which does not take word order into consideration. Often two- or three-word sequences, so-called bigrams and trigrams, are also used. While they often lead to slightly higher performance, the number of features dramatically increases, which usually also complicates the interpretation.
- *f>4*: Only words (types) that appear at least five times (i.e. have more than four tokens) are used. A smaller threshold may lead to slightly better performance but to considerably more features, often with reduced generalizability, as rare words are strongly affected by sparse data problems. A model that is trained on rare features tends to overfit the data and actually performs more poorly on new, similar data.

- *L2 regularization*: Regularization is a standard method to prevent models from overfitting. Very strong feature weights are punished. Schreiber-Gregory (2018) summarizes regularization as follows:

  Statistical theory and machine learning have made great strides in creating regularization techniques that are designed to help generalize models with highly complex relationships (such as multicollinearity). In its most simplistic form, regularization adds a penalty to model parameters (all except intercepts) so the model generalizes the data instead of overfitting (a side effect of multicollinearity). (Schreiber-Gregory 2018: 6)

- *10-fold cross-validation*: N-fold cross-validation is a further method to reduce the risk of overfitting. For N=10, the training happens in 10 iterations. Each time, a different tenth of the data is left out and the performance is evaluated on the held-out part. The final model is an average of the 10 individual model.

Due to computer memory limitations, we had to restrict ourselves to a random subset of 10,000 Old Bailey trial proceedings out of the total 50,000 for this case study. We obtained 13,715 features. Classification accuracy of the ternary decision (17xx, 18xx, 19xx) is 96.9 per cent and the improvement over random choice (kappa) is 94.2 per cent. Unlike in standard machine learning approaches, we are interested not only in classification accuracy but also in interpreting the feature weights. The top fifty features of the earliest period (17xx), with obvious non-interesting features such as year numbers manually filtered, are given in Table 5.2, on the left side.[1]

This approach shows changes (i.e. differences to other centuries) in linguistics, but it also includes a mixture of extra-linguistic changes stemming from different reasons: court language and proceedings, and societal changes.

Table 5.2 reveals changes in legal language, proceedings and punishments. Many early trials (left column) were given a brief *summary* at the end (rank 2), and the verb *try* (rank 1) is used in the sense of *prosecute*. The punishment of *transportation* (rank 3) was very frequent in the seventeenth and early eighteenth century, as was *whipping* (rank 147).[2]

Many of the high-ranking features refer to types of crime (*stealing*, rank 24) or stolen goods (*linen, leather, guineas, silver, cloth*). By comparison, the results for the later data look very different. Yet, some differences between the earlier and the later data are consequences of the protocol style. After 1780, the lawyers' questions

Table 5.2 Strongest Text Classification Features Indicating 17xx Trials (Left) and 19xx (Right)

Rank	Feature for 17xx	Freq.	Feature influence	Rank	Feature for 19xx	Freq.	Feature influence
1	tried	849	33.810	1	sentence	142	23.468
2	summary	1478	20.747	2	division	71	17.257
3	transportation	1347	19.580	3	verdict	114	17.173
5	<PLUSSIGN>	895	17.398	5	prosecuted	191	11.502
6	sworn	735	16.391	6	k.c.	23	11.128
8	by	2291	15.204	7	again	98	11.093
9	linen	553	14.011	8	convictions	90	10.894
10	indicted	4317	13.310	9	released	26	9.429
12	deposed	728	11.783	10	oath	98	8.627
13	<QUESTIONMARK>	1572	11.776	11	proved	119	8.452
16	acquitted	1468	10.241	12	male	7	8.289
17	last	1621	9.868	15	edith	9	7.889
18	leather	189	8.496	16	bodkin	20	7.841
21	imprisoned	69	8.069	18	police	151	7.467
22	but	2162	7.830	19	pleaded	189	7.456
23	of	4278	7.735	21	rentoul	21	7.207
24	stealing	3622	7.582	22	michael	4	6.973
25	fined	67	7.382	23	10s.	23	6.970
26	<COMMA>	4317	7.281	24	articles	62	6.841
27	for	4321	7.175	25	15s	22	6.557
28	guinea	384	7.170	26	ernest	27	6.474
29	fact	460	7.113	28	defended	96	6.369
30	lawyer	945	7.070	29	hard	188	6.205
31	guineas	422	6.776	30	page	20	6.088
32	indictment	630	6.482	31	otherwise	21	6.042

(*Continued*)

Table 5.2 (Continued)

Rank	Feature for 17xx	Freq.	Feature influence	Rank	Feature for 19xx	Freq.	Feature influence
34	privately	354	6.386	32	christopher	4	5.951
35	carried	669	5.812	34	hurley	0	5.828
36	st.	1174	5.749	35	benjamin	12	5.796
37	desired	629	5.734	36	dwelling	6	5.744
38	val	416	5.732	37	frederick	69	5.731
39	silver	887	5.725	38	wilkinson	10	5.669
40	march	485	5.722	39	p.m.	94	5.635
41	the	4291	5.571	40	agnes	1	5.579
42	lb	141	5.547	41	confessed	49	5.579
43	cloth	390	5.455	42	march	81	5.464
44	him	2253	5.265	43	second	79	5.394
45	bill	125	4.964	44	labor	175	5.392
46	otherwise	266	4.947	45	job	21	5.269
48	lost	973	4.809	46	defamatory	9	5.196
49	marrying	17	4.693	47	labourer	39	5.150
50	<AMPERSAND>	324	4.685	48	then	159	5.146
				49	benefit	23	5.028
				50	fish	9	5.005

are not recorded consistently, which explains the high frequency of question marks (rank 13) in the early data (17xx). The ampersand and plus signs are shorthand ways of protocolling the trials; *val.* (rank 38) is shorthand for *value(d)*. The protocols are typically shorter in the earliest century, which gives higher weight to words referring to the procedure (*sworn, indicted, deposed, acquitted, imprisoned, fined, lawyer*) and possibly also abstract nominal style (*the, of, for, fact*). Further changes in court proceedings can be seen by looking at other centuries. For example, in the early period it was uncommon to use cross-examinations, and the use of the term *sentence* for *verdict* arises in the twentieth century; professional *police* forces were also established then, as the right column of Table 5.2 shows.

Some of the typically expected lexical changes can also be found: *upon* is at rank 526 of the earliest century, *ought* at rank 168, but finding such differences in some of the not extremely highly frequent words involves sifting through hundreds of features.

In the data of the earliest century, character judgements like *maliciously* (rank 111 of 13,715), *honest* (rank 144), *corrupt* (rank 180), *character* (rank 239), *wickedly* (rank 476), *jealous* (549), *wise* (743), *wicked* (947), *trust* (1,049), *evil* (1,331), *deceitfully* (rank 1,505), *dishonest* (rank 1,538), *rogue* (rank 1,987), *villain* (4,516), *felonious* (rank 3,680) are most frequent, so are moral stance like *proper* (rank 169), *improperly* (rank 385), *unnatural* (787), religious concepts like *god* (rank 389) *confession* (444) and *hell* (1,139). Swearwords are usually censored; it is thus difficult to assess their frequency.

The changes described in this section also involve societal attitudes. The purely data-driven approach used here shows us societal changes even more clearly than linguistic ones. This indicates, on the one hand, that societal changes may have been stronger than linguistic ones. If so, investigating these societal factors would be a desideratum for any multifactorial linguistic study. On the other hand, we see that the OBC is also suitable for the exploration of society and linguistic style, which we did in Section 4.3. Stylistic differences, for example the expression of moral attitudes and subtle lexical choices, equally involve linguistic form and content. Studying both in combination leads to a more complete picture.

5.3 Hands-on: American speeches with *LightSide*

As a hands-on exercise on document classification, we apply document classification to the detection of salient lexical differences in a comparison of US American parties. For this, we can use CORPS-II, a corpus of over 3,000 political speeches (Guerini et al. 2013). The relevant part for our studies has been made available for download on the companion website for this book.

While powerful classification algorithms such as logistic regression with bag-of-words features are computationally intense, there are user-friendly tools which allow users without any programming skills to use these approaches. *LightSide*, which uses the state-of-the-art machine learning tool *WEKA*, even offers graphical support throughout. *LightSide* can be downloaded for free.[3] It runs on Mac OS X, Windows and Linux. The *LightSide* manual (Mayfield et al. 2014) also gives useful instructions but is partly outdated.

Its installation is complicated by the fact that it needs a slightly older version of Java. Detailed installation instructions are given in Box 5.1.

Box 5.1 Installation instructions for *LightSide*

Installing *LightSide*

The following document describes the installation of *LightSide* on a Macintosh computer running OS 10.15.7 (Catalina).

Summary

The installation and execution of *LightSide* can be tricky, due to the following reasons:

- Although *LightSide* is a nice, user-friendly GUI tool, it needs to be started from the command line.
- You need to install the Java development kit (JDK).
- The current version (JDK 16) does not work. In my case, the older JDK version 8 works.
- Java has been bought up by Oracle. Downloads of older versions are not straightforward.
- The *LightSide* manual reflects the state of affairs a few years ago.

1. Installing the right version of Java JDK

Java has a pre-installed runtime environment (JRE) and a development kit (JDK). The latter is needed to develop programs or run programs from the command line, as we will have to.

You need to install the Java development kit to run *LightSide*, but the current version (JDK 16) gives an error message. For me, JDK version 8 works very well.

First, check if you have JDK installed. For this, use the command-line tool (aka shell) in /Applications/Utilities/Terminal). Type

java -version

If you have no JDK installed, the following dialogue pops up. We will discuss in a moment how to install JDK version 8.

Figure 3. Dialogue if no JDK is installed.

If you have a JDK installed, in the following example, JDK 16, you will get:

gschneid@gerolds-imac ~ % java -version

java version "16" 2021-03-16

Java(TM) SE Runtime Environment (build 16+36-2231)

Java HotSpot(TM) 64-Bit Server VM (build 16+36-2231, mixed mode, sharing)

In this example, we have JDK version 16, but we need an earlier version, such as version 8.

You can either download it from Oracle, where you need to register, or you can get it from the openlogic open JDK foundation.

Figure 1. The open logic Open JDK download site.

Install it as you usually install Mac OS programs.

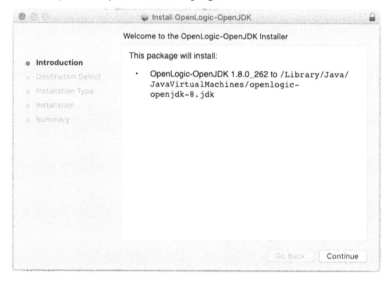

Figure 2. Installation dialogue

After successful installation, you can check if your Java JDK is now the appropriate version. For this, let's again use the command-line tool (aka shell) in /Applications/Utilities/Terminal)

gschneid@gerolds-imac lightside % java -version
openjdk version "1.8.0_262-internal"
OpenJDK Runtime Environment (build 1.8.0_262-internal-b10)
OpenJDK 64-Bit Server VM (build 25.262-b10, mixed mode)

Note that 'version 8' and 'version 1.8' are just synonyms, or '1.16' and '16' as well.
    Power users may want to have several versions of Java installed alongside and switch between them. That is possible. The tool libexec/java_home tells you about your Java JDK versions:

gschneid@gerolds-imac lightside % /usr/libexec/java_home -V
Matching Java Virtual Machines (1):
1.8.0_262, x86_64: "OpenLogic-OpenJDK 8" /Library/Java/JavaVirtual
    Machines/openlogic-openjdk-8.jdk/Contents/Home
/Library/Java/JavaVirtualMachines/openlogic-openjdk-8.jdk/Contents/
    Home

If you have several JDK versions, you can switch between them (see, e.g., https://medium.com/@devkosal/switching-java-jdk-versions-on-macos -80bc868e686a). The following command switches to version 8:

export JAVA_HOME=`/usr/libexec/java_home -v 1.8`

Check again with

java -version

if you are now set to version 8.

2. Installing and starting *LightSide*

Download *LightSide* from its home:

http://ankara.lti.cs.cmu.edu/side/

Be kind to drop a few lines on why you want to use it :-)

I have downloaded version 2.3.2

Figure 3. *LightSide* download page

I then recommend to move it to the 'Applications' folder, but if you prefer you can run it from anywhere (keep a record of where, though).

Figure 4. Moving *LightSide* to the "Applications" folder

Now we can start. For this, you can either double-click 'LightSide.command' or start the shell script 'run.sh' from the command-line tool.

Double-clicking 'LightSide.command' probably brings up the following warning:

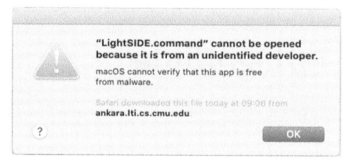

Figure 5. Refusal to open with double-click.

Right-click instead (or command-click) to bring up the context menu. Select open and 'yes' in the following dialogue:

Figure 6. Dialogue with context-click

LightSide.command is a wrapper script which starts run.sh, so you are doing exactly the same thing if you type

bash run.sh

In the command line, the latter option displays warning messages and errors directly in the command line, which may facilitate debugging.

The first startup may take a good while.

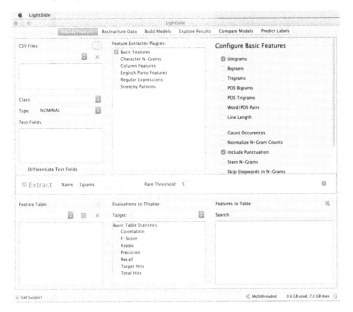

Figure 7. *LightSide* Application

If it all works, you should then see the *LightSide* Application window, as here.

All the user needs to do in order to apply *LightSide* is to bring the corpus into appropriate format (comma-separated, we will show how to do that in Section 5.3.1) and select among the various options, such as setting a frequency threshold and using only words or bigrams. We recommend starting with just words and a high threshold, as the computer may crash if the memory load becomes too high. Gradually, the complexity of the task may then be increased.[4]

5.3.1 Creating a .csv file

In order to process the texts, they need to be in a simple comma-separated format, with the class in one and the text in another column. A good option is to produce this format by means of Excel or OpenOffice. Once you have filled the data into the

Excel table, save the table as a comma-separated value (csv). Excel is careful to put quotes around fields containing commas, particularly the text field. Depending on your language settings, you have to be careful with encoding, where Excel's options are restricted, and make sure that the separator used between different data points is really a comma and not a semicolon. In German settings, the comma is also used as a decimal point, which then triggers Excel to use the semicolon as a field separator and produce a format that *LightSide* cannot read.

In the following, we provide the relevant subset of CORPS-II in a format that *LightSide* needs as the file

SEL_perparty_v2.csv

5.3.2 Loading the corpus

In the tab 'Extract Features', click the load file symbol on the top left and load SEL_perparty_v2.csv. The following figures show just 'Basic Features' and word monograms 'Unigrams', the classical bag-of-words setting. You may experiment with bigrams, trigrams and so on later. The class to be predicted is 'party', which

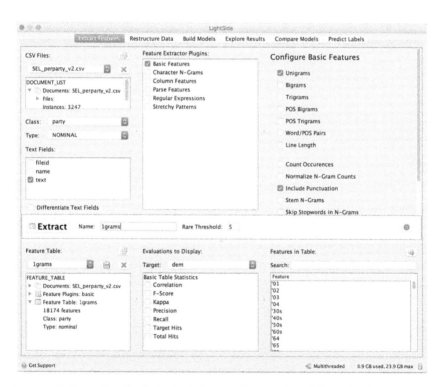

Figure 5.3 Extracting the features of Democrats versus Republicans in *LightSide*.

is a 'nominal' feature. Hit 'Extract' and wait for the computer to do its job. The screenshot after this step is shown in Figure 5.3.

5.3.3 Training the classifier

Now, we are ready to train the classifier. Change to the 'Build Models' tab to do so. To train the classifier, we can use logistic regression and the standard settings: L2 regularization and 10-fold cross-validation (see Sections 5.1 and 5.2 for explanations).

After you hit 'Train', your computer will put a lot of processing power into the training process, and the speed of the fan may also increase. The gauge on the right of the 'Train' button tells you about the progress. You can use multithreading to speed up, but this also entails that the computer may become unresponsive for a while. If your data set is too large, the computer may even crash if its memory is too low; however, this typically happens only if you use a slightly older computer.

After the computer has trained the final model, which is an average of all the n folds, it displays the results. Naïve Bayes classifies about 95 per cent of the speeches correctly and logistic regression about 98 per cent on this data set. In my own case, I obtained 97.9 per cent accuracy with logistic regression and a Kappa value of 95.8 per cent. Accuracy is the number of correctly classified documents, and Kappa shows the increase over a random choice. As one class, *dem(ocrat)*, is a bit larger, returning this class would lead to an accuracy of slightly above 50 per cent.

5.3.4 Interpreting the results

Next, let us explore the results. In the 'Explore Results' tab, we can see the confusion matrix at the top in the centre. The rows are the actual annotations and the columns the classification by the system. We can see in Figure 5.4 that in our case twenty-four documents that were actually *dem* are mistakenly classified as *rep*.

On the right (see Figure 5.4), we can explore the features, that is, the words and how much they lean towards one document class or the other. Here we have selected Republican features. Next to some trivial features (e.g. *Nancy* referring to Nancy Reagan) we see favourite topics, for example *freedom, god, nation, terror, taxes*. We can also see contractions (*'ve, 're*), indicating that the speeches are intended to be close to spontaneous spoken language, possibly transporting the image of the speaker being 'he is one of us'. We only see the few top features here, but as there are over 18,000, the top hundreds or the top thousand are strong features that invite to be interpreted. In order to make sure that the words are used in the way that we

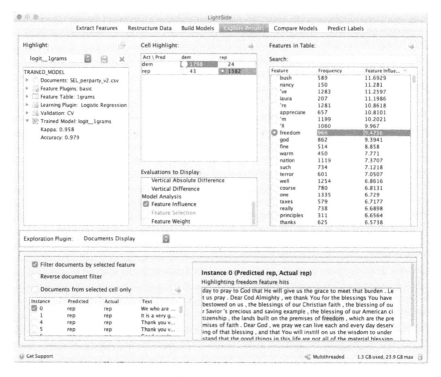

Figure 5.4 Exploring the results of Republican versus Democratic features in *LightSide*.

assume, we should always check actual instances. At the bottom of Figure 5.4, two documents containing the currently selected feature 'freedom' are displayed.

5.4 Hands-on: American speeches in R with *quanteda*

We have seen in Section 4.2 how a text collection can be loaded and keywords are calculated for us once the corpus is in the correct format. We will start in the same way in this hands-on exercise. It may be useful to outline the general procedure first and explain the different types of objects that *quanteda* offers.

5.4.1 Working with *quanteda*

In Section 4.2.2, we used the *readtext* library to load a text collection. We will also do so here, then create a document-term matrix, calculate the keywords with the *quanteda* library and then use this document representation to perform document classification, also with *quanteda*. A part of what we present is also described in a compressed form in Welbers et al. (2017). For reference purposes, experienced users can also obtain help from the *quanteda* cheat sheet compiled by Stefan Müller.[5]

The *readtext* and *quanteda* library come from the same developers and are tightly integrated. In order to perform text classification, we will also need the *quanteda. textmodels* library. We will see that other libraries, in particular the *stm* (structural topic modelling) library, also use the same type of objects that *quanteda* uses: objects in R, like in any object-oriented language, are variable types with complex precisely defined structures. The advantage of objects is that these variable types allow one to do complex and often CPU-intense tasks in a unified simple way, for example the calculation of TFIDF values in Chapter 4. The internal structure of the objects is optimized for speed and memory consumption. The disadvantage of objects is that they often behave differently from the simple types such as string, vector, data.frame, and so on, that we are used to in R. Simple, safe commands such as head to inspect the structure may not work. Typically, the objects make sure that the screen is not flooded with too many lines of data. Objects can be inspected by using the *str* function or in R Studio in the 'Environment' tag, where an overview of every loaded variable is available.

The relevant objects of *quanteda* and the related libraries are:

- *readtext* object: a text collection that has been read in from a file or folder. The readtext function offers a simple way to load entire folders into a variable (Section 4.2.2).
- *corpus* object: an object that contains corpus lines. It is particularly suitable for corpus search queries with the *kwic* command (keyword in context, Section 1.2). It can also keep the metadata that we loaded in with *readtext* by means of the *docvars* function. The corpus function allows us to create a corpus object from various sources, in particular a readtext object (Section 4.2.3) or a data .frame. If converting from a data.frame, the most typical R table format, we need to specify the column which contains the text with the *text_field* argument.
- *tokens* object: an object in which each word in the text, that is, the tokens, is represented. The conversion function tokens allow a number of classical tokenization options, such as removing punctuation, numbers, symbols or web addresses. Lowercasing and stemming may take place in this object or also in the following *dfm*.
- *dfm* (document-feature matrix) object: a table containing the frequency (or the TFIDF value) of each word for each document (Sections 4.2.2 and 4.2.3). The function which converts tokens or corpus objects into document-feature matrices, *dfm*, has a number of options to reduce the complexity and increase classification performance. Words can be mapped to lowercase (to lower), truncated (stem) and stopwords, that is, function words may be removed (remove).

It is a good idea to familiarize yourself with these functions by reading their help pages, that is, to load the libraries into R and call up their help functions:

```
help(readtext)
help(corpus)
help(tokens)
help(dfm)
```

5.4.2 Hands-on: Classifying US American speeches

We are now ready to perform our hands-on exercise, namely to classify US American speeches from the collection by Guerini et al. (2013), the corpus CORPS-II from Section 1.9.9. The research question that we want to answer is this: Can we predict the party affiliation (Republican or Democrat) given just the speech? In addition to finding overused words, document classification will also tell us whether the difference is reliable, which we can assume to be the case if classification performance is high, and bring to the surface the most discriminative words in contradistinction to side effects. In computational linguistics terms, we are applying supervised document classification for political profiling. Our classification is called supervised because the corpus has two categories on the basis of annotated or pre-existing knowledge.

The relevant part for our studies has been made available for download on the companion website for this book.

5.4.2.1 *Loading and pre-processing*

First, make sure that the necessary libraries are installed and loaded. The code is given in Box 5.2.[6] Then, load the datafile into the variable *rt*. Make sure to adapt the path. Next, we inspect the variable rt. Like all *quanteda* objects, it is protected: there is usually no danger of flooding your screen with the contents of an entire corpus, or worse still, an entire document-term matrix.

The output tells us what we are dealing with: a *readtext* object consisting of 3,247 documents and 3 document variables. We also see the first six rows of the object, which shows that we are dealing with a two-dimensional matrix, which in the R context is also called a data frame. What may be surprising is that although the object is described as having three document variables, the data frame has five columns.

If we look at the CSV file of the corpus, we can see why this is the case. The CSV file contains four columns, labelled 'party', 'fileid', 'name' and 'text', respectively. First, the object 'rt' to which we assigned the data created an additional column, labelled 'doc_id'. In this variable, the row number of each row in the CSV file is stored. If we were to load in a second document and append it to the 'rt' object, it would be clear which row of data comes from which corpus.

Second, the column 'text' is not a document variable but the actual text, as we have set it with text_field option. The tokenization, creation of the document-term matrix, and so on, will be applied to this field.

Before we can proceed to the document classification, we need to go through a few steps. Step 1, we need to turn the data frame rt into a corpus object. Step 2, we need to convert into a token object and use the opportunity to delete punctuation marks. Step 3, we lowercase all words. In the more radical and possibly contested Step 4, we reduce words to their stem. This has the effect that *obligations* and *oblige* are reduced to the same stem. While this step maps semantically closely related words to the same stem, stemming is sometimes going too far. For example, if *party* is reduced to *part* (which happens in some stemming algorithms), stemming has cut too many word endings. As a rule of thumb, if stemming is used classification performance increases slightly if the corpus is small, but decreases slightly with large corpora where the sparse data problem is less acute. As Step 5, we remove the stopwords. Observe that steps 3 to 5 could equally well have been performed while converting to the next object, the document-term matrix. As step 6, we convert to the document-term matrix. In step 7, we remove rare words. In step 8, we calculate the TFIDF values. Now we are ready to classify!

Box 5.2. Loading the US American speeches, converting to corpus, token and document-term matrix, weighting by TFIDF

```
## install what you have not installed yet
#install.packages("readtext")
#install.packages("quanteda")
#install.packages("quanteda.textmodels")

# load the libraries
library(readtext)
library(quanteda)
library(quanteda.textmodels)

# load CORPS-II into the variable rt: adapt the path!
rt   =   readtext("/Data/CORPS_II_RELEASE202/SEL_perparty_v2.csv",
    text_field="text")

rt ### to inspect
readtext object consisting of 3247 documents and 3 docvars.
# Description: df[,5] [3,247 × 5]
   doc_id              text                party fileid    name
   <chr>               <chr>               <chr> <chr>     <chr>
```

```
1 SEL_perparty_v2.csv.1 "\"We who are\"..." rep   akeyes-95    Alan_Keyes
2 SEL_perparty_v2.csv.2 "\"It is a ve\"..." rep   akeyes-98    Alan_Keyes
3 SEL_perparty_v2.csv.3 "\"Thank you \"..." rep   akeyes1-2-00 Alan_Keyes
4 SEL_perparty_v2.csv.4 "\"Thank you \"..." rep   akeyes1-6-96 Alan_Keyes
5 SEL_perparty_v2.csv.5 "\"Thank you \"..." rep   akeyes1-6-98 Alan_Keyes
6 SEL_perparty_v2.csv.6 "\"Thank you \"..." rep   akeyes10-96  Alan_Keyes
# … with 3,241 more rows

## Step 1: create corpus object
fulltext = corpus(rt)

fulltext # to inspect

Corpus consisting of 3,247 documents and 3 docvars.
SEL_perparty_v2.csv.1 :
"We who are Christians usually think about Christ in terms of..."

SEL_perparty_v2.csv.2 :
"It is a very great honor and pleasure for me to be here and ..."
...

## Step 2: tokenize
toks <- tokens(fulltext, remove_punct = TRUE)

## Step 3: reduce all words to lowercase
toks = tokens_tolower(toks)

## Step 4: stemming
toks = tokens_wordstem(toks)

## Step 5: remove stopwords
toks = tokens_remove(toks, pattern = stopwords(language = "en",
source = "snowball"))

## Step 6: create the document-term matrix
dtm <- dfm(toks)
dtm  # to inspect
dim(dtm) ## dimensions: 3247 x 32072

## Step 7: remove rare words (f < 5)
doc_freq = docfreq(dtm)
dtm = dtm[,doc_freq >= 5]
dim(dtm) ## dimensions: now down to 3247 x 11785

## Step 8: weighting by TFIDF
dtm = dfm_tfidf(dtm)
```

Before we move on to the classification, I would like to point out that the options, that is, arguments that we have chosen, are not compulsory, just reasonable practice. For example, not removing punctuation or not lowercasing leads to more but typically unhelpful features. Not removing rare words leads to a much larger, slower and overfitting model. Removing at a higher threshold (e.g. ten or fifty words) leads to a much smaller model, probably with a lower performance, but if your corpus is so large that R takes very long to calculate or crashes increasing this threshold will be the first reasonable improvement.

In Step 8, we converted to TFDIF weighting, a step whose sense may be far from obvious. The reason is that very frequent words have a large effect on the document vector, which is unfortunate as they are less telltale for the content of the document. The TFIDF value, as keyword metric, exactly gives high weights to the words that are most typical for a given document, and TFIDF usually leads to better classification performance. If you have very short documents, for instance tweets, TFIDF-weighting may, however, work less well than just using raw counts, so this step is better skipped in some circumstances.

5.4.2.2 *Document classification with Naïve Bayes and logistic regression*

Finally, we are now ready for the interesting part: the classification step. A supervised algorithm needs to learn from annotated data, and we have annotated data. So we could simply train the algorithm with all the data. While this would lead to the best possible performance, how could we then evaluate how good the performance is? If we test the classification model on the texts that it has already seen during the training phase, we get results that are not reliable: first, testing what you already know is child's play, second, it is an unfair comparison, third, it cannot tell you how much your model overfits and thus, fourth, gives you no reliable estimate on how the model would perform on new data. The typical answer is to test on 80–90 per cent of the data and assess the performance on the rest. R does not have n-fold cross-validation built in like *LightSide*, so we first just use one split between training and testing (and at the end suggest an improvement).

We have a corpus with 3,247 speeches, so why not take 2,800 random documents for training (86 per cent), which leaves us with 447 documents (14 per cent) for testing. The code is given in Box 5.3. We use the *dfm_sample* function (a sample function specifically for *dfm* objects) to create the training part and the *setdiff* function to create the testing part, making sure that the test set is the exact complement to the training set. The training step only needs one line: the *textmodel_nb* function (*nb* is short for Naïve Bayes) creates the model. And the first document classification model we are going to train is Naïve Bayes, using the function *textmodel_nb* from the library *quanteda.textmodels*. The name Naïve Bayes derives from the fact that the model applies Bayes' theorem with a strong, that is, naïve, independence assumption: the model assumes that the class of any feature is independent of the class of every other feature in the set and is equally important. While this is pretty simplistic, or even naive, it works well enough in practice. We will see that logistic regression can overcome this assumption.

Now that we have the model, what should we do with it? We can use it to predict classes with the *predict* function, on whatever speech, seen or unseen. If we predict the classes of the test set, we can assess how well the model predicts, that is, we can evaluate it. *head(pred_nb, n=20)* shows us the first twenty predictions. We can now compare these to the correct classes that we had in the original data. The comparison of these first twenty documents looks promising. In order to count how many cases were correct, we can again use the versatile *table* function (which we have used to create wordlists in Chapter 3).

The table is a so-called confusion matrix (as we have seen it in *LightSide* in Section 5.3); it tells us how often the model makes the right predictions and how often it confuses the classes, and in which way round. The rows give us the classes predicted by the model, the columns the party label from the correct class in the test data. We can see that in my case fifteen speeches that actually are Republican are erroneously predicted as Democrat, while thirteen speeches that are actually Democrat are predicted as Republican. The correct speeches are in the diagonal. To assess the accuracy of the model, we divide the values in the diagonal by all the values in the table. In my case, I obtained 93.7 per cent accuracy. Observe that due to the random sampling of the data you will almost certainly get slightly different values.

Box 5.3 Training and evaluating the model

```
train_dtm = dfm_sample(dtm, size=2800)    ## create training set
test_dtm = dtm[setdiff(docnames(dtm), docnames(train_dtm)), ] ## testset

nb_model = textmodel_nb(train_dtm, y=docvars(train_dtm, "party"))

pred_nb = predict(nb_model, newdata=test_dtm) ## predictions on testdata

head(pred_nb, n=20)         ## see the first 20 predictions
head(docvars(test_dtm, "party"),n=20) ## see the first 20 annotations

confmat_nb  =  table(prediction  =  pred_nb,  party  =  docvars(test_dtm,
      "party"))
confmat_nb  ### this prints the confusion matrix
        party
prediction dem rep
      dem 249 15
      rep 13 170
accuracy_nb = (confmat_nb[1,1]+confmat_nb[2,2]) / sum(confmat_nb)
accuracy_nb  ## print accuracy
```

5.4.2.3 *Predictive features*

LightSide allowed us to inspect the features to find out which words are typical for which party. Can we also do so in *quanteda*?

The answer is, fortunately, yes. The complex object of the classification model (our variable nb_model) contains values for each word. Let us start with an example where we may have clear expectations. How does the use of the word *God* differ between the two different parties?

```
nb_model$param[,"god"]
dem rep
0.0003677036 0.0007196737
```

Presence of the word *god* seems to point to Republican politicians twice as strongly as to Democrats.

As a next step, we probably want to look at the features more systematically. We can, for instance, sort them in descending order, giving us the strongest features at the top:

```
>head(sort(nb_model$param["rep",],decreasing=T),n=30)
        tax    terrorist         bush         iraq        kerri        terror
0.0026690698 0.0025817658 0.0024134355 0.0021934956 0.0021048338 0.0018606578
       iraqi      freedom        senat         enemi         vote  afghanistan
0.0014515993 0.0014134816 0.0013746416 0.0013547095 0.0013520946 0.0013263236
         war       attack      militari           re         must          peac
0.0013142571 0.0013082427 0.0012270117 0.0011243966 0.0011061986 0.0010593458
      govern        women        georg       weapon       saddam         secur
0.0010499840 0.0010498461 0.0010318257 0.0010307759 0.0010265713 0.0010248987
        forc           ve           11        spend          men         feder
0.0009950923 0.0009782643 0.0009708466 0.0009698244 0.0009672233 0.0009661798

>head(sort(nb_model$param["dem",],decreasing=T),n=30)
      health        insur          kid       school        colleg         crime         educ
0.0017417733 0.0016042614 0.0014966476 0.0013832774 0.0012904518 0.0012446254 0.0011894560
          re         care          got        thing     communiti          bill         parti
0.0011524499 0.0011454772 0.0011438044 0.0011311372 0.0011049884 0.0010621374 0.0010614515
      compani     children       economi      student        invest           tax           mr
0.0010492605 0.0010383141 0.0010231211 0.0010126890 0.0010115202 0.0010042278 0.0010041212
     everybodi          lot        money      deficit        nixon       tonight      problem
0.0009958826 0.0009870878 0.0009643331 0.0009638867 0.0009630375 0.0009614364 0.0009561305
        chang            t
0.0009507279 0.0009482375
```

The output highlights the policy focus of the Republican and Democratic parties. Many of the strongest Republican features directly reflect aspects of Republican policy priorities. There are strong flavours of national security in the top thirty features, among them 'terrorist', 'enemi', 'war', 'attack', 'militari' and several more. There are features pointing to fiscal policy, with 'tax' and 'money'; former Republican presidents, with 'georg' and 'bush'; and we can be quite certain that the feature '11' refers to 9/11.

For Democrats, there are features pointing to Medicare, with 'health', 'insur', 'care', likely also 'bill' (although it will probably also be a reference to Bill Clinton, which would look exactly the same as a result of our pre-processing); education is a big theme as well, with 'school', 'colleg', 'educ' and 'student' featuring prominently; and there is also a sense of inclusion, with features like 'communiti', 'everybodi' and 'tonight'.

We should state here clearly that these feature tables are great to obtain a high-level overview, first on whether the model managed to roughly identify the key features and second on what the content of a corpus is, like the party programs here, but obviously no conclusions should be drawn merely on the basis of these keywords, but they offer good starting points for what to look for in the text and where to dive in with close reading.

Finally, an important technical remark is due. While the Naïve Bayes algorithm gives equal weight to all features, and this is one reason why the word *naïve* is part of its name, there are several methods to assign weights to features in a post-hoc fashion, that is, after the naïve model has been trained. In *quanteda*, the reported weights are so-called posterior conditional probabilities, the probability of a given word to appear in the class that we consider, in terms of conditional probabilities *p(class|word)*. There are also extensions that aim to include feature weights during the training step (e.g. Lee et al. 2011), but a more frequent method to include feature weights is probably to use different algorithms, such as logistic regression.

5.4.2.4 *Alternative models: Logistic regression*

Logistic regression, which we used with *LightSide*, is also available in *quanteda*. The difference between Naïve Bayes and logistic regression is that every feature is given its optimal weight during the training. Results with logistic regression are typically a bit better, but the training of the model takes longer. Box 5.4 summarizes the commands that need to be different if logistic regression is used. The function for the training is called *textmodel_lr*, the rest of the code uses different variable names to allow a comparison, given in the last two lines.

Box 5.4 Logistic regression and comparison to Naïve Bayes

```
lr_model = textmodel_lr(train_dtm, y=docvars(train_dtm, "party"))
pred_lr = predict(lr_model, newdata=test_dtm)
confmat_lr = table(prediction = pred_lr, PARTY = docvars(test_dtm,
    "party"))
confmat_lr  ## accuracy of logistic regression
confmat_nb  ## accuracy of Naïve Bayes
```

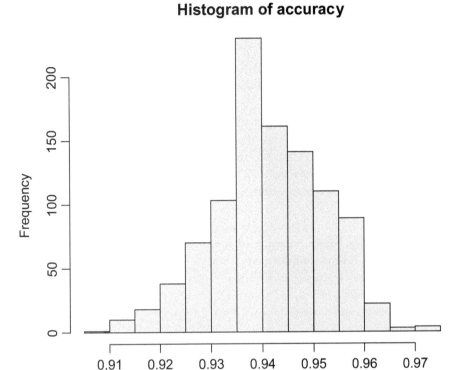

Figure 5.5 Fluctuations and robustness: Distribution of accuracy of 1,000 runs with Naïve Bayes.

5.4.2.5 *Robustness and fluctuations*

Due to the random sampling, every run of the program reports slightly different results. We could fix the random seed (with the function *set.seed*) to ensure reproducibility, but this would also sweep the problem under the rug. In *LightSide*, fluctuations are very small due to n-fold cross-validation. In *quanteda*, there is no built-in n-fold cross-validation function. A good proxy to obtain more robust evaluations is to train several times, each time with a different random sample, then report the mean of the accuracy as a reliable accuracy figure and its standard deviation as an assessment of worst and best-case scenarios, or simply which fluctuation that we need to expect.

Training several times is achieved most easily with a loop. Make sure to keep all accuracy values in a list, indexed by the loop number. The (normal) distribution of 1,000 Naïve Bayes runs is given in Figure 5.5. The mean accuracy is 94.1 per cent and the standard deviation is 0.1 per cent. With logistic regression, we obtained a mean accuracy of 95.6 per cent and a standard deviation of 0.08 per cent.

Further Reading

Grimmer and Stewart (2013): An excellent introduction to and overview of content analysis from the perspective of political science with a strong focus on supervised classification (Chapter 5), but also explaining several unsupervised approaches (e.g. topic modelling, see Chapter 7). It also summarizes many case studies. Highly recommended unless you are an expert in document classification and political science.

Welbers et al. (2017): An introduction to using *quanteda* for text classification and pre-processing. Highly recommended, as reference and in order to get a different perspective. The code contains typos, so use the one shown in this chapter instead.

Mayfiled et al. (2014): The *LightSide* Manual. Highly recommended to get to know all the functions of *LightSide*, and many practical hints, such as how to increase the memory allocated to *LightSide*.

Topic Modelling

6.1 Theoretical background

In Chapter 5, we have seen document classification. Yet, interpreting feature spaces of thousands of items, which is needed in document classification, is demanding and possibly confusing, and the fact that synonyms and related words are completely ignored is a disadvantage for semantic investigations. We can learn topics from the context by relying on the Firthian hypothesis (Section 1.2), which has become popular, thanks to the quote 'You shall know the meaning of a word by the company it keeps' (Firth 1957: 179). It expresses that 'words with similar distributional properties have similar meanings' (Sahlgren 2006: 21), words which often co-occur have similar meanings. Quantitative linguists exploit the Firthian hypothesis in order to detect collocations (e.g. Evert 2009). Sahlgren (2006) shows that the size of the observation window plays a crucial role in finding out about such collocation patterns of a word. He discusses that using adjacent words (or very small observation windows) delivers classical collocations, that is, syntagmatic relations, while extending the window to include increasingly more context delivers results on the paradigmatic axis, that is, synonyms, antonyms and associations. This is exploited by the hugely successful paradigm of distributional semantics (e.g. Baroni and Lenci 2010), which we will introduce in Chapter 8.

The insights into the relationship between words, documents and contexts have also given birth to the method of topic modelling (Blei 2012). Topic modelling and document classification exploit the fact that documents usually display a semantic coherence which parallels the strong semantic unity of the discourse of a topic. Topic modelling, thus, even extends the semantic context beyond the level of a single document to the level of topics of similar documents. Specific topics are very likely to generate the use of specific words. One of the most popular methods, Latent Dirichlet Allocation (LDA), works as follows.

LDA optimizes p(*topic*|*document*) * p(*word*|*topic*) for all given documents in a collection. It thus combines document classification (p(*topic*|*document*)) as used in Chapter 5 and keyword generation (p(*word*|*topic*)), which we have seen in Chapter 4. In the approach of topic modelling, *documents* and *words* are given, and the *topics* are fitted iteratively by the model, starting from a random configuration. By contrast, in document classification, the classes are manually annotated and thus given. For topic modelling, the main parameter that the users have to set is the number of topics that they want to mine for.

In R experiments, we will also use structural topic modelling (STM), an extension to LDA which uses available metadata to steer the algorithm. In particular, the relationship between the classes and the metadata can be considered. For instance, is a topic more important in an early period or for a certain political party, gender, media type, newspaper, country and so on?

For many well-studied domains, the mapping from words to concepts is available in the form of thesauri, which have been developed carefully and are often inspired by corpus research. A tool for mapping words to concepts is the rule-based system *WMatrix*[1] (Rayson 2008). This approach performs well on general newspaper texts; however, more specific genres and historical texts often end up with unsatisfactory analyses, as many of the words have undergone strong semantic shifts or have domain-specific readings. Thus, topic modelling offers a viable alternative if large amounts of domain data are available.

A particular appeal of topic models is that they are completely data-driven, and no annotated data is needed as in document classification. Document classification is a prototypical *supervised method* – the learning is supervised to fit the provided, annotated classes. Topic modelling is a prototypical *unsupervised method*: all results are derived from the data, and no metadata is used.

While the annotated categories that we used for document classification (party affiliation or period) are uncontested, there are many borderline cases if one uses categories such as genres, styles, newspaper sections or semantic categories, and different annotators would categorize these differently. In other words, inter-annotator agreement may be low, and even the number and labels of categories are often contested, and can depend on one's social, educational or political background, and they are influenced by pre-conceived theories. By contrast, topic models are free from these constraints and conform with the vision of a purely data-driven science, as it is expressed by John Sinclair, a pioneer of corpus linguistics.

> We should strive to be open to the patterns observable in language ... and rebuild
> a picture of language and meaning which is not only consistent with the evidence
> but also exploits it to the full ... the first stage should be an attempt to inspect the
> data with as little attention as possible to theory. (Sinclair and Carter 2004: 10)

But topic models have also come under criticism: first, reliance on data places very high demands on the balancedness and representativeness of the data. An early warning, also from the corpus linguistics tradition, is voiced by Tognini-Bonelli (2001):

> since the information provided by the corpus is placed centrally and accounted
> for exhaustively, then there is a risk of error if the corpus turns out to be
> unrepresentative. (Tognini-Bonelli 2001: 88)

The voices of enthusiasm and criticism mirror the views on largely data-driven approaches such as those we have discussed in Section 1.3 in the context of culturomics (Kitchin 2014, Prensky 2009). Topic models do not deliver solutions, but just patterns at very different levels. Many of the patterns relate to the found topics, but some also show stylistic differences or are due to biases in the selection of data. As a practical concern, the performance of data-driven methods largely relies on, and strongly correlates to, the size of the data. Very often, topic modelling is applied to corpora that are basically too small. While it is hard to give a lower boundary as exact figure, corpora smaller than a few hundred thousand words are hardly suitable; several millions are usually needed to obtain good results.

Second, topic models are difficult to evaluate. We have just mentioned performance, but how can we measure that? Tognini-Bonelli's quote sounds like a categorical distinction: as if there were representative and unrepresentative corpora. In reality, every corpus is partly representative and also the most carefully balanced corpus is only representative up to a point, and only of a certain variety, population group, text type or the keywords that we used to collect a corpus. Even the largest corpora, such as web-scrapes, while they do not have a sparse data problem, still overrepresent certain genres and do not represent native English very well, as the majority of writers are L2 English speakers. Since representativeness is a matter of degree, a quantitative assessment (of how much, that is, how much does a given corpus represent the given genre in which we are interested and how much does our topic model represent the categories found in them) becomes central.

But topic models are hard to evaluate, as we cannot easily compare them to a manually created uncontested reference, a so-called *gold standard*, like in document classification. Let us review some suggestions that have been made to evaluate topic models in the following.

Röder et al. (2015) suggest an automated evaluation method using distributional semantics (Chapter 8) to assess the similarity of keywords using cosine distance. The topic model in which the cosine distance between the top *n* words of each topic is lowest on average is assumed to be the best one. But this approach also has shortcomings. It relies (a) on another unsupervised and partly related method (distributional semantics) which leads to a circularity of the argument, and (b) aims to measure semantic similarity of the keywords, which is one aspect, but partly fails to assess associations, which is another important aspect of meaningful topics.

Quinn et al. (2010) and Grimmer and Stewart (2013) suggest to distinguish between *semantic* validity, in which the internal coherence of individual topics is assessed, and *predictive* validity, in which a given topic is assessed in comparison to external reference, that is, other topics and expected events.

Semantic validity can be judged manually by scanning the keywords and judging how coherent they are, and by evaluating how easily and consistently human annotators can label the topics. Predictive validity measures how well variation in topic usage corresponds with expected events (or other metadata) and how distinct the topics are from each other. Correspondence with events can be assessed by looking for peaks in the frequency graphs that reflect important historical facts. We can further find out how distinct topics are by checking if they have little overlap, for example, if human annotators can easily give a different label to each topic. We find that Quinn et al's (2010) method is a reasonable operationalization for an evaluation, even though it fails to give us exact numerical data, which in practice makes it hard to assess which of the two suggested topic models that were created using slightly different parameters is better.

Third, even running a topic model on the same data with the same parameters does not guarantee an equal outcome. Many algorithms, including the one used in *mallet* and *stm* (LDA = Latent Dirichlet Allocation), which we introduce in the following, start from a random configuration. This means that the results differ from one run of the algorithm to another. This is, on the one hand, bad news for reproducibility (although we can set random seeds) and bad news for building trust in the algorithm. On the other hand, it is also a chance: it allows us to run a topic model several times, and if we see that the large majority of generated topics are reconstituted form each time, this is an indicator of robustness.

Fourth, as the algorithm is more complicated, topic models are more of a 'blackbox' algorithm, and it is hard for us to understand what really happens under the hood. Convincing results, compatible results using other methods, compatibility to existing theory and careful close reading (Moretti 2013) are, therefore, important elements to build trust.

One characteristic of data-driven approaches is that they partly revert the roles of hypothesis building and application. Traditionally, theory building and hypothesis building come first and these are then tested on the data. In the most extreme form of data-driven approaches, no theory is used and all the categories are shaped by the patterns found in the data. In this sense, topic models are a method that belongs to the fourth paradigm (Section 1.3, Hey et al. 2009, Kitchin 2014). But the human researcher still has to interpret the output, which is not necessarily easier than forming a theory in the beginning. In practical terms, theory building and hypothesis building are usually inspired by data, and metadata reflecting categories and theories may be added to topic models, and topic models contradicting established theories need to be scrutinized carefully with other methods. While for some researchers, mixing the orders of theory-building and application comes close to a sacrilege, paradigms have started to shift. A data-driven paradigm is used in system biology (Ananiadou 2006):

> In the data-rich but hypothesis-poor sciences, including functional genomics and most of biomedicine, the normative hypothesis-driven, deductive scientific method becomes increasingly difficult to sustain. . . . As a complement to hypothesis-driven deductive science, we are now witnessing the emergence of data-driven inductive methods of scientific discovery. These are characterized by the rapid 'mining' of candidate hypotheses from the literature. (Ananiadou et al. 2006: 571)

The use and systematic comparison of different methods (e.g. topic models and document classification) and/or perspectives (e.g. theory-driven and data-driven) are establishing itself under the label of *triangulation* (Munafò and Smith 2018):

> Triangulation is the strategic use of multiple approaches to address one question. Each approach has its own unrelated assumptions, strengths and weaknesses. Results that agree across different methodologies are less likely to be artefacts. Isn't this how science is meant to operate?
>
> (Munafò and Smith 2018: 400).

Also in linguistics and content analysis, data-driven approaches are used increasingly. Schwartz and Ungar (2015) state that they are more flexible in detecting changing patterns over time, as they bring to the surface patterns arising from the data. Thus, Schneider (2022a, 2022a) uses a data-driven approach to historical linguistics. Schneider (2020b) presents a triangulation of methods to trace the concept of poverty from 1470 to 2000 and coins the term *system history* for such approaches. Our following case study is set up in a similar vein, using a different source of data and the method of topic modelling, which is discussed in this chapter, but also comparing to the case study with the same corpus in Chapter 5.

6.2 Case studies

In the following, we use the completely data-driven method of topic modelling (Blei 2012) to explore two studies. For our experiments we are using Mallet (MAchine Learning for LanguagE Toolkit).[2]

6.2.1 Old Bailey Corpus

Changes in society go beyond exchanging one word for another. While investigating word-based features in Section 5.2 allowed us to describe some changes, we can further use an approach that also takes synonyms and associations into consideration, and thus allows us to detect trends and conceptual changes in society and reveal shifting topics. In this study, we focus on which topics are important at which period. We trace various types of crime, ranging from manslaughter to theft and royal offences. We investigate increase and decrease over time, and ask whether spikes can be detected at any period. The OBC is a very good source for such research as it enables us to track societal problems like poverty and crime, thus giving poor people a voice, although in very specific settings.

Stylistic differences, for example the expression of moral attitudes, social standing and subtle lexical choices, which we have investigated in Section 5.2, involve linguistic form and content to an equal degree. Studying the one without respecting the other would lead to a one-sided impression. We are thus obliged to also consider the context, in particular changes in society, legal language and legal proceedings. Historical pragmatics, the study of historical changes in language use, according to Taavitsainen and Jucker (2015), has undergone a number of important changes in thought style, increasing the importance of social context. The latest change is the turn towards interdisciplinarity, with linguists, sociologists and historians collaborating. In this perspective, connecting disciplines, such as stylistics, moves to the core: 'linguistic stylistics and corpus stylistics should be mentioned as particularly relevant and fruitful sources of inspiration for historical pragmatic studies' (Taavitsainen and Jucker 2015: 16). This sine qua non condition is also stressed in Culpeper and Kytö (2010): 'pragmatics takes the view that language is a societal phenomenon, and also emphasise use, uses and contexts' (Culpeper and Kytö (2010: 8). We shed light on the social context in Section 5.2; now we focus on the semantic context.

Societal findings show, among other things, that theft (e.g. *stealing*, see Section 5.2) decreases and deception increases. But the types of crimes, such as a highway robbery, home servants, mutiny, seafaring, forgery and corruption, are changing. While these findings may not be surprising for insiders and historians, data-driven approaches like topic modelling allow us to extract these insights automatically from the data. Thus they do not only provide further quantitative support to previous hypotheses but also allow users to automatically analyse such changes without following up specialized research literature on the context.

While investigating word-based features in Section 5.2 allowed us to describe some changes, we need an approach that also takes synonyms and associations into consideration to detect trends and conceptual changes in society, and reveal shifting topics. We employ topic modelling in the following to do so.

Topic models give us a chance to detect the topics of criminality in society and in the courtroom, and how they change over time. As the entire protocol contains valuable background information, which is particularly important for a semantic analysis, we are using not only the utterances but the entire protocol, including important meta-information, for example the category of the indictment, the same data as in Section 5.2.

6.2.1.1 A detailed example

We are now going to discuss one topic model in some detail. It is a run with fifty topics. The keywords of the topics are given in Table 6.1. Our manual interpretation of the topic is given in the second column. Our decision on which manual label to give to a topic was based on the keywords and on reading the most prototypical document for each topic. In about forty topics, a clear semantic class arises. In four topics, which we have labelled *RAGBAG*, the keywords are so unspecific that no convincing interpretation arises. These are topics which either contain many high frequency and thus unspecific nouns (*time, thing, man, day,*

Table 6.1 Topic Model with Fifty Topics of OBC

ID	WEIGHT	MANUAL	KEYWORDS
0	0.0042	POISONING	smell acid bottle bones premises smelt factory quantity medicine night poison day arsenic examined smells state water stomach pills
1	0.0725	*RAGBAG*	house time told thing man day sworn asked master court desired woman night till give put brought long home
2	0.0208	CHEQUES/ BANKING	letter cheque letters office received writing order wrote gave examined cheques signed money book write produced found asked clerk
3	0.0372	PICKPOCKETS	handkerchief pocket person hand gentleman pocketpicking book theft indicted found felt put guilty picked defence transport stealing turned property
4	0.0363	GOLD/SILVER	silver spoons gold ring spoon pair rings buckles plate things property house table tankard diamond tea forks set goods
5	0.0358	DECEPTION	evidence indicted deception notguilty false intent prosecution fraud ticket perjury offered case defraud indictment trial noevidence court guilty pretences
6	0.0201	HORSES	horse horses coach stable cab mare cart coachman chaise man drove road harness yard rode pony saddle stables drive
7	0.0306	WATCHES	watch chain gold silver seal found person watches gave property key seals stealing house pocket lost clock case night
8	0.0702	POCKETING	hand hold man put pocket round time side laid arm turned immediately made heard left called hands ran held
9	0.0978	categories	aged guilty theft indicted goods clock john subcategory imprison shop months live policeman simplelarceny gave confined asked missed constable
10	0.0390	POLICE	examined station man police made charged men charge asked months told arrested back statement years identified guilty left gave
11	0.0678	DAYTIMES	clock house night morning home left till day past ten time bed evening live hour minutes eleven room twelve
12	0.0324	METALS/ FORGERY	work found copper iron metal pieces tools piece house made wood shop brass things worked mark produced put timber
13	0.0431	*RAGBAG*	time made case thing evidence man court sworn great make part person order read gentlemen present law writing letter

Table 6.1 (Continued)

ID	WEIGHT	MANUAL	KEYWORDS
14	0.0337	WAREHOUSE/ GOODS	bag warehouse parcel tea weight sugar pounds found bags pound put chest tobacco bacon soap lb parcels lbs goods
15	0.0627	DRUNKENNESS	house beer woman asked man pot drink pint bar night drinking called liquor gave glass drunk clock sober drank
16	0.0551	MONEY	money pocket shillings purse found half silver guineas put guinea shilling sovereigns sovereign pence gave hand halfpence searched till
17	0.0745	ARREST	ran man stop thief heard running run back stopped yards boy sight cry pursued hold street door corner coming
18	0.0291	HEAD INJURIES	struck head examined blow knocked man face fell hit back house drunk policeman strike time ground heard hand ran
19	0.0207	WINE CELLAR	basket cellar bottles wine bottle butter bread cheese cask loaves put candles casks master oil gallons brandy baker dozen
20	0.0747	THEFT	found stealing guilty indicted property things theft defence brought deposed house lost transport grandlarceny told summary produced owned sold
21	0.0153	FIRE	fire lead house burnt place pipe found premises shop fixed part building piece floor smoke put water set hole
22	0.0139	VIOLENT MURDER	deceased murder death wound died heard kill body dead side struck head time blood man fell blow beat strike
23	0.0231	sell / deliver	goods sold books book order examined bought business paper stock received made paid delivered price amp invoice sell shop
24	0.0521	HONEST CHARACTER	years man character heard time good honest thing house live knew months work ago lived long year business day
25	0.0640	ROOMS	room door stairs bed house found back wife floor heard kitchen open parlour asked table clock put opened passage
26	0.0486	SHOPLIFTING	shop piece yards silk cloth pieces counter handkerchiefs asked door lace cotton back goods woman yard brought bought mark
27	0.0670	CLOTH	things linen gown pair goods bundle shirt sheets house wife property apron silk woman cloak sheet shirts petticoat room

(Continued)

Table 6.1 (Continued)

ID	WEIGHT	MANUAL	KEYWORDS
28	0.0790	COURT verdict	guilty imprison months pleadedguilty theft pleaded confined aged indicted years simplelarceny imprisonment goods convicted sexual twelve hard john labour
29	0.0307	HIGHWAY ROBBERY	hat pistol robbed violenttheft money highway fear men putting prisoners man highwayrobbery robbery taking life death indicted person night
30	0.0551	categories	prisoners examined policeman station found clock custody back minutes yards asked side time past conducted morning standing prosecution road
31	0.0843	*RAGBAG*	time examined house told day person made asked swear gave left court knew heard magistrate called recollect till custody
32	0.0576	PAWN	box found pawnbroker things pawned room house property left articles gave key pledged duplicate missed trunk duplicates produced boxes
33	0.0203	LIVESTOCK	sheep meat field skins found house morning butcher beef fowls bought market pigs live mutton pork clock skin animaltheft
34	0.0228		time told remember made day examined paper left room asked put place back evidence wanted case business people heard
35	0.0164	CHILDREN	child time children found death examined body day told bed baby state asked doctor died made appeared mother water
36	0.0599		told found man money call time depos made gave put brought wife till heard give half indicted death open
37	0.0524	FASHION	pair coat shoes boots stockings waistcoat breeches leather shop found things cloth clothes trowsers coats pairs property goods stealing
38	0.0478	*RAGBAG*	man men time coat minutes swear face side light person heard court round knew dark hat asked looked yards
39	0.0225	FORGED NOTES/ FRAUD	note notes bill money book writing bank paid bills pound received gave forged clerk house pounds paper person pay
40	0.1572	THEFT	indicted stealing theft guilty grandlarceny transport summary property notguilty theftunder acquitted val feloniously found evidence theftfromplace privately fact goods

Table 6.1 (Continued)

ID	WEIGHT	MANUAL	KEYWORDS
41	0.0501	FAMILY	wife father mother husband married years sister son brother daughter live house lived woman told home girl living boy
42	0.0610	BREAK-INS	house door found window open night morning clock broke breaking burglary glass broken heard entering locked key opened back
43	0.1298		sworn property stealing indicted guilty theft aged john defence grandlarceny feloniously found house officer gave clock produced asked constable
44	0.0155	WOUNDING/ SHOOTING	knife wound cut hand blood stabbed wounding found shot left revolver intent wounds fired side heard harm murder bodily
45	0.0156	SHIP	board ship boat captain vessel barge shore mate rope water deck time cabin river men side man gun ships
46	0.0824	actions	asked told money gave man bought give sold pay sell wanted paid brought buy back shop knew morning day
47	0.0248	FALSE COINS	gave bad shilling crown found shop put change good counterfeit coin asked sixpence half till money shillings back piece
48	0.0237	HAY TRUCK	cart van sack sacks hay yard waggon man put coals carman morning load truck examined back wharf stable oats
49	0.0202	BOOKKEEPING	paid money account received book business pay made company time receipt signed office bill examined books amount shares week

person) or can be found in most documents from the court trial domain (*court, guilty, indicted, property, things, theft, defence*).

As we can see from Table 6.1, society and linguistics are tightly related. Topic 24 (*honest character*) relates to reputation and moral attitudes. It peaks early and falls off after 1800, giving way to more scientific and less subjective assessment. Moral discussions typically involve modal verbs. Their frequency drops considerably, which suggests that moral discussions are indeed decreasing in the data. A de-contextualized linguistic study on modal verbs would risk reporting flawed results.

In the following, we look at excerpts from the most prototypical trials for these topics. All the chosen excerpts come from trials for which topic modelling suggested the illustrated topic as central to the complete trial.

6.2.1.2 *Prototypical documents*

In this section we look at prototypical documents from selected topics, bridging the gap between distant reading and close reading (Moretti 2013). This step is important to verify if our manual labels are appropriate and if the topics really contain what our interpretation of the keywords suggested. Note that important meta-information, such as the method of punishment (e.g. *royalOffences*), has been taken over from the text.

Topic 0, POISONING:
18910209-215 [Witness] I am a registered medical practitioner at 29, King David Lane, Shadwell — I received from Mr. Morton this bottle – I examined its contents – apart from analysis I came to the conclusion that it contained phosphorus – it is a poisonous substance – a grain or 1 1/2 grains of phosphorus is sufficient to cause death – there would be 4 or 5 grains in this bottle, sufficient to destroy life

Topic 5, DECEPTION:
19110328-45 SALZINGER MAX (29, musician) guilty pleadedGuilty deception fraud Manchester, in the County of Lancaster, feloniously causing to be inserted in a register of marriages a certain false entry of a matter relating to his marriage with Martha Gobel, to wit, a false entry of the age of the said Martha Gobel. miscPunish Prisoner was released on his own recognances in £50 to come up for judgment if called upon.

Topic 8, POCKETS AND PICKPOCKETING:
18040111-43 I put my hand into the drawer in the counter, and missed my money directly; I asked him what he had done with my money; you villain, says I, you have got my money in your pocket; he put his hand in his pocket, and took out two shillings and a penny; I said, you have got one shilling more in your pocket; he said, he had not a farthing in the world more; he put his hand in his pocket, and pulled out a shilling among some halfpence.

Topic 12, METALS/FORGERY:
18000528-7 EDWARDS JONES, alias DIGHT, and MARY CAMPBELL, alias DIGHT, were indicted for that royalOffences coiningOffences they, on the 24th of April, a piece of false and counterfeit money to the likeness of a shilling, falsely, deceitfully, and traiterously did forge, counterfeit and coin.

Topic 14, WAREHOUSE/GOODS:
18000219-38 the prisoner was employed, with some others, to house some chests of sugar; he had been up about an hour, I had reason to suspect him before, and

I kept my eye upon him; as he came down stairs, I saw some sugar upon his jacket; I immediately went to him, and asked him to let me see what he had got in his pocket; I laid hold of his pockets, and found them to be full of sugar; . . . Prisoner's defence. I have nothing to say. guilty GUILTY. (Aged 22.) imprison Confined one month in Newgate, and fined 1s.

Topic 15, DRUNKENNESS:
17630413-31 About a month ago I had some people in my house drinking beer, there came two foreigners in my house, after they had been knocked down, that had met with some English sailors in the street, they had quarrelled; there came almost two hundred English sailors, the prisoner was one of them, they stripped my house entirely. The prisoner went into my cellar and drank four pots of porter; after that I saw him go up stairs, and break the lock of one of my chests; the rest of the sailors came to knock me down.

Topic 17, ARRESTING THE SUSPECT:
18210912-32 the prisoner pretended to stumble in the kennell, he snatched the prosecutrix's ridicule from her hand, and ran up the alley, I pursued him, three or four little boys came from the doorway, and ran by his side for some way. I kept him in sight, till he was stopped. He made a desperate resistance by kicking and fighting.

Topic 18, HEAD INJURIES:
18741123-47 the moment Wragg said 'Kick the b — — brains out' Duffy seized me, struck me on the side of the head and knocked me down, and the other prisoners all came round and kicked me and struck me with their whips until one of them said 'I think we have given the b — — enough.'

Topic 24, HONEST CHARACTER:
17600416-3 [Lawyer] What is his general character? Rogers. [Witness] A very honest sober young man. William Herbert. [Witness] I live in Rupert Street, and have known him betwixt four and five years. Q. [Lawyer] What is his character? Herbert. [Witness] He is a very honest man for what ever I have heard. Thomas Pollard. [Witness] I have known him from his birth; he was born in the house where I have lived forty years, and I never saw any thing amiss of him; he is a very honest industrious man. John Collier. [Witness] I am a peruke maker; I knew him four or five years before he work'd with Mr. Pitman. Q. [Lawyer] What has been his behaviour? Collier. [Witness] He is very honest as far as I know or have heard. John Pool. [Witness] I have known him about three years. Q. [Lawyer] What is his general character? Pool. [Witness] I always look'd upon

him to be a very honest man. I am a cabinet-maker. He bought ten pounds worth of goods of me, to furnish a room, and was to pay me so much a week, which he did very honestly; it is almost paid. guilty Guilty. transport [Transportation].

Topic 26, SHOPLIFTING:
18120115-59 the prisoner came to the shop accompanied by another woman, the other woman asked to look at some silk handkerchiefs, I produced forty or fifty silk handkerchiefs. . . . I took the prisoner into our accompting-house, she produced five pieces of silk handkerchiefs from under her coat.

Topic 27, CLOTH:
17501017-30 Thomas Price was indicted for theft grandLarceny stealing 2 linen aprons, value 2 s. 3 linen hoods; one linen cap; one pair of lawn ruffles; 3 dimitty stomachers, and other things , the goods of persons unknown. Sept. 28. notGuilty Acquitted

While topics 26 and 27 have a clear focus, they are closely related. This makes it difficult to distinguish. If in a temporal analysis the one increases while the other decreases, it is difficult to interpret what this should mean.

Topic 39, FORGED NOTES/FRAUD:
18100411-141. GEORGE DAVEY was indicted for that royalOffences coiningOffences he on the 18th of December, without lawful excuse had in his custody and possession a forged bank note for the payment of two pounds. To this indictment the prisoner pleaded. guilty pleadedGuilty GUILTY. transport Transported for Fourteen Years. Second Middlesex jury, before Mr. Recorder.

Topic 46, verbs of action:
18300218-124 I did not hear him at the time he was taken, say he had bought it; I asked him to let me look at it – he said he should not. GEORGE DOWDING. [Witness] I stopped the prisoner last Saturday, at seven o'clock, and asked where he got the umbrella from; he would not tell me – I endeavoured to get it from him: he struggled very much – he did not say he had bought it; I took him to Bow-street.

Topic 47, FALSE COINS:
18610128-208 [Witness] I am the landlord of the General Havelock beerhouse, Woolwich – yesterday week, between 11 and 12 o'clock in the morning, the prisoner came in there and asked for a pint of half-and-half – I drew it for him, and, upon that, he threw down a fourpenny piece – I supposed it to be bad, the moment I saw it, and prevented him from drinking the beer – the prosecutor and

a constable came in in less than three minutes – I gave the prisoner in custody, and gave the policeman the fourpenny piece

Summing up, we can see that the topics offer a good overview of the subject areas that appear in the corpus and thus also give an insight into society. The topics mirror types of offences, descriptions of the characters of suspects and scenes of arrestation. As a next step, we could compare how far these topics occur in other legal corpora, or general reference corpora, or how they develop over time inside the OBC – this is what we will do in Section 6.2.1.4.

6.2.1.3 *Granularity*

Some topics are closely related, for example 12, 39 and 47. While topic 12 describes the fabrication of forged money, 47 is more concerned with its circulation, and 39 contains forgery of bank notes rather than coins. When topics are very closely related, there is a true problem of interpretation in topic modelling: Does the suggested split between two related topics reflect a real difference, or is it an artefact of the data? This increasingly turns into an issue if the number of topics is very high. Conversely, if only a few topics are chosen, a very coarse granularity often does not express many of the topics that we are hoping to find in our data. Choosing an approximately appropriate number of topics is one of the biggest challenges when working with topic models.

6.2.1.4 *Temporal development*

The temporal development of these three topics is given in Figure 6.1. While in earlier periods there are more references to the production of coins, in the later periods there are more convictions of people who are caught trying to spend them. Due to progress in technology, it was increasingly easy to produce forged coins in larger numbers, shifting the convictions from the producers to the users. Coining offences contributed only 0.4 per cent of all offences in 1720–70, rising to 2 per cent in 1770–1820 and to 6.5 per cent in 1820–70, according to the OBC metadata.

Not only coins but also notes were forged, as topic 39 shows. The topic shows a strong peak from 1800 to 1820. Searching history reveals that during the so-called Bank Restriction Period, forgery of notes reached a peak.

> Between 1797 and 1821 the Bank of England issued its smallest denomination notes to date, for the values of just one and two pounds sterling. Although these were not the first small denomination notes to circulate in England, they were certainly the first to do so on anywhere near approaching what might be

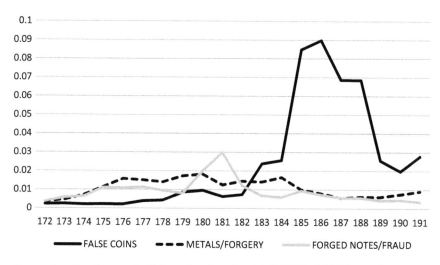

Figure 6.1 Development of the related topics 47 (FALSE COINS), 47 (METALS/FORGERY) and 39 (FORGED NOTES/FRAUD) in OBC.

considered a national scale. Previous accounts of this period have generally suggested that as Bank Notes were now falling into the hands of so-called ignorant and illiterate people, this created an opportunity for established counterfeiters to turn their attention to this new form of currency crime en masse. Although the suspension of gold payments that led to the issue of these new notes was intended as a temporary measure, the legislation continued to be renewed by Parliament, and resumption of payments in gold did not fully occur for over two decades. The circulation of this new paper increased almost continuously between 1797 and 1821, with the period witnessing what Randall McGowen has called 'an epidemic of forgery', during which over 2000 people were prosecuted for forgery and the uttering of forged notes. (Mockford 2014: 4)

Our observed trend, that money forgery is strongly increasing, is confirmed by the metadata of convictions (see Section 4.3). But the trends of note forgery in the Bank Restriction Period and the shift towards convicting persons for the utterance of forged money could only be detected by a deeper analysis of the texts, such as our method of topic modelling.

While the topics of forging money steeply increased, other criminal offences seem to stay more stable. Let us look at the worst crimes, killing, murder and manslaughter, which are covered by topics 0, 22 and 44. These three topics are compared in Figure 6.2. We have added topic 18 (HEAD INJURIES), which is different as only a smaller fraction of the victims died. Comparing 0, 22 and 44 we notice that killing people by beating and striking (0) seems to decrease, while the spread of firearms leads to a steep increase in shootings (44); stabbing

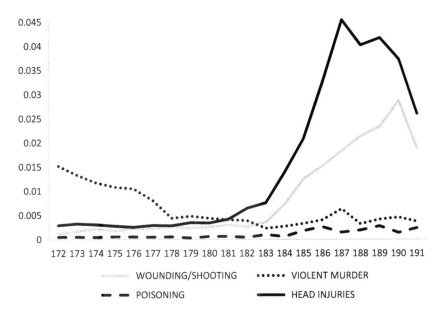

Figure 6.2 Development of the related topics 0 (POISONING), 18 (HEAD INJURIES), 22 (VIOLENT MURDER) and 44 (WOUNDING/SHOOTING) in OBC.

also increases (44) – although not necessarily involving a lethal outcome. Technological advances bring firearms, but the production of poison (0) is also easier, leading to more cases of poisoning, although the level remains lower than shooting (44).

Figure 6.2 also gives one the impression that although people were killed at all times, the period from about 1780 to 1840 was relatively calm. This impression is also confirmed by the number of prosecutions (Section 4.3): while killing contributes to 3 per cent of all cases in the period of 1720–70, it drops to almost 1 per cent in 1770–1870, rising again to 4 per cent in 1870–1920. Also, in absolute numbers, we see first a decrease and then a small increase after 1870. Reasons for the decrease are unclear but probably related to the slowly increasing wages, education and quality of life, the effects of the civilizing process, strengthening state powers, the Protestant Reformation and modern individualism. Roth (2001) confirms a steady decrease in homicides from 1600 to 1800 across all regions of England and many European countries.

The most modern topics in Table 6.1 are POLICE (10), CHEQUES/BANKING (2), BOOKKEEPING (49), and DECEPTION (5). POLICE (10) is a late topic because a regular police force was only introduced in 1829 and their influence only gradually increased. CHEQUES/BANKING (2) and BOOKKEEPING (49) show the advance of modern banking techniques and administration. A well-organized administrative system also invites a high number of DECEPTION attempts (5).

Some of the topics that are initially important decrease considerably or almost disappear over time. Examples are GOLD/SILVER (4), HONEST CHARACTER (24), CLOTH (27), HIGHWAY ROBBERY (29) and, a bit later, HORSES (6) and LIVESTOCK (33). As a sign of hope, DRUNKENNESS(15) is also decreasing. We compare these topics in Figure 6.3, without detailed discussion, as the developments are largely expected: for example, HONEST CHARACTER is decreasing as the limited value of character judgements and a good repute is increasingly being recognized. CLOTH (27) is partly shifting to its related but later topic of FASHION (37) and GOLD/SILVER (4) to WATCHES (7).

Several of the topics in Table 6.1 are very unspecific; they contain keywords that are generally frequent (e.g. *time, thing, man, make* in topic 13 or *house, time, thing, day* in topic 1) or keywords that are typical of the courtroom domain (e.g. *aged, guilty, theft, imprison* in topic 9). We have given them the label RAGBAG. Most of these topics are strongest in the early decades,

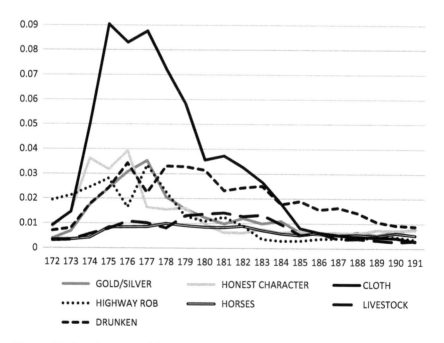

Figure 6.3 Development of the relatively early topics GOLD/SILVER (4), HONEST CHARACTER (24), CLOTH (27), HIGHWAY ROBBERY (29), HORSES (6) and LIVESTOCK (33) and DRUNKENNESS(15) in OBC.

which are dominated by theft. Yet, records of what was said in the trials are rare and incomplete in the early data. This means that many trials look very similar and the bias of differing protocol styles, in particular the fact that dialogues are largely missing in the early data, adds a skew which, as far as we can see, cannot be explained by historical trends. These topics show us the strong limitations of both the skewed corpus and the problem of the method of topic modelling. Yet, the data and the method provide us with interesting and comparatively easily obtainable results, and may manage to give us an overview of the period.

Topic modelling gave us some insights into the topics surrounding criminal behaviour and the courtroom. We also discovered societal changes: killings are decreasing, shootings are increasing, fashionwear instead of fabrics are stolen and highway robbery almost disappears. What has not disappeared, however, is that English society shows a marked, and probably widening, difference between rich and poor, and the divide between social classes is very pronounced.

6.2.2 Topics in Charles Dickens' writings

As the second case study, we consider topics from Charles Dickens' writings. We have downloaded the following eight Dickens' novels from Project Gutenberg and describe how readers can do so themselves.

- *A Christmas Carol*
- *David Copperfield*
- *Great Expectations*
- *Hard Times*
- *Nicholas Nickleby*
- *Oliver Twist*
- *The Pickwick Papers*
- *A Tale of Two Cities*

There are typically no direct comments, no abstract discussions of poverty in Dickens' novels but a very descriptive and suggestive, often ironic, style – which may be particularly difficult for any automatic content analysis method. Think of the famous beginning of *Oliver Twist*:

> *Although I am not disposed to maintain that the being born in a workhouse, is in itself the most fortunate and enviable circumstance that can possibly befall a human being, I do mean to say that in this particular instance, it was the best thing for Oliver Twist that could by possibility have occurred. The fact is, that there*

was considerable difficulty in inducing Oliver to take upon himself the office of respiration,– a troublesome practice, but one which custom has rendered necessary to our easy existence; and for some time he lay gasping on a little flock mattress, rather unequally poised between this world and the next: the balance being decidedly in favour of the latter. Now, **if, during this brief period, Oliver had been surrounded by careful grandmothers, anxious aunts, experienced nurses, and doctors of profound wisdom, he would most inevitably and indubitably have been killed in no time. There being nobody by, however, but a pauper old woman, who was rendered rather misty by an unwonted allowance of beer; and a parish surgeon who did such matters by contract;** *Oliver and Nature fought out the point between them. The result was, that, after a few struggles, Oliver breathed, sneezed, and proceeded to* **advertise to the inmates of the workhouse the fact of a new burden having been imposed upon the parish,** *by setting up as loud a cry as could reasonably have been expected from a male infant who had not been possessed of that very useful appendage, a voice, for a much longer space of time than three minutes and a quarter.* (Charles Dickens 1838. *Oliver Twist*, London: Bentley. Emphasis added)

We have thus run a topic model on the novels given above. To make sure that the topic model does not mainly follow individual novels, we have replaced all proper names (according to the *Tree-Tagger*) by the placeholder 'np'.

The raw output of the topics in these novels, without manual interpretation, is given in Table 6.2. The topics which are easily interpretable are given in boldprint. We can see topics describing *horses and carts,* allegedly *honourable company managers, poor* as term of *affection in the family,* the *copyright* line, descriptions of *body parts, light & dark, vernacular speech, writing, descriptions of rooms* and scenes of *drinking and eating.* Particularly these two, but also affection in the family, follow the new style of literary realism, describing everyday scenes of the working classes.

Many topics are easy to interpret: topic 1 is about travelling, for example with horse carriages, 4 the copyright line, 5 family and endearment, 6 descriptions of body parts (so typical of literary realism, 9 light and darkness, 10 direct speech with dialect and sociolect features, 11 about letter writing, 14 about day times, 16 descriptions of rooms and houses, 17 cozy everyday dinner scenes, 19 about money. Topics 6, 9, 10, 16 and 17 are typical of literary realism.

Looking at the topics that are assembled in Table 6.2, we sometimes also need to interact with the texts in order to see what is going on: topic 3 contains scathing criticism and irony, referring to the debauchery and incompetence of the rich factory managers who exploit. Topic 5 seems to be about poverty, mainly in terms

Table 6.2 Topics Arising with Topic Modelling from the Selected Dickens Novels

ID Weight	Keywords
0 0.48126	great time lady young gentleman mind state friend person made conversation moment part appeared object place
1 0.0952	**coach scrooge horse uncle horses carriage chaise guard road cart box stopped coachman door baron roads passengers**
2 0.28014	man cried back head boy men hands round dog blood moment made dead hold arms cry hand body feet
3 0.12916	<u>gentlemen</u> company people ladies great gentleman public men man friends <u>honourable manager</u> general party stage
4 0.01806	**work works electronic terms agreement donations copyright copy full access paragraph trademark laws set fee**
5 0.44488	**heart father life child love** <u>poor</u> **day mother hope world knew young thought tears years long mind dear brother**
6 0.59361	face eyes hand **looked** head **sat hands man chair** back **turned side round stood time put** arm **voice made**
7 0.20197	coat man hat black hair gentleman head white red large half great boots green small eye round pair legs
8 0.79153	np dear don good aunt returned make head asked ll mother cried thought thing mind suppose pretty time poor
9 0.20018	**light night place air wind water great people dark sun sea cold stone passed streets long men high lay**
10 0.06381	**wery em ain gen replied afore ll wos wot father ere fur sir ve thou good man vith inquired**
11 0.13364	read book paper letter **pocket put** office **clerk papers pen gentlemen prisoner business case writing court desk wrote**
12 0.27174	np sir man replied gentleman ma lady stranger beg returned ll don speak hear pardon call hope business rejoined
13 1.14976	np replied friend inquired friends observed give exclaimed end master returned long smile cried hat called whisper
14 0.43416	**time night day home morning house back long found evening place made thought left good hour days half bed**
15 0.38283	made family great good manner business life fact present man make opinion short question confidence sister thing
16 0.2931	**door room house back window open street light stairs opened bed shut candle fire night walked upstairs dark looked**
17 0.14005	**glass water table wine dinner tea bottle drink fire bread hot good put drank half waiter cold drinking punch**
18 0.13506	**money madame defarge twenty hundred man pounds time year wife years good business thousand pound shop day pay**
19 0.2213	boy gentleman young replied lady man dear fat ll inquired jew doctor half boys sir em good girl woman

of family affection. Kailash (2012) and in fact most literary critics praise Dickens for his social criticism and for giving the poor workers. We will come back to Dickens' views on poverty in Chapter 8. There are typically no direct comments, no abstract discussions of poverty but a very descriptive and suggestive style.

6.3 Hands-on

6.3.1 Topics in society across time in CLMET, with mallet

For the first hands-on exercise, we want to investigate social and historical change with the help of the tool mallet and the CLMET corpus (Section 1.9.4), which spans the time period from 1710 to 1920, split in three periods of seventy years each. As CLMET is a genre-balanced corpus, it is particularly useful for this task, allowing us to focus on changes over time while we get less side-tracked by genre biases. It will allow us to go beyond simple observations of topics to comparing the periods, such that there may be fewer religious texts in the latest periods or that scientific inventions or movements in art may shift people's perspectives.

 The tool mallet has extensive online help on its website.[3] It can be downloaded from the site directly.[4] It runs in Java, so installation is usually simple. An installation guide for Mac OS is given in Box 6.1. Option A (installing the GUI) is even simpler to use, but the GUI (graphical user interface) supports fewer functions: for instance, the flag *--optimize-interval* which we recommend is not supported. We thus follow the command-line option in the following. If you just want to get a first impression, using the GUI will also bring you one step further in your journey.

Box 6.1 Installing Mallet

Installing Mallet
The following document describes the installation of Mallet on a Macintosh computer running OS 10.15.7 (Catalina).

 There are two options: Using a GUI with a Java tool or installing the command-line tool.

A. INSTALLING THE GUI

Download the Java Archive (jar) from
https://code.google.com/archive/p/topic-modeling-tool/downloads.

If you have a Java installation, double-clicking the TopicModelingTool.jar should start Mallet.

B. INSTALLING THE COMMAND-LINE TOOL

Summary

- You need to install the Java development kit (JDK).
- Install Mallet from the Mallet website.
- Call it from the Mac Command line (Terminal).

1. Install Java JDK

Follow the steps described in the installation of *LightSide*.

2. Download Mallet

On the Mallet website,

http://mallet.cs.umass.edu/download.php

You can download mallet-2.0.8.zip.

Depending on your settings, the .zip file is expanded automatically (you can set this, in Safari it is in General: 'Open safe files after downloading').

3. Move the mallet folder to an appropriate place

This step is facultative, but it is not a good idea to run everything from the downloads folder, which would be getting increasingly messier. I have moved to the Applications folder for the following description.

4. Start the Terminal and test

Open the Terminal by double-clicking its icon in /Applications/Utilities.

A text window pops up. At the prompt you can enter UNIX commands. Switch to the correct directory (with the *cd* command). Then you can test the mallet application, which is in the bin/directory. The easiest way to test it is by using the *help* option. All of these steps can be seen in the following example dialogue.

```
mallet-2.0.8 — -zsh — 102×61

ns/mallet-2.0.8 — -zsh

Last login: Sun Apr 11 11:11:45 on ttys003
gschneid@gerolds-imac lightside % cd /Applications/mallet-2.0.8
gschneid@gerolds-imac mallet-2.0.8 % ls
LICENSE        bin         dist         sample-data    test
Makefile       build.xml   lib          src
README.md      class       pom.xml      stoplists
gschneid@gerolds-imac mallet-2.0.8 % bin/mallet --help
Unrecognized command: --help
Mallet 2.0 commands:

    import-dir        load the contents of a directory into mallet instances (one per file)
    import-file       load a single file into mallet instances (one per line)
    import-svmlight   load SVMLight format data files into Mallet instances
    info              get information about Mallet instances
    train-classifier  train a classifier from Mallet data files
    classify-dir      classify data from a single file with a saved classifier
    classify-file     classify the contents of a directory with a saved classifier
    classify-svmlight classify data from a single file in SVMLight format
    train-topics      train a topic model from Mallet data files
    infer-topics      use a trained topic model to infer topics for new documents
    evaluate-topics   estimate the probability of new documents under a trained model
    prune             remove features based on frequency or information gain
    split             divide data into testing, training, and validation portions
    bulk-load         for big input files, efficiently prune vocabulary and import docs

Include --help with any option for more information
gschneid@gerolds-imac mallet-2.0.8 %
```

Extensive help is also available by using the –help flag of mallet. Assuming that Mallet is installed in /Applications/mallet-2.0-7/bin/ (adapt your path), help is obtained with:

```
/Applications/mallet-2.0.7/bin/mallet --help
```

6.3.1.1 *The distributed CLMET plain texts*

In our first experiment, we use the CLMET corpus as it is distributed. We take the plaintext version. The folder corpus/txt/plain/ contains 333 files, 88 from the first period (1710–80), 99 from the second period (1781–1850) and 146 from the third period (1851–1920).[5]

Two commands are needed to run a topic model: importing the corpus and then training the topics. Importing the corpus (import-dir) either requires a folder (in which the files are the documents) or a single file (in which each line is a document). As CLMET is distributed in 333 files, we use the folder method:

```
/Applications/mallet-2.0.7/bin/mallet import-dir --input plain/
--output PLAIN_ALL.mallet --keep-sequence --remove-stopwords
```

After the –*input* flag you need to set the correct path. The flag –*keep-sequence* is always required for topic modelling, and –*remove-stopwords* removes English stopwords. For other languages or additional stopwords, the options –*extra-stopwords* allows one to extend the list of stopwords.

Now we are ready to train the topics. The default number of topics is 10. This can be set with the flag –*num-topics*. The online help suggests: 'The default (10) will provide a broad overview of the contents of the corpus. The number of topics should depend to some degree on the size of the collection, but 200 to 400 will produce reasonably fine-grained results.' We thus start with 10 and increase the number slightly in the second experiment. The option -*optimize-interval* allows Mallet to use topics of different total weight. This allows the program to adapt better to the found topics and we recommend using it with the value of 10, which is usually fine. The rest of the command line saves the results to files.

```
/Applications/mallet-2.0.7/bin/mallet train-topics --input PLAIN
_ALL.mallet --optimize-interval 10 --num-topics 10 --output-doc-
topics  PLAIN_ALL.doc-topics.10.txt  --output-topic-keys  PLAIN
_ALL.keys.10.txt --output-state PLAIN_ALL_output-state.10.gz
```

When running this command, Mallet iteratively shows its progress and how the topics are adjusted. The final topics and keywords are also saved into the file that we have set with the flag –*output-topic-keys*. The output of topic modelling is a mixture of topic classification and keyword generation (Section 6.1). In our case, we obtained the following result:

```
0    0.10102 page type sir lady lord 11 mrs mr dear good love
miss man enter em tho harry give ha
1    0.29128 man good day men time great put make poor back half
thing people head things long water till made
2    0.16309 mr lord sir letter great king day duke time lady
george good made house year life friend years john
3    0.32148 mr time man sir good made make lady mrs great
thought letter dear give heart father house miss love
4    0.20725 mr time mrs man back miss room good thought face day
house eyes looked made long hand mother life
5    0.19937 great country people part time money trade england
state government price public made men present house greater
war years
6    0.29414 thou heart life love man eyes thy long hand time
night moment heard day voice light king thee world
7    0.09069 water found south great west island time sea made
north ship small land day large page miles degrees feet
8    0.12844 footnote emperor roman rome people empire church
war hundred thousand death years st city public arms king age
prince
9    0.26738 nature man mind things men time human sense life
general great true fact case good world form matter thing
```

The numbering of the topics on the left is (as always) arbitrary. In your runs, you will see similar topics but different topic IDs. Some topics are simple to interpret. Number 5 is about trade and money, number 6 about love, number 7 about discoveries, number 8 about history, number 9 about philosophy. We could thus give the topics clear manual labels. Topics 0 to 4 are more difficult to interpret. Topics 2 and 3 contain the word *letter*, which reveals what the core cluster of the topics is and also explain the terms of address (*mr, sir, mrs, lady, miss, king, duke*) and formal or truly heartfelt wishes (good, great, *day, give, heart, love*). The word *enter* in topic 0 and the spoken-like words (*em, tho, ha*) give away that this topic represents theatre plays. Topic 1 is very unspecific. It contains unspecific, frequent words (*man, good, day, time, put, make*). At the same time, it is one of the weightiest topics (the number at the beginning of the second column). This topic soaks up all unspecific information. This often happens, and we could perhaps call it a ragbag topic.

Topic 3 is also partly a ragbag topic. This is one possible explanation to distinguish it from topic 2. Generally speaking, it is unsatisfactory if topics overlap. How good is the topic model that Mallet suggested, then? Evaluations of topic modelling usually involve two parts: first, how coherent are the found topics, second, how well are they distinguished from other topics? As stated earlier, Quinn et al. (2010) and Grimmer and Stewart (2013) suggest to distinguish between *semantic validity*, in which the internal coherence of individual topics is assessed, and *predictive validity*, in which a given topic in distinction to external reference, that is, other topics and expected events, is assessed.

The assessment of semantic validity can be performed manually by scanning the keywords and judging how coherent they are, and how easily and consistently human annotators can label the topics. Predictive validity, by contrast, measures how well variation in topic usage corresponds with expected events (or other metadata) and how distinct the topics are from each other. We can assess distinctness by asking ourselves how many topics could have the same manual label.

In order to check topics against expected events (to assess predictive validity), we would need to know the period or year of the documents that are related to particular topics. The file saved with the option *--output-doc-topics* shows us for each document to which degree it is associated to which topic. The number of lines of this file is always one longer than the one of input text. It is one line longer because a header with a brief explanation is added.

We show an excerpt from the top of that file in Figure 6.4. We see in the first line that the file CLMET3_1_3_277.txt belongs most strongly to topic 1, with 32.55 per cent of its textual mass, and to topic 4 second (with 28.25 per cent). At the bottom of the excerpt, the file CLMET3_1_2_104.txt belongs most strongly to topic 9, with 55.99 per cent. We gave the manual label philosophy to topic 9. Reading the text shows that the Mallet keywords and our label are very appropriate. The first text lines are:

```
(base) gerold-schneiders-macbook-pro:txt gschneid$ more PLAIN_ALL.doc-topics.10.txt
#doc name topic proportion ...
0       file:/Data/CLMET_distribution/corpus/txt/plain/CLMET3_1_3_277.txt        1       0.3255969541967904      4       0.28256551701803695
08269056083     9       0.020410389545801537    5       7.614153341384011E-4    3       1.1929724411793231E-4   0       3.954528258454689E-5
647714498E-6
1       file:/Data/CLMET_distribution/corpus/txt/plain/CLMET3_1_3_263.txt        0       0.551968005765011       4       0.41535400720933
482710520299    1       0.005859794851013836    6       0.004692295906796055    7       0.002196069651681692    5       1.6051410592042876E-4
167625023E-6
2       file:/Data/CLMET_distribution/corpus/txt/plain/CLMET3_1_3_288.txt        4       0.7209942723493442      2       0.13850406107169627
264661846434    3       0.013227025983865692    9       0.010869047538745262    5       0.00380475918078577     6       3.3692522251657745E-4
280741037E-6
3       file:/Data/CLMET_distribution/corpus/txt/plain/CLMET3_1_1_20.txt         3       0.5417294085542901      0       0.234125848936837
005800974442    2       0.016502843389777533    8       0.01558721000059281     5       0.01384101787617718     1       1.308294529045913E-4
9215011188E-6
4       file:/Data/CLMET_distribution/corpus/txt/plain/CLMET3_1_1_34.txt         3       0.6372206139400576      0       0.13781551977722717
3409768806      2       0.03861612044686218     9       0.013446074533789735    6       0.009436749657919043    4       1.0665589816467005E-4
952500433E-6
5       file:/Data/CLMET_distribution/corpus/txt/plain/CLMET3_1_3_303.txt        4       0.7809728805760733      1       0.07900400638122048
39105672409     5       0.03187949493271599     3       0.01974406527859912     2       0.008166609407297465    7       0.004471663147353054
3653506196E-5
6       file:/Data/CLMET_distribution/corpus/txt/plain/CLMET3_1_2_110.txt        3       0.3432970933392166      2       0.3192521547005231
40553693025     9       0.06573566121148544     5       0.02223824362362525     4       0.004930450197228562    7       0.0031653859093079676
5236485898423
7       file:/Data/CLMET_distribution/corpus/txt/plain/CLMET3_1_3_317.txt        2       0.46434898057218904     1       0.3060037378328881
66887571307     6       0.03915299381531975     9       0.0023182272996326993   3       3.2869165503916363E-4   5       2.0384611419923038E-4
709706825E-5
8       file:/Data/CLMET_distribution/corpus/txt/plain/CLMET3_1_2_104.txt        9       0.5599997023584229      6       0.1542597313832 5852
01711961524     8       0.041597438638098706    2       0.02291937689136 3013     1       0.02023056006745078     7       0.003208896619941589
```

Figure 6.4 Screenshot from the output of the file *PLAIN_ALL.doc-topics.10.txt* to which we have saved with the flag *--output-doc-topics.*

ESSAY I. OF BODY AND MIND.

THE PROLOGUE.

There is no subject that more frequently occupies the attention of the contemplative than man: yet there are many circumstances concerning him that we shall hardly admit to have been sufficiently considered.
(CLMET3_1_2_104)

Systematically collecting this information would allow us to assess which topics are used more in which period, in which genre and so on. It also allows us to find prototypical documents for each topic. Open the *output-doc-topics* document with Excel, making sure to import spaces as column delimiters. Then you can sort first by the column with the strongest topic and secondarily with its score.

6.3.1.2 *Pseudo-documents and a bit of help*

Although the topic model applied on the distributed data performed reasonably well, the fact that two topics are very similar is not very convincing. There are several issues which could be improved. We will tackle some of them in the following.

- Random initial state: as each run delivers slightly different results, it is a good idea to run the algorithm several times to get an impression which topics are robust and which only appear sometimes. You are encouraged to do so.
- Distribution across the metadata: in addition to seeing which topics exist, it would be interesting to see how they are distributed across the metadata, for example how they differ across genres or between the periods. We will address topic prevalence by period in this section by adding the period information as a pseudo-word, at the beginning of each document, as a very simple way to add structural support. At the same time, this adds a bit of cyclicity to our arguments. We will see a methodologically cleaner method in Section 6.3.2.
- Topic changes within the document: Mallet assigns several topics to every document, in fact even all topics but to varying degrees. In reality, a document, particularly if it is long, typically develops various topics throughout. The various sections will differ considerably. This argument does not apply if we have a corpus of tweets, but in CLMET, we have (relatively) few but very long documents. Thus, also in terms of data sparseness, it is reasonable to split long documents. We split each document

each 100 lines. From the 333 initial documents, with a total of 2.3 million lines, this gives us 23011 pseudo-documents.

- Granularity: with a large corpus like CLMET, it is often possible to get fairly fine-grained topics, with 100 topics or more, but then the interpretation work increases, including interaction with the individual texts, and also the danger of getting very similar topics increases. For space reasons, we need take a compromise. As a rule of thumb, it is advisable to start with ten topics, then increase, but the number of topics should stay an order of magnitude smaller than the number of documents, otherwise the topics start to reflect individual documents. At the other extreme, asking for very few documents, for example two or five, does not necessarily lead to clearer separation. In our next experiment on the further pre-processed corpus, we will use fifteen topics.

This pre-processed corpus is available for download from the companion website for this book.[6]

We have used the following command:

```
Applications/mallet-2.0.7/bin/mallet train-topics --input CLMET
3_1_1to3_forMallet100.Periodtextmarked3.mallet      --optimize-
interval 10 --num-topics 15 --num-top-words 30 --output-doc-
topics     CLMET3_1_1to3_forMallet100.Periodtextmarked3.15.txt
--output-topic-keys    CLMET3_1_1to3_forMallet100.Periodtextmar
ked3.keys.15.txt --output-state CLMET3_1_1to3_forMallet100.Per
iodtextmarked3_output-state.15.gz
```

With this command, we have obtained the following results. The pseudo-words referring to the periods are given in boldprint, and we have added a suggested label in italics at the end of each line. Otherwise the following is the exact output, saved in the file CLMET3_1_1to3_forMallet100.Periodtextmarked3. keys.15.txt.

```
0    0.35419   time made man person present found mind manner
great part received house mr conduct power reason subject
immediately character make opinion means place occasion thought
nature life appeared pleasure Philosophy & Reason

1    0.09261   mr author de dr poet book works footnote written
smith great poetry year life work published la wrote poem years
genius letters st letter history read vol john coleridge Poetry

2    0.25022   long air light time place side round day great
water night white trees house feet half found beautiful sun passed
black back large road green left small made dark Landscapes
```

3   0.05391   south ship sea west island water north found land great captain degrees east made miles small time shore minutes day board islands boat wind men large species feet ships *Discoveries*

4   0.18423   mr mrs miss day time good lady dear letter mother house father thought made home young make morning poor told room long friend sir great wife **clmetptwo** hope left *Letters*

5   0.05088   emperor footnote roman empire rome war people city thousand hundred years church arms death **clmetpone** tom army troops reign public constantinople italy age ancient son romans prince military st *History*

6   0.07733   nature general case time fact matter object objects idea form mind thing true sense things present cases existence science number effect laws part ideas means parts body motion pg *Philosophy & Science*

7   0.07781   man king men horse time great knight hand made back good replied master head left cried sir side john heard knew moment night toby set de horses day found *Cavalry*

8   0.10131   lord king mr sir duke great prince de house queen royal french earl court england day france paris william george lady letter made parliament majesty english men time people *Nobility*

9   0.1636   mr **clmetpthree** room face mrs door eyes back man looked hand ll thought lady time head woman miss voice good night father moment asked ve dear mother knew made *Descriptions (Rooms, bodies)*

10   0.22638   man men life world great things good nature people human mind god power work moral true society sense time make truth children page spirit thing women character fact made *Philosophy, God, Society*

11   0.12767   sir mr lady mrs good dear **clmetpone** letter man miss make madam give father time thing love thought told great honour heart made lord poor mother young woman hope *Letters*

12   0.18065   good man ll put make day time boy young half poor till tom give head water thing people ve great ye house back men round **clmetpthree** fellow fine jack *Informal spoken, contractions*

13   0.17871   thou love heart thy life thee father god death eyes hand heaven man soul **clmetptwo** lord world mother voice child night poor thought tears face words day mind lady *Prayers & Love*

14   0.0966   country great money trade part price people england land capital time labour produce greater government years year state present number pay made bank public increase quantity interest large wages *Trade*

Some topics partly overlap, like in our last section. Philosophy (Topics 0, 6 10) and Letters (4, 11) appear several times. Topic 0 relates to philosophy more from the perspective of reason, nature – rationalism and scholastic thinking, while in topic 6 the words *effect* and *object* suggest more empirical methods. Topic 10 with keywords *god, moral, society* and *character* seems to focus on matters of society and moral judgement. The two-letter topics are harder to distinguish.

In six topics, the pseudo-word of the period (in bold) also appears among the top thirty keywords. The letter topics 4 and 11 indicate that the formal address *sir* decreased. Topic 5 indicates that history and heroism were strongest in the earliest period. Topic 9 shows that detailed descriptions of rooms and bodies are much stronger in the latest period. This seems to be a clear reflection of the new style of literary realism (Kailash 2012, Mahlberg 2013, see also Chapter 2 and Section 6.2.2). Topic 12 looks unspecific at first sight, but it contains contractions (*ll, ve*) and dialectal forms (*ye*) from informal speech, again signs of literary realism in novels and plays. Topic 13, prayers and love, is stronger in period two.

6.3.2 Comparing Barack Obama to Donald Trump with *stm*

The library *stm* in R is a popular way to perform topic modelling in R. Its advantage is that it has built-in mechanisms to compare the distribution of topics across the metadata, such as time periods (Section 6.3.2), political parties (as we have done in Chapter 5), news source and so on. In this hands-on, we will compare Barack Obama's topics and style to those of Donald Trump.

The corpus of US American speeches that we worked with in Chapter 5 did not include Barack Obama or Donald Trump yet, so this study can also be seen as an update. As corpus, we use a part of the Corpus of American Speeches compiled by Karl Fogel (Section 1.9.11). We compare Barack Obama to Donald Trump.

The relevant part for our studies has been made available for download on the companion website for this book, as the file *TrumpVSObama2.csv*. This .csv file can also be used to load into *Lightside* to compare individual lexical features of Trump and Obama.

Topic models are not part of the *quanteda* package, but there is a package called *stm* (structural topic models) which uses *quanteda* corpus objects. With the library *readtext*, we can read in the .csv file directly (Welbers et al. 2017: 248). In Box 6.2 we read the corpus into the variable *rt*, specifying that the column with the heading *TEXT* contains the text. Adapt your path according to your own preferences. The resulting readtext object has 6858 lines, corresponding to paragraphs in Barack Obama's and Donald Trump's speeches. The one document variable *SPEAKER* tells us if Obama or Trump is the speaker. As *stm* works with quanteda *dfm* objects, we need to convert, first using the *corpus* function and then the *dfm* function, which we both know from Chapter 4.

As with document classification (Chapter 5), it is recommended to discard rare words. Additionally, we also discard words that occur in fewer than 0.25 per cent of all documents with the option *min_docfreq*. Topic models are sensitive to reasonable settings. The *stm* function then trains the topic model. We chose K = 10 topics and a maximum of 100 iterations.

Box 6.2 First structural topic model with *stm* in R.

```
## load with readtext, adapt your path
rt=readtext("/Data/presidential-speeches
    master/TrumpVSObama2.csv",text_field="TEXT")

rt
readtext object consisting of 6858 documents and 1 docvar.
# Description: df[,3] [6,858 × 3]
   doc_id              text                SPEAKER
   <chr>               <chr>               <chr>
1 TrumpVSObama2.csv.1 "\"I stand he\"..." Obama
2 TrumpVSObama2.csv.2 "\"Forty-four\"..." Obama

fulltext = corpus(rt)
dtm <-
    dfm(fulltext,tolower=T,stem=T,remove_punct=T,remove=sto
    pwords("english"))
dtm_trimmed = dfm_trim(dtm, min_termfreq=5, min_docfreq=0.0025,
    docfreq_type="prop")
stmOut = stm(documents=dtm_trimmed, data=docvars(dtm_trimmed), K=10,
    max.em.its=100)
plot(stmOut)
```

The resulting topic model, the output of plot(stmOut), is given in Figure 6.5. The length of the bar on the left indicates the weight of the topic, and its keywords are on the right.

The results look, frankly, unconvincing. Although we have used generally reasonable parameters, the topics are not distinctive. What can we do?

Top Topics

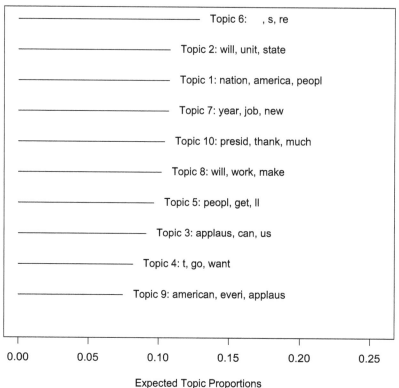

Figure 6.5 Output of our first *stm* topic model of Obama's and Trump's speeches.

First, the fact that many very frequent words (e.g. *go*, *year*), in fact only very frequent words are keywords, indicates that the problem are not rare words (which we have filtered), but rather the fact that we should filter very frequent words up to a point. There is an option called *max_termfreq* which filters word above the indicated threshold. We may also have chosen a threshold that is too high for *min_docfreq*. Also, our number of topics was very low, and the stm default of only three keywords makes it hard to interpret topics. Our next run uses the following commands:

```
dtm_trimmed = dfm_trim(dtm, min_termfreq=5, max_termfreq=500,
    min_docfreq=0.0001, docfreq_type= "prop")
stmOut = stm(documents=dtm_trimmed, data=docvars(dtm_trimmed),
    K=20, max.em.its=100)
plot(stmOut,n=8) ## see the topic, with top 8 keywords
```

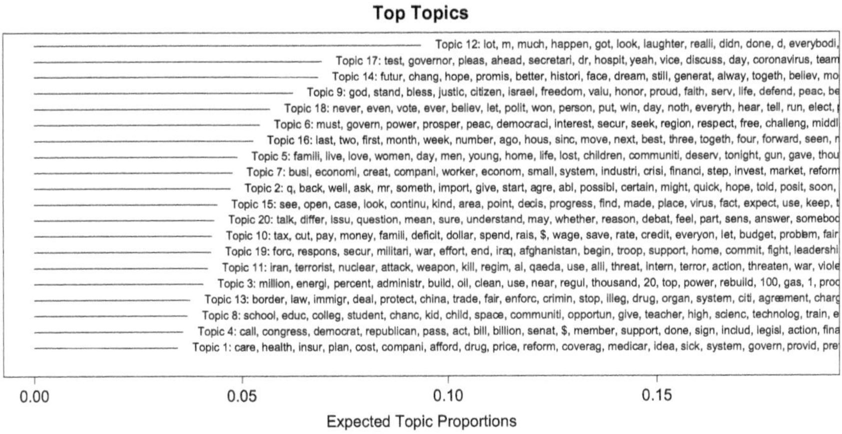

Top Topics

Topic 12: lot, m, much, happen, got, look, laughter, reali, didn, done, d, everybodi,
Topic 17: test, governor, pleas, ahead, secretari, dr, hospit, yeah, vice, discuss, day, coronavirus, team
Topic 14: futur, chang, hope, promis, better, histori, face, dream, still, generat, alway, togeth, believ, mo
Topic 9: god, stand, bless, justic, citizen, israel, freedom, valu, honor, proud, faith, serv, life, defend, peac, be
Topic 18: never, even, vote, ever, believ, let, polit, won, person, put, win, day, noth, everyth, hear, tell, run, elect, p
Topic 6: must, govern, power, prosper, peac, democraci, interest, secur, seek, region, respect, free, challeng, middl
Topic 16: last, two, first, month, week, number, ago, hous, sinc, move, next, best, three, togeth, four, forward, seen, r
Topic 5: famili, live, love, women, day, men, young, home, life, lost, children, communiti, deserv, tonight, gun, gave, thou
Topic 7: busi, economi, creat, compani, worker, econom, small, system, industri, crisi, financi, step, invest, market, reform
Topic 2: q, back, well, ask, mr, someth, import, give, start, agre, abl, possibl, certain, might, quick, hope, told, posit, soon,
Topic 15: see, open, case, look, continu, kind, area, point, decis, progress, find, made, place, virus, fact, expect, use, keep, t
Topic 20: talk, differ, issu, question, mean, sure, understand, may, whether, reason, debat, feel, part, sens, answer, someboc
Topic 10: tax, cut, pay, money, famili, deficit, dollar, spend, rais, $, wage, save, rate, credit, everyon, let, budget, problem, fair
Topic 19: forc, respons, secur, militari, war, effort, end, iraq, afghanistan, begin, troop, support, home, commit, fight, leadershi
Topic 11: iran, terrorist, nuclear, attack, weapon, kill, regim, al, qaeda, use, alli, threat, intern, terror, action, threaten, war, viole
Topic 3: million, energi, percent, administr, build, oil, clean, use, near, regul, thousand, 20, top, power, rebuild, 100, gas, 1, proc
Topic 13: border, law, immigr, deal, protect, china, trade, fair, enforc, crimin, stop, illeg, drug, organ, system, citi, agreement, charg
Topic 8: school, educ, colleg, student, chanc, kid, child, space, communiti, opportun, give, teacher, high, scienc, technolog, train, e
Topic 4: call, congress, democrat, republican, pass, act, bill, billion, senat, $, member, support, done, sign, includ, legisl, action, fina
Topic 1: care, health, insur, plan, cost, compani, afford, drug, price, reform, coverag, medicar, idea, sick, system, govern, provid, pre

0.00　　　0.05　　　0.10　　　0.15
Expected Topic Proportions

Figure 6.6 Output of our second *stm* topic model of Obama's and Trump's speeches, with improved parameters.

The result of this new command is given in Figure 6.6.

Now, the majority of topics are interpretable, for instance 17 is Covid, 14 is the bright future, 9 is religion, 6 is peace, prosperity and democracy (what politicians promise), 16 is about numbers, 5 about family, 7 about economy, 10 about money and taxes, 11 about terrorism, 3 about sustainable energy, 13 about immigration and China, 8 about education and 1 about health care. Topic 1 probably is a topic of Obama's. But how can we test such an assumption?

As the topics now look more convincing, we would like to know whether they are more closely related and thus probably more relevant to a specific US president. The *stm* library explicitly offers the option to detect trends in the metadata, for example which topic is more clearly associated with Trump or Obama. The function is called *estimateEffect*; it estimates a regression where the predicted class is the proportion of each document about a topic in an STM model, and the covariates are document-meta data.

Unfortunately, the alleged compatibility between *stm* and *readtext* ends here, and we receive error messages due to the trimming. Fortunately, *quanteda* offers a function called *convert* which delivers a compatible object by converting a quanteda *dfm* object to the *stm* format.

The commands needed to recalculate a topic model and the estimateEffect function is given in Box 6.3. To illustrate how a replicable topic model can be created, we have fixed the random seed.

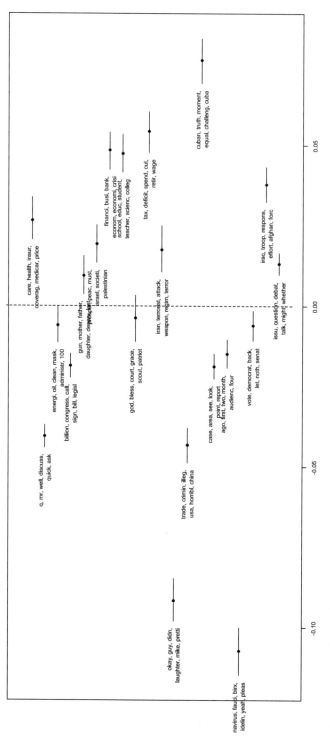

Figure 6.7 Prevalence of topics between Trump (to the left) and Obama (to the right), according to *estimateEffect* of the *stm* library.

Box 6.3 R Code for calculating the effect, that is, the prevalence of the metadata *SPEAKER*, which is Obama or Trump

```
dtm_trimmed2= convert(dtm_trimmed,to="stm", docvars=docvars(fulltext))
stmOut2 = stm(dtm_trimmed2$documents, dtm_trimmed2$vocab, K=20, seed =
    6687529, max.em.its = 100, data=dtm_trimmed2$meta, prevalence =~
    SPEAKER, verbose = F)

est_effect = estimateEffect(~SPEAKER, stmOut2,
    metadata=dtm_trimmed2$meta)
plot.estimateEffect(est_effect, "SPEAKER", method = "difference",
    cov.value1 = "Obama", cov.value2 = "Trump", labeltype = "frex",
    n = 6, verbose.labels = F, model=stmOut2)
```

The comparison, which is the output of the *plot.estimateEffect* function, is given in Figure 6.7. The dot represents the mean, and the line is the confidence interval. The ordering of the topics is numerical. We can see that topic 1, health care, is indeed more closely related to Obama. The topic of Cuba is the one leaning most strongly towards Obama, the Covid topic the one most strongly associated with Trump, during whose presidency the pandemic occurred. We see as other topics close to Trump topic 12 (laughter and audience reactions) and topic 13 (immigration and China). The keyword calculation method is unfortunately a bit different, which complicates the comparison. The option *labeltype* can also be used to display just the label number (*labeltype = 'number'*, the default).

Further Reading

Jabobi et al. (2016): A detailed case study using topic models to trace topics of nuclear technology in *The New York Times* from 1945 to 2015.

Rüdiger et al. (2022): Their comparison of algorithms finds that sampling-based LDA, which is used in Mallet, performs best, and it 'dominates all other algorithms' (Rüdiger et al. 2022: 12). They also describe that it is almost impossible to find an optimal number of topics automatically.

Schneider (2020): A study of the concept of poverty from 1470 to 1920 with LDA topic modelling. Poverty was always a problem, but the focus shifts (a) from a religious virtue to philosophical considerations. In the religious discourse, a shift from prayers to the institution of the church can be observed, and also the rise of England as a trading nation and the style of literary realism are apparent.

Schneider (2022b): The concept of poverty is further scrutinized by running to separate topic models on the early period from EEBO (1470 to 1700) and CLMET (1710 to 1920). The study gives special attention to distant reading and close reading in interaction. The turn from the romantic hero to everyday life and literary realism becomes all the more apparent.

Schmidt (2012): A critical assessment from a digital humanities perspective, warning us that topic models are compromises at many levels, which highlights the need for careful evaluation and close reading. The author is pessimistic that even if topic modelling works, literary scholars will still be put off by the blackbox character and the lack of parsimony of the algorithm.

Kernel Density Estimation for Conceptual Maps

7.1 Theoretical background

Topic modelling forms classes of topics from the words of documents, but the distances in the distributional space between words and topics are not visible. In order to visualize the relationship between keywords within a topic, it is useful to measure and display the semantic distances in maps of concepts, first and foremost, between all the words, but ideally also between the topics suggested by topic models. Kernel density estimation (KDE) is a well-established smoothing method (e.g. Zucchini 2003). Yet, its application in digital humanities or computational linguistics is less well known than topic modelling. Some of the rare references are Kaufmann (2020) and Eve (2022). Like distributional semantics (Chapter 8), it exploits the Firthian hypothesis (see Section 1.2) and learns semantic concepts from the textual context. In this approach we use KDE to create maps. We call them *conceptual maps*, but there is no broadly accepted established term yet. They are also known as *mind maps* (Buzan and Buzan 1993), although these are typically drawn manually. In other words: we can say that the method of creating term–term matrices with kernel density estimation and then plotting similar words together, using a spring-attraction algorithm, is an automated method to draw mind maps, or maps helping us to construct mind maps, in a fully data-driven fashion. We introduce the method in the following.

Firth (1957) and Harris (Harris, 1968, 1970) noticed that words which frequently co-occur, or which occur in similar contexts, are similar or related in meaning. For example, *horses, saddle* and *ride* appear mostly in the same location, both in the real world in large collections of materials with detailed descriptions and in varied perspectives in sufficiently large corpora. If we calculate mutual co-occurrences across texts, we obtain a data-driven measure of similarity. Kernel density estimates are functions of these mutual co-occurrences which are learnt from corpus data. Then, visualizations of similarities of words are done in the form of such networks which we call conceptual maps. In order to obtain smoothed results, approximating functions are used which gloss over data fluctuations.

Distributional methods open up a family of new methods – distributional semantics and word embeddings (Chapter 8) are the best-known ones. According to Sahlgren (2006), small observation windows deliver syntagmatic relations (such as linguistic collocations), while large observation windows (e.g. ten or twenty words to the left and right) deliver paradigmatic and associative relations – the words that could appear instead of those used in the text. With even larger window sizes, the influence of the individual document and the topic grows larger. If the window size coincides with the documents, we would perform document classification. Even larger observation windows also reflect the similarity of adjacent documents. This does very often not make sense, but if the documents in a collection are sorted by meaningful categories – in many cases the documents are sorted diachronically – we can profit from context far beyond documents. Topic models do assume context beyond the document, that is, the same topic is witnessed by many documents, but the ordering of the documents is irrelevant. Our next method takes the document sequence into consideration: the observation windows are so large that the global ordering of the documents in the entire collection plays a central role. As a consequence, the entire semantic space can be interpreted globally, for instance the left end may be showing the topics in the earliest documents, up to the right end mirroring the latest documents in our collection. If our ordering of the documents fails to reflect a differentiating semantic feature, however, the results are largely random and do not offer any insights.

Conceptual maps use kernel density estimation (Zucchini 2003), a smoothing method which makes sure that it works with relatively small data sets and which further boosts the effect of the global ordering in the text collection to calculate word–word associations by means of the Python library *textplot* (McClure 2015). David McClure's former website illustrates the impact of different smoothing parameters.[1] In *War and Peace*, for the word *Napoleon* a 500-word bandwidth shows strong fluctuations. With a bandwidth of 10,000 words, which seems to be roughly the 'sweet spot' in this case, associations are picked up reasonably well, as shown in Figure 7.1. Even larger bandwidths run the risk that every word is related to every other words, so that true signals are no longer detectable. In our own experience, the setting of this parameter is both relatively robust, producing reasonable results with similarly large corpora between 5,000

Last but not least, the bandwidth controls the smoothness of the underlying probability density functions. For example, here's "napoleon" in *War and Peace*, with a 500-word bandwidth

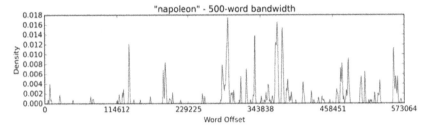

This is probably too low. The idea is that the density function should extract a kind of statistical "trend" for a word – it should smooth out the noise, but not so much that it papers

10,000 seems like a sweet spot for *War and Peace*:

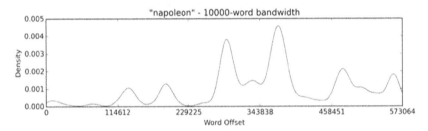

Figure 7.1 Screenshots from David McClure's former website, illustrating the smoothing parameter 'bandwidth' with values of 500 and 10,000 words.

and 20,000 words, and crucial: bandwidths of only 100 words adapt too much to individual sentences. With very short texts, such as interviews, such small bandwidths may also be desirable because they visualize single occurrences of words and make it possible to literally *plot plots*, that is, to create a plot of the plot of a novel.

To create the conceptual maps, we apply the spring-attraction algorithm ForceAtlas2 (Jacomy et al. 2014) in *Gephi* (v. 0.9.5), which creates maps of the most frequent terms based on the KDE results.

An obvious serious challenge of the method is, however, that strongly different parameters lead to quite different maps, and it is very difficult to assess which is better. As a trend, small bandwidths boost individual events, while large bandwidths bring more general associations to the surface. As *Gephi* starts with a random configuration, results are not fully reproducible. While we find them quite robust, because maps are usually similar, the left–right, and top-down orientation is arbitrary, also mirrored versions of the same semantic content are created with an equal likelihood.

Comparing distributional semantics and kernel density estimation, they mainly differ in their smoothing method. Distributional semantics typically employs dimensionality reduction techniques, such as PCA (principal component analysis), SVD (singular value decomposition) or t-SNE (t-distributed stochastic neighbor embedding). These methods make the calculations tractable by reducing the spaces of features from tens often thousands to a few hundreds, and the resulting non-sparse matrices are also a smoothing method. While their semantic granularity is often surprisingly fine, the method does not consider the order of the documents. Here, kernel density estimation can possibly profit from a new perspective on the data and add situational knowledge, and changes across very long distances, from the beginning to the end of the story or the gradual, subtle development across an entire corpus. This is indeed the case in a large collection of historical texts that cover long time spans. We have observed that maps created with distributional semantics are typically locally very accurate, but not globally interpretable, while conceptual maps are globally interpretable: the extreme left and right corners, or top and bottom, are usually also semantic opposites.

There are a number of predecessors and approaches related to conceptual maps. For instance, raw co-occurrence counts instead of smoothed kernel density estimates are used in Automap (Diesner and Carley 2004). Van Atteveldt (2008) suggests a probabilistic model. What is special about the approach of McClure is that the entire document space is considered instead of a small observation window and that the smoothing approach of kernel density estimation alleviates data sparseness problems.

7.2 Case studies

In this section, we present two case studies, one from religion, focusing on the associations of spirituality, faith and religion, and the other from politics and sociology, focusing on attitudes to and associations of migration.

7.2.1 Religion, spirituality and faith

Religion has been one of the most prominent cultural phenomena in the entire history of humanity, a source of personal identification, meaning, motivation, inspiration, but also contest, war, discrimination and church scandals. We wanted to investigate the associations of the term *religion* in the interplay with the terms *spirituality*, which is less affected by worldly abuses, closer pure transcendence and meditative inspiration or practical relaxation, and *faith*, which is personal and dear to many believers.

7.2.1.1 *Spirituality*

While there is a large overlap between religion and spirituality, there are also considerable differences. Emblen (1992) systematically investigated four definitions of religion and those ten terms connected to ten of spirituality which were those most frequently cited in the nursing literature from 1963 to 1989. For religion, the six most frequent key terms were *person, system, beliefs, organized, practices* and *worship*, while for spirituality, they were *person, life, principle, animator, being, God*. Only the top keyword overlaps. Emblen (1992) concluded that contrary to the common assumption of close interrelatedness between religion and spirituality, the differences in conceptualizations are vast. Often *religion* is attributed to everything negative (patriarchal power structures, extremism, authoritarianism, dogmatism), while *spirituality* is connoted positively as the subjective, often mystical core or the essence of religion, which by definition is positive and through practice and personal experience unfolds powerful personal, collective and therapeutic efficacies. The semantics of spirituality might serve here as a bridge between religious and secular world views (Bender and McRoberts 2012, Peng-Keller et al. 2022).

7.2.1.2 *Faith*

The personal experience, which seems to be a central difference between religion and spirituality, is often referred to by the term *faith*, which we add to our investigation as a third term. In their discussion of the differences between faith, religion and spirituality, Paul Victor and Treschuk (2020) write that '[f]aith is more personal, subjective, and deeper than organized religion and relates to the relationship with God' and how individuals are touched by God and their religious experiences. It is also often described as psychological human universal, for example, '[f]aith, from a more naturalistic, psychological perspective, is merely the innate drive to search for meaning, purpose and significance' (Popcak and Popcak 2014). Newman (2004) presents faith as the underlying force behind both religion and spirituality.

> [I]n my model, spirituality and religion are a function of faith. Both religion and spirituality require faith as a foundation (. . .). In other words, faith is the guiding principle by which individuals are either religious or spiritual. Faith

serves as both the source and the target of their religion or spirituality. Devotion to religion or perception of growth in spirituality may be seen as a measure of greater valence of understanding one's faith. (Newman 2004: 106)

7.2.1.3 *Word usage as a most radical definition*

What typically complicates discussions of terminology further is that some terms tend to evade exact definitions. This certainly applies to spirituality, and the variety of concepts and its semantic travel across time (Peng-Keller 2019), but also to faith, due to its personal, individual, idiosyncratic and intimate nature. Newman (2004) summarizes that '"[f]aith" is nearly impossible to define. It means something different to each individual. Faith is understood to be intensely personal and often seen as extremely private' (Newman 2004: 102). Fowler (1981) in his discussion of faith stresses that faith exhibits the qualities of a mystery. 'Faith . . . is perplexing, because we are internal to it' (Fowler 1981: 32).

Kim et al. (2020:64) suggest that research on religion and spirituality can be classified into two general approaches: theoretical, top-down approaches, which assume *a priori* dimensions, and empirical bottom-up methods. The philosophical distinction between rationalism and empiricism lends itself well to mirror this distinction. Top-down approaches are typically rationalist, and monotheistic religions may have a tendency to adapt a view of God-given truth that can be discovered. The societal perspectives, in which individuals have quarrels, observations and associations that can be measured, summarized and compared, are often investigated by bottom-up methods.

Wittgenstein, in his philosophy of language, rejects top-down definitions of words and argues for a usage-based approach: 'the meaning of a word is its use in the language' (Wittgenstein 1953 §43). This view has literally been implemented by distributional semantics (Lenci 2008, Chapter 8), and usage-based methods are very frequent in linguistics (Goldberg 1995, 2006, Bybee 2007). More recently, usage-based approaches to studying the conceptualization of religion have also been proposed (Neubert 2016). Neubert's suggestion for a radically discursive constitution seeks to include everyday usages of the terms into their definition.

> Die Suche nach einer wissenschaftlichen Definition geht jedoch weiter und stößt immer von Neuem auf die Frage, wie Religionsverständnisse in breitere soziale Diskurskontexte eingebunden sind.
>
> The search for a scientific definition, however, needs to go further and keeps encountering the question of how conceptions of religion should be embedded into larger discursive concepts.
>
> (Neubert 2016: 15)

He then concludes that its everyday use could also be explicitly used as the starting point of the definition or exploration of religion and its associated terms.

> Da empirisch also am Ausgangspunkt religionswissenschaftlicher Theoriebildung dieses Alltagsverständnis liegt, könnte man dieses bei konsequenter Theoretisierung auch explizit zum Ausgangspunkt machen.
>
> Because this everyday conception of religion is the starting point for scientific theory formation in religious science, it could also be explicitly made its initial point, following a consistent theoretisation.
>
> (Neubert 2016: 15)

Tweets are one such everyday usage and conception, but we need to bear in mind the caveat that some of the most obvious associations are often not explicitly mentioned. We thus expect to find a picture of a vibrant social debate rather than a complete definition.

7.2.1.4 Data

If frequency in a text collection moves centre stage, and even the categories arising from it, then the choice of text plays a crucial role: our results would be different had we selected different text sources. As we intend to reflect views and associations of 'religion' and 'spirituality' in contemporary society, unfiltered by editorial, intellectual, expert or institutional bias, it is best not to rely on reviewed articles and other genres of 'gated' discourse, but instead to use the loud and unfiltered market square of Twitter data. We collected tweets containing three keywords – 'religion', 'spirituality' and 'faith' – using the R library *rtweet*. The randomly chosen collection period was between March and April 2021. We collected between 32,000 and 52,000 tweets from each keyword, in total 138,000 tweets, with a total of about 4.5 million words. For data processing, we removed stopwords but kept hashtags, except for the hash symbol.

7.2.1.5 Results: A pact with the devil

Let us now turn to the conceptual maps that are created fully automatically. In Figure 7.2, we see *faith* and its co-occurring words at the top, *spirituality* on the left and *religion* on the right. Faith is particularly close to *hope, god, Jesus* and the word of the *Bible*. The *Bible* connects faith to religion, which seems to surround abstract concepts such as the institution of the *church, state,* but also calls for *freedom* and *respect*. In addition to listing some of the world's important religions including *Islam, Hindu* and *Christian, politics* highlights the conflicts in which the church has been involved with and as these are often ignited with

Figure 7.2 Conceptual map of *spirituality, faith* and *religion* with 100 terms.

reference to different beliefs, such as *hate* and *race*, they also appear here. The frequent negations (*doesn, don, isn*) mirror complaints, for instance that (other) religions *don't* respect our values, or warnings, namely that hate *doesn't* solve any problem.

Spirituality is not linked to such conflicts and is not considered to be responsible for any controversies. It appears surrounded by *mediation* and *happiness*, a pure concept of the *soul* and *mind* (compare Figure 7.2).

The conceptual map, shown in Figure 7.2, largely confirms and quantifies intuitions that have been described on the roles of religion and spirituality, as, for instance, summarized by Neubert (2016):

> 'Spiritualität': in vielen Kontexten 'Religion' positiv gegenübergestellt wird – entweder als positive Überhöhung und 'wahres Wesen' von 'Religion' oder aber als in positiver Weise individualistisch, innerlich und heilsorientiert, wogegen 'Religion' negativ mit Organisation, Hierarchie, Dogmatismus und Weltlichkeit verknüpft wird. (Neubert 2016: 127)
>
> 'Spirituality' is often juxtaposed to religion as positive – be it as positive idealisation or the true essence of religion, or as positively individualistic, intimate and healing, whereas 'religion' is negatively connected with organisation, hierarchy, dogmatism and profanity.

Beyond this confirmation, the conceptual map invites further interpretations. What connects *spirituality* to *faith* is *love, truth, God* and his *work.* As connecting elements between spirituality and religion, we see *faith* on top and *society, culture, science* at the bottom. We can even observe the juxtaposition of *word,* close to *Bible, god* and *faith,* to *world,* with its constant *change,* hard to *understand,* the locus both of *science* and *culture* – the juxtaposition of vita *activa* and *vita contemplativa* is reflected here.

Such a distant simplifying map or perhaps even automated caricature heeds the warnings by Moretti (2020) that distant reading, the 'pact with the devil', should be backed up by close reading. Let us, thus, after close-reading Moretti (2020) in our extended quote in Section 1.5, close-read some typical examples of the tweets.

Two examples concerned with *spirituality* which mirror several keywords are:

1) What will really give me joy is finding a meditating circle in Abuja. People that are into yoga, spirituality, meditation, art, music, books and the like. That's my niche.

2) It's okay to be an atheist. It's also okay to be religious. A perfect human being is a mix of science and spirituality. Science cannot answer a lot of questions. Practices like yoga and meditation were once seen as religious. But science is proving their benefits. Be open minded.

Two examples representing *religion* which mirror several keywords are:

3) i hate living in the north of ireland, i hate the majority of the people in the north of ireland, i hate the politics and religion in the north of ireland. get me the fuck out of here now!

4) Feels weird seeing people drawn to a faith I hate. Perhaps the distance and esotericism is a big factor. I'm generally drawn to buddhism but I am aware that as a religion it has some weird stuff Spirituality =/= religion. The latter is filled with politics and defiles life.

Two examples of the use of *faith* which mirror several keywords are:

5) You have the gift from God to chose what you put your faith in Paul ('THE GIFT OF FREE WILL'). Just like Adam and Eve had . . . they will never live again anywhere! I respect that gift god gave you and he hopes you make the right chose before he gets rid of ALL Corruption!

6) Adding or removing 'blind' from faith doesn't change anything. Faith (as commonly defined) is a belief without evidence, faith itself is the evidence. Atheism is simply not being convinced that gods exists. Claiming that we hope no gods exists is a lie.

The topics that are addressed in these tweets, and further topics surrounding the discourses of religion, spirituality and faith, are visualized in the conceptual map in Figure 7.3.

Conceptual maps provide useful and easily interpretable visualizations of concepts. However, the concise overview also carries with it the danger of oversimplification of the investigated concepts. One way to counteract the danger of such oversimplification is to include more terms in the map, both to add more detail and to reduce the danger of foregrounding possible incorrect word senses.

We give a conceptual map with 200 terms in Figure 7.3. In this conceptual map based on Twitter data, even *fuck* and *kill* appear close to religion, and the general impression of a systematic difference between *spirituality, faith* and *religion* persists.

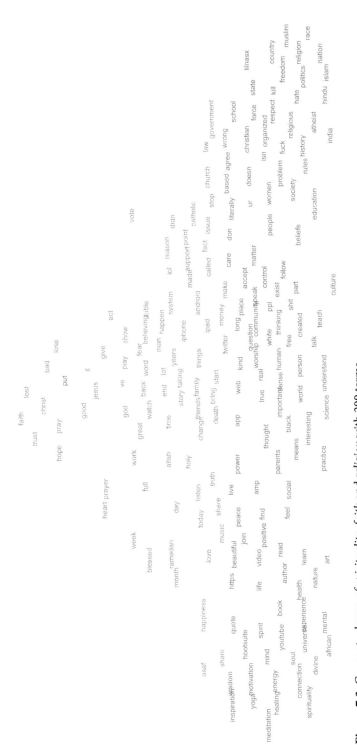

Figure 7.3 Conceptual map of *spirituality, faith* and *religion* with 200 terms.

7.2.2 Migration

After the hotly debated topic of religion we are heading to the next hot spot: the topic of migration. The topic of migration is an emotional one for many people, and Schneider and Reveilhac (2022) investigate how associations of *migration* have changed in *The New York Times* (*NYT*) from 1987 to 2007. For this study, articles containing the query words *migration, migrant, immigrant, emigrant, foreigner, asylum seeker* and *refugee* were collected. The collection was split into an early period from 1987 to 1999 (19xx) and a late period from 2000 to 2007 (20xx). Both periods are approximately equal in size. The associations found with terms from the migration context are illustrated in Figure 7.4.

The results, given in Figure 7.4, show that the perception of migration that was represented in *The New York Times* centred on a shift from *war aid, refugee camp* and *asylum* seekers in the twentieth century (19xx, as indicated in the top of the map) to a politicized topic (*congress, senate*), and *legal* discussion (lawyers, illegal) and court battles on migration *status*, particularly with *workers* coming across the *Mexican* border in the twenty-first century (20xx), indicated at the bottom of the map).

7.3 Hands-on

After the case studies, you are probably eager to test the method of conceptual maps yourself. Two tools need to be installed for these experiments: the Python library *textplot* – which can then also be called from the command line in Mac and UNIX – and the application *Gephi*.[2] The installation of the professional GUI application *Gephi* is usually simple, and other tools, for example *cytoscape*, can also be used instead. The installation of textplot can be more demanding, as it needs a Python installation and a manual change in the code. The details of how to install these programs are given in Box 7.1.

Box 7.1. Installation of the Python library *textplot*

Installing textplot and *Gephi*

The following document describes the installation of textplot.

Installation of *Gephi* should be trivial, just install it like any standard app on Mac or Windows.

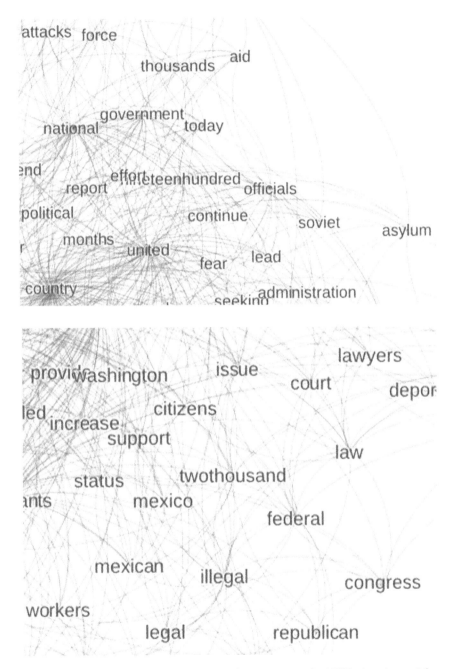

Figure 7.4 Conceptual map with 200 most frequent terms for *NYT* migration articles, witnessing the shift from war aid to political and legal battles. Nineteen hundred on the top, two thousand on the bottom.

This installation has been tested on a Macintosh computer running OS 10.15.7 (Catalina), with Python version 3.8. You need to have Python3 installed on your computer.

1. Install textplot

Install the textplot library like a standard Python library. Typically, this is done using pip from the command line:

pip install textplot

If you want to do manual installation, you can alternatively also get textplot from github:

https://github.com/davidmcclure/textplot

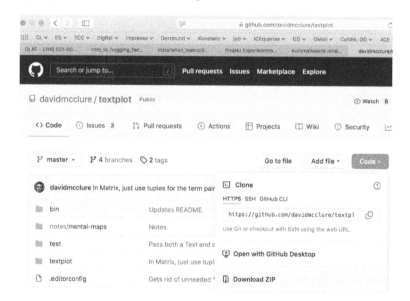

In 'Code' on the right, select 'Download ZIP'.

Depending on your settings, the .zip file is expanded automatically (you can set this, in Safari it is in General: 'Open safe files after downloading').

2. Correct a library call

In earlier versions of Python, the function 'comb' was in scipy.misc, now it is in scipy.special. If you try to start textplot, you get an error message.

You need to edit the file textplot/matrix.py where your Python libraries are installed.

To find out where textplot was installed, either check what pip tells you during the installation, or you can ask for it (and you see my installation path)

```
$ pip show textplot
Name: textplot
Version: 0.1.1
Summary: (Mental) maps of texts.
Home-page: https://github.com/davidmcclure/textplot
Author: David McClure
Author-email: davidwilliammcclure@gmail.com
License: MIT
Location:    /Volumes/Macintosh_HD_1TB/Users/gschneid/opt/anaco
nda3/lib/python3.8/site-packages
Requires: click, clint, matplotlib, networkx, nltk, numpy,
pytest, scikit-learn, scipy
```

Change

from scipy.misc import comb

to

from scipy.special import comb

as shown in the screenshot

After that, you should be able to start textplot, also directly from the command line. You can test if it works with the command

textplot generate --help

as shown in the screenshot.

Installing *Gephi* should be easy. Get it from

https://gephi.org

and install it like any program.

You may have to set your security settings to allow execution.

On Windows computers, execution needs to happen via Python. On the website, instructions on how to use it in Windows, compiled by Silvio Liesch, are given.

7.3.1 CLMET

On the one hand, we want to introduce as many different applications as possible from different domain applications, ranging from literature to linguistics and politics to religion (Section 7.2.1); on the other hand, returning to familiar topics and corpora can also give us a chance to see what different approaches bring to the surface.

For the first hands-on exercise, we want to investigate social and historical change with the help of the textplot, *Gephi* and the CLMET corpus (Section 1.9.4), which spans the time period from 1710 to 1920, split in three periods of seventy years each. As it is a genre-balanced corpus, it is particularly useful for this task, allowing us to focus on changes over time while less side-tracked from genre biases. For this reason, we have already used CLMET for topic modelling in Section 6.3.

We are using the version from Section 6.3.1.2, where period is added to the documents as pseudo-words, offering additional structural hints, which helps the formation of a global structure at the cost of adding a potential cyclicity to one's argument. If you use conceptual maps on own projects, adding meta-information and sorting your corpus by the crucial metadata are important steps, because the observation windows that kernel density estimation use are often much larger than individual documents.

The file that we will need for our task is called

```
CLMET3_1_1to3_forMallet100.Periodtextmarked2.csv
```

It can be downloaded from the book's companion website.

The *textplot* tool call from the command line is well documented. You can call help via

```
textplot generate --help
```

and

```
textplot --help
```

The main function of textplot is *generate*, with an input file as raw text and an output file in the *.gml* format, a term–term matrix. Additionally, several parameters can be set via flags.

The map shown in Figure 7.6 was created with the following call to textplot:

```
textplot generate --term_depth 500 --skim_depth 7 CLMET3_1_1to3
_forMallet100.Periodtextmarked2.csv  CLMET3_1_1to3_forMallet100
.Periodtextmarked2.t500.skim7.gml
```

Here, we explicitly ask for the most frequent 500 words to be used for the map and a term to be linked maximally to seven others. This parameter can be changed by simply changing the term *depth figure* in the call from 500 to your own preferred term depth. A low skim_depth parameter creates a map with more distinct corners, a more rugged and semantically easily interpretable coastline if we interpret the map as an island, but it can lead the map falling into several dissociated pieces that drift away like continents. A further frequently used flag is –*bandwidth* which allows one to use more (higher value) or less (lower value) smoothing. A high bandwidth brings out global trends more strongly, that is, developments from the beginning of the corpus (or the story) to the end, while a low bandwidth adapts to details, up to mirroring the individual texts but also increasingly being plagues by sparse data. In some cases, the quality of the map crucially depends on finding a 'sweet spot' or at least a reasonable range of this parameter. Reasonable ranges are typically between 1,000 and 20,000.

It is typically a good idea to start with a small number of terms (and then increase) because the interpretation of small maps is easier, and the calculation takes less long, and we can experiment with reasonable settings for other parameters, such as *bandwidth* and *skim_depth*.

These parameters are illustrated in great detail on the former website of David McClure; it can fortunately still be reached via web archive (see Section 7.1 for the link). The basic information is also available from the github distribution site, and Eve (2020) also summarizes the steps that need to be taken.

Once the term–term matrix has been created, we can import it into *Gephi*. Select 'File: Open' and take the .gml file which you have created, as in our example

```
CLMET3_1_1to3_forMallet100.Periodtextmarked2.t500.skim7.gml
```

Should you not have managed to create the file, it is also available for download from the book's companion website.

Choose 'undirected' as graph type.

You can inspect the loaded term–term matrix under the tab 'Data Laboratory'. In our case, in 'Nodes' we see *eyes* with ID 43. In 'Edges' we see that this ID is linked to IDs 43 (face), 45 (hand), 65 (asked), 71 (fell), 99 (woman), 115 (door), 117 (table), 125 (light), 49 (turned) and more. We can sort the table by any column. The strongest edge weight, for example, is 0.756, between nodes 6 (*day*) and 31 (*made*).

More interestingly, let us create a map. In the 'Overview' tab, you will see an initial random layout. Select 'Force Atlas' (which is a more precise but slower option) or 'ForceAtlas2' (which is very fast). Once you press 'run', the graph

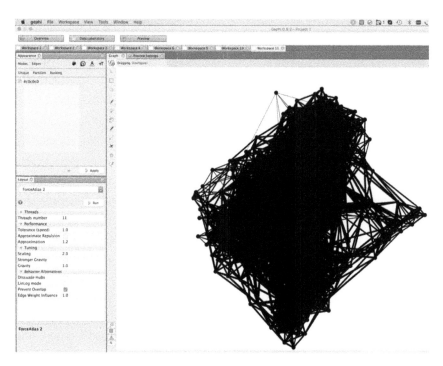

Figure 7.5 Screenshot after running 'ForceAtlas2' in the 'Overview' tab.

unfolds, and you can see the spring-attraction algorithm at work. Wait for a moment until it stabilizes. You can now see the general outline of the use of the terms.

As we want to be able to read the words better, tick 'Prevent Overlap' in the pane under 'ForceAtlas2' and run again for a moment. A screenshot of the current situation is given in Figure 7.5.

In Figure 7.5, you can already see the shape of the final map given in Figure 7.6. In order to create the final map, you need to switch from the 'Overview' to the 'Preview' tab in *Gephi*. At first, the preview screen does not display anything, you need to press 'Refresh'. You will probably see a graph without text. If you still see nothing, try 'reset zoom' and set 'preview ratio' to a high value (100 per cent). If all fails, export a PDF, the exported PDFs will usually be correct even if the screen stays blank. In order to see the labels, make sure to tick 'Show Labels', select a small font and choose small thickness and high opacity for the edges, so that one can clearly read the labels. Figure 7.7 shows the settings that were used for generating the map in Figure 7.6.

Close to *clmetpone*, the pseudo-word representing the first period, we see *prince, king, court* (monarchy) and also *virtue, moral conduct* (a bit higher),

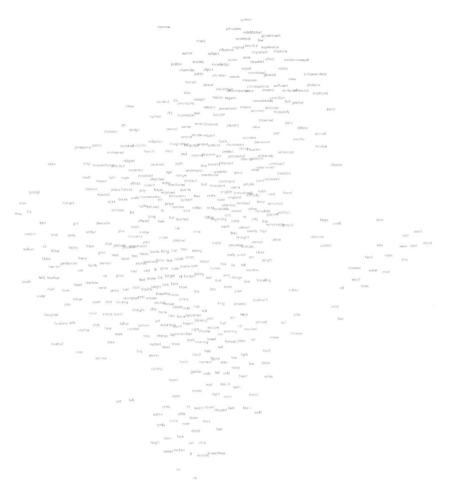

Figure 7.6 Conceptual map of CLMET with period information as pseudo-words *clmetpone*, *clmetptwo* and *clmetpthree*.

and (a bit lower) *god* with *thee*, *thou*, *thy* coming from prayers (which often are centred around *hope*, *happy*, *bless* and *heaven*). Further down, we see family words (*sister*, *uncle*, *mother*, *father*, *child*) and terms of address (*sir*, *lady*, *dear*) from letter writing and the pseudo-word *clmetptwo*.

The vicinity of the words *play* and *story* to *clmetptwo* gives us a further hint: on the one hand, everyday experiences are getting more important and on the other, plays and novels are an important mirror of society and everyday life. We have already seen in Section 6.3.1.2 that letters and family are particularly present in the second period, and prayers stay important.

Towards the pseudo-word *clmetpthree* (at the bottom), sensory everyday impressions (*felt*, *talk*, *touch*, *heard*) are getting ever more important and

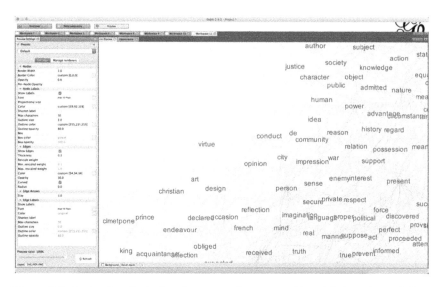

Figure 7.7 Setting for displaying the map in Figure 7.6: Show labels with small font, edges with low opacity.

descriptions of impressions (*watch*), movements (*walk*), bodies (*face, eyes*) and rooms (*door, garden*). A bit further to the right, we see colours (*black, white*) and *light* and *dark*, and further to the right, *sun*.

We can thus trace a clear movement from prayers, morals and virtues towards everyday life, first family and then increasingly a new way of seeing and observing, traces and possibly causes of literary realism and impressionism. Journeys, explorations and discoveries follow further to the right, upwards, witnessed by *horse, road* and finally *north, west, south, island*. We have almost closed the circle to *To the Lighthouse*, where journeys mainly happen introspectively.

The left hemisphere of the map offers a time machine from the earlier *clmetpone* to the later *clmetpthree*, while the right hemisphere of the output contains clusters of topics that were important in several periods, such as discoveries which we have just mentioned (rightmost). For the topics that are closer to *clmetpthree*, we can assume a higher importance in the last period. *War* and *history* (high, slightly to the left) occur in all periods but are a bit more in focus in period one – the *cities* are affected hardest. *Nation* and *government* bridge this to *trade* and *produce*. Philosophy (*principle, universal system, nature*) and science (*experience, effect, result, subject*) follow at the very top of the graph.

Due to the random character of the initial layout, you may also obtain slightly different results. Obviously, rotated versions and mirrored versions can arise. You can use the 'Rotate' function in the layout pane in order to change the display. A new random arrangement can also be forced with 'Random Layout' in the layout pane. Then one can use Force Atlas again. Comparing the output of several runs also allows one to detect patterns that are less robust.

Finally, graphs can be exported in various formats (bottom left in Figure 7.7). In our experience, complex graphs can only be exported to PDF.[3]

7.3.2 US American political speeches

Let us apply conceptual maps to speeches of US American politicians, using the CORPS-II corpus again (Section 1.9.9), which we have used already for document classification (Chapter 5).

```
textplot generate --term_depth 500 --skim_depth 7 --bandwidth
2000 SEL_perparty_v2.csv SEL_perparty_v2.t500.skim5.bw2000.gml
```

The map that arose in our experiment is given in Figure 7.8. The pseudo-word *dem*, indicating topics of the Democratic Party, appears at the left bottom, closest to *university, education* and *children*. The pseudo-word rep is surrounded by *liberty, military* and *action*. Observe that the adjectives *democratic* and *republican* appear close together in a different place, near *election, society, campaign* and *candidate*, so these are united in technical and organizational aspects rather than in terms of party programs. Further, the adjective *democratic* is also ambiguous, as capitalization is removed; we cannot distinguish between the party and form of government.

Some names of presidents also appear in specific places in the map. *Nixon's* impeachment in 1973 also makes him appear in this technical election corner and his long-term opponent *Kennedy*. Kennedy was assassinated in 1963; he was Nixon's opponent in the 1960 election. *Bush* is remembered for his stance on terrorism in the aftermath of the 9/11 attacks. *Clinton* appears close to *kids* and *welfare*. These were important topics for Bill and Hillary Clinton, and more than half of the occurrences of *welfare* in our CORPS-II subset come from them.

Nevertheless, we need to bear in mind that to reduce Bill Clinton to welfare or George W. Bush to terrorist defence is of course a simplification – the only question is whether it is a simple characterization or a gross oversimplification. In either case, it is what they will be remembered for in history.

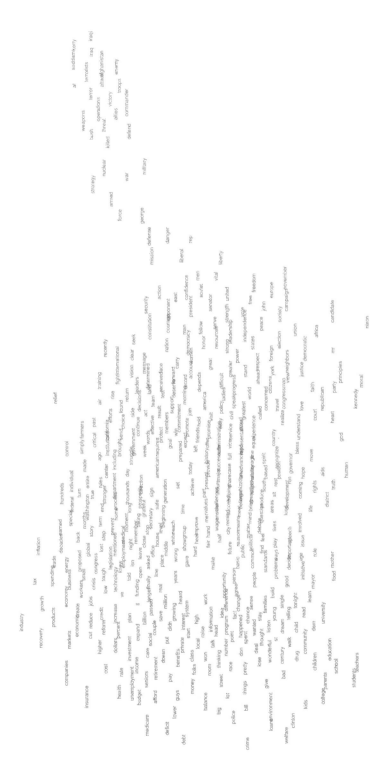

Figure 7.8 A conceptual map of US American politics from CORPS-II.

Further Reading

As the method of creating conceptual maps from smoothed term–term matrices via kernel density estimation is still quite rarely used, the list remains shorter than those in other chapters. This is an area of research which offers exciting opportunities.

Ourednik (2022): A website dedicated to turning text into maps, with code in R – everything from word clouds, term–term matrices, PCA to self-organizing maps (SOM). The perfect preparation to or extension after this chapter.

Kaufman (2020): A content analysis of Henry Kissinger, former US foreign minister from 1973 to 1977 and a respected political voice until now. He was probably the most influential politician in the Nixon area and played an important but contested role in the Vietnam War. On the one hand, he was awarded the Nobel Prize for Peace in 1973 and played an important role in pragmatic diplomacy in the Cold War era and in negations between Israel and Palestine; on the other hand, his role in the Vietnam War and the bombing of Cambodia is contested.

Schneider (2020): A study of the concept of poverty from 1470 to 1920. Poverty was always a problem. The conceptual map confirms a focus shift from a religious virtue to philosophical considerations that we have observed with topic modelling. Further details become visible, for example the word *poor* appears close to terms of *affection* and *family* (*brother, wife*), and that *honour* and *virtue* are important in the early periods.

Schoch (2022): A tutorial dedicated to creating network visualizations inside R. Using *textplot* and *Gephi* is great, fast and relatively easy, but advanced users may miss the options to do everything in one script, set a random seed to ensure reproducibility and exploit the vast space of visualization options. As Schoch (2022) warns, the *igraph* package 'may take some time to familiarize yourself with the syntax'. Also, knowledge of *ggplot* is advisable to be able to profit from all the details. The tutorial is extensive and shows a wealth of examples and gives many detailed hints.

Distributional Semantics and Word Embeddings

8.1 Theoretical background

Distributional semantics (and the related word embeddings) is based on the so-called Firthian hypothesis (see Chapter 6). It expresses that 'words with similar distributional properties have similar meanings' (Sahlgren, 2006: 21) and that words which often co-occur have similar meanings.

Given the large size of corpora, the results of distributional semantics are very accurate. While native speaker accuracy may not be in reach yet, Karlgren and Sahlgren (2001) show that distributional semantic approaches can easily pass the word similarity test of the TOEFL test; it thus reaches the level of the intuition of an advanced language learner. Distributional semantics and word emdeddings have revolutionized computational semantics (Baroni and Lenci 2010, Turney and Pantel 2010).

How does the principle of distributional semantics work? In Chapter 5, we encountered bag-of-words representations, in which document-term matrices are used. In its simplest form, distributional semantics uses term–term document matrices, a table in which both columns and rows are formed by the word types. A matrix of the short paragraph is given in (18)

(18) Dogs can bark and run. Hyenas bark and run. Cats rather miaow, but they also run.

After excluding stopwords and using the word *lemmas*, we operationalize the context as an observation window of two words to the left and two to the right. The resulting counts are given in Table 8.1.

This is of course an extremely short and simple example. But Table 8.1 shows already that *dog* and *hyena* are much more similar than *cat*, because of the shared context. Technically speaking, the context vector of the line for *dog* has

Table 8.1 Term–Term Matrix of Example Paragraph in (18)

	dog	bark	run	hyena	cat	miaow
dog	1	1	1	1		
bark	1	3	2	2		
run	1	3	2	2	1	1
hyena	1	2	2	1		
cat			2		1	1
miaow			2		1	1

```
icegb <- scan(file="/Lehre/Statistics_2015/11_Language_Models_1-gram
icegb_written.words",sep="\n", what="raw");
context = data.frame(Totals=double())
# for (word in [6:length(icegb)-5]) {
for (wordcount in 6:100) {
        for (wordcount2 in wordcount-5:wordcount+5) {
                word = icegb[wordcount];
                word2= icegb[wordcount2];
                if (is.null(context[word,word2]))
                        { context[word,word2] = 1 }
                else {
                        context[word,word2] = context[word,word2]+1}
        }
}
```

Figure 8.1 Simplest implementation of distributional semantics in R.

a vector similar to the one of *hyena*. In a term–term vector space similar to the document-term space seen in Chapter 5, the cosine measure of *dog* and *hyena* is thus higher than the one between *dog* and *cat*.

We could calculate these matrices ourselves, for example in R, by using the code shown in Figure 8.1, which calculates a term–term matrix of the first 100 words in a corpus. The loop has been restricted to the first 100 words (line 5) instead of the entire corpus (line 4, commented out) to make it executable and testable on a feasible subset. You could try this code on the first few lines, but commenting out line 5 and using line 6 instead would lead to difficulties with any large corpus.

In practical terms, the resulting tables and the vector spaces are so complex that they can hardly be handled. We saw in Chapter 5 that in a realistic collection, we easily find ten thousand word types above a reasonable frequency threshold. Accordingly, we need a table with 10,000 rows times 10,000 columns and a vector space of 10,000 dimensions. The code in Figure 8.1 is not practically useful to try to apply it to a large corpora.

In addition to being inefficient, this simple implementation of distributional semantics has further disadvantages. One is that most cells are simply zero, and the data is very sparse. As we have observed in Zipf's law (Section 3.1.2), most words are rare. This has the effect that many similar documents will not be reliably detected because they use semantically related but different words. In other words, word-based approaches do not manage to abstract from words to concepts, as topic modelling does.

There are several ways to obtain less sparse matrices, and they are usually used in combination. A first improvement is to use larger context windows. In addition to leading to less sparse matrices (simply because a bigger context contains more words), this has beneficial characteristics for finding associations. *Syntagmatic* relations, which are the subject of collocation research, can be extracted from texts on the basis of pure adjacency or with the help of small observation windows, while larger observation windows increasingly deliver *paradigmatic* relations like synonymity and associations, as Sahlgren (2006) explains. 'Paradigmatically related words are words that do not themselves co-occur, but whose surrounding words are often the same' (Sahlgren 2006: 66), and in order to capture these indirect relations via shared co-occurrences, large observation windows are needed. Sahlgren (2006: 98) reports that a window size of nine words before and after produced the best results, that is, a total context window of almost twenty words.

A second improvement is that representations with fewer dimensions are less sparse and thus have the potential to detect shared contexts better (Sahlgren 2006: 70, 103). Instead of taking topic ID number from topic modelling, other statistically well-known approaches are used, for example singular value decomposition (SVD), which is also known as Latent Sematic Analysis (LSA, Deerwester et al. 1990). Put simply, the algorithm works as follows: in the original vector space (say of 10,000 rows times 10,000 columns), it finds the projection (or angle or perspective to use humanly more interpretable terms) which represents, that is, approximates, the complete vector space best. Then it keeps this representation and calculates the difference between it and the full space, which is again a vector space. Then, on this difference vector space, it again finds the best projection, and so on. Typically, the approach is stopped after K=100 to 500 iterations, thus obtaining a vector space of K times 10,000 dimensions, which is more manageable and less sparse, and which particularly manages to bring semantically closely related and associated words together in the vector space (Sahlgren 2006: 70), thus managing to detect which words are semantically similar or have similar associations.

Distributional semantics has come under criticism because it fails to make a distinction between synonyms, antonyms, hypernyms and so on. While this observation is valid from a *prescriptive* perspective and from a *descriptive* perspective, these relations are not axiomatic, and the broad notion of semantic similarity seems perfectly plausible. Miller and Charles (1991) point out that people instinctively make judgements about semantic similarity without the need for further explanations of the concept – as an example, they mention antonyms.

Distributional semantics, however, needs very large amounts of data and genre-balanced corpora to come up mainly with synonyms (terms that are similar or even identical in meaning), antonyms (opposites) and hypernyms (cover terms). If small corpora and corpora from limited domains are used, the approach rather delivers associations than synonyms. Also with very large corpora, this restriction does not completely disappear. While this would be a serious shortcoming for the compilation of a semantic dictionary, it in fact is a beneficial advantage if we want to find associations inherent in the text:

> The kind of co-occurrence marking the relationships among the words that encode the discursive concept belongs to computational distributional semantics. Co-occurrence in this model captures association: a notion of relatedness that is much looser than that captured in formal synonymy (. . .) or strict collocation (. . .). (Fitzmaurice et al. 2017: 25)

Sahlgren (2006) quantifies the optimal context window sizes from very small for syntagmatic collocations to larger for paradigmatic relations and to very large for associations. 'It is evident that different window sizes are optimal for different tests; narrow windows spanning only a few surrounding words seem optimal for the thesaurus comparison, the synonym test, and the part-of-speech test, while wider windows seem optimal for the association and antonym tests' (Sahlgren 2006: 122).

These facts can be exploited in the automatic analysis of texts. Although we should not expect to see complete definitions or solutions to all problems, the correlations between frequency of contextual occurrence and how our minds perceive and process the world are very strong. We briefly present two of these correlations, one from psycholinguistics and the other from political science. These correlations are obtained from totally different perspectives, which offer further robustness to the hypothesis that quantitative models and cognition are related, and that quantitative models can be used as proxies to cognitive models.

From a psycholinguistic perspective, reading times are a good indicator of the time taken to understand a word or sentence and integrate it into the discourse. How well a word is integrated into the discourse can be determined by the method of surprisal. Surprisal is the expected frequency of a word in its context and there are calculation methods for it (Levy and Jaeger 2007). That surprisal has a psycholinguistic reality is shown by Smith and Levy (2013), who find a strong, logarithmic correlation between surprisal and reading time, across six orders of magnitude, from very rare to very frequent words.

Working from the perspective of political science, Ghanem (1997) states that a strong correlation has been generally recognized and that frequency may be the best single predictor, thus also confirming the tacit hypothesis of culturomics that frequency and popularity are strongly correlated.

> Agenda-setting studies have focused on how frequently an issue is mentioned in the media. The frequency with which a topic is mentioned probably has a more powerful influence than any particular framing mechanism. (Ghanem 1997: 12)

So far, we mainly talked about distributional semantics, and we mentioned that word embedding is a similar method. Distributional semantics uses vector space models, in which the semantic distances are calculated by means of cosine similarity. Word embeddings use different methods, in particular they use neural networks. A main difference is that the models used are predictive models (Baroni et al. 2014). They have been shown to generally perform better than vector space models with cosine similarity. The method that we use in the following case studies and hands-on parts also relies on a predictive model, *word2vec* (Mikolov et al. 2013).

The discussion of whether word embeddings are inherently better than distributional semantics is still going on. In reality, the discussion has partly been backgrounded by the advent of new, more complex models that perform even better, but are harder to handle and interpret: large language models (LLM), for instance BERT and GPT-2, which we will discuss in Chapter 9.

The performance of an individual method also strongly depends on the task. Arguably, for instance, the relatively simple method of kernel density estimation, which does not use distributional semantics or neural networks, performs very well the task of creating conceptual maps, which is discussed in Chapter 7.

A further important notion for applied research is whether a method is good enough. In document classification with logistic regression (see Chapter 5), the evaluation showed an accuracy rate of about 98 per cent for the detection of the party affiliation of the speaker. While it is possible that the latest methods, particularly BERT or GPT (see Chapter 9), could increase the accuracy to 98.5 per cent or 99 per cent, the question whether the extra effort pays off needs to be considered: first, the application of these models is more difficult, and calculation times are much longer. In practical terms, this makes a difference of several working days for a student or for a researcher. Second, it is unlikely that the few documents which a more accurate model will classify differently would lead to a significant shift in results and insights, for instance that the weights of individual features (see Chapter 5) or the cosine distances between words, which we have used in this chapter, would change considerably. Third, deep learning methods are typically only better once a lot of training data is available, which is often not the case in social science, or once we have enough data the training times can be forbiddingly long on users' personal computers (see Chapter 9). For instance, Cam-Stei (2019) describes an application where we obtained worse classification results with word embedding than with TFIDF vectors (which we have used in Chapter 5), while Kilimci and Akyokus (2018) report improved classification performance when using a large pre-trained word embedding model for dimensionality reduction. Sixth, if you are interested in absolute performance in order to advance science you should aim to use the latest and most advanced methods, irrespective of their cost, while if you take an application-oriented perspective focusing on reasonable results, a good-enough method coupled with careful interpretation and close reading is probably more valuable.

8.2 Case study and hands-on: Associations of poverty in Dickens

So, let us return to distributional semantics and word embeddings and assume an application-oriented perspective. If we accept the assumption that distributional semantics at least partly and significantly correlates with the associations of readers and authors, let us try to use this correlation. For our first case study, we take up the writing of Charles Dickens again and his visions of society.

After tracing the concept and associations of poverty across time (Section 7.4, Schneider 2022b), we wondered what poverty means for Dickens. Does he present a view that differs from his contemporaries? Does he present a vision of society in which the poor were seen with respect and great promise? We have seen *poor* as a keyword in Section 6.2.2, though in terms of family affection. Kailash (2012) and most literary critics praise Dickens for his social criticism and for giving the poor a voice – Can we find this respect and social criticism in Dickens' work by using content analysis methods?

Let us give a computational answer by computing a distributional semantic model trained on our selected works by Dickens. Following Sahlgren (2006) we have used a large context window of twenty words. We have applied the *R* library *WordVectors*.[1] Under the hood, this library uses *word2vec* (Mikolov et al. 2013), a neural network version (word embeddings) to calculate semantic spaces. We used the library to query for synonyms of *poverty*. As mentioned, distributional semantics is also likely to report association, or even antonyms, particularly in ironic writing. To explore this, we can then compare Dickens' synonyms to those of other corpora from the period, that is, CLMET mid and late period. The synonyms of *poverty* that we can find in Dickens' work and in the work of his contemporaries are given in Table 8.2. While his contemporaries (in CLMET Period 2 and 3) mainly associate *misery, squalor, destitution* and *disgust* with poverty, Dickens thinks of the *wrongs* and *oppressions*, the *grief* and *hardship*, and of the grotesque *debauchery* and *cupidity* at the opposite end of the social strata.

In this light, Charles Dickens' works seem all the more visionary, as his contemporaries and even later generations largely had different views.

8.3 Hands-on

The *R* library *WordVectors*, which we have just used for our case study in Section 8.2, is easy to use and allows you to calculate your own semantic spaces. It cannot be installed with a single install.packages command, but the installation instructions on its github website are comprehensive.

https://github.com/bmschmidt/wordVectors

Just follow them, in the section 'Quick Start'. Basically, you need to install the package *devtools* which then enables one to directly install and compile packages from github. In order to install devtools, you may have to install a development tool first. On Mac, this is *XCode* which you can obtain from the App Store; on Windows, you need *Rtools*.[2]

You need these tools in order to be able to compile packages yourself. Sooner or later, when you install more exotic libraries which you can find via Google or a code snippet that was suggested to you, you will be asked whether you want to install from sources because binaries for your version are not available on CRAN – then you need a development tool anyway. So, if you have not installed one yet, this is a good investment into the future.

For our experiments, we need a couple of further libraries, namely *Rtsne, tsne, dplyr, ggplot* and *ggrepel*. All of these can be installed simply using the *install. packages* command.

Table 8.2 Synonyms of *Poverty* in Dickens, Compared to Contemporary Periods of CLMET

Bold=empathy and social criticism   Italics= disgust and misery

	Distr. Sem. SYNONYM Dickens words 1619929		1780-1850 CLMET p2 words 1640497		1850-1920 CLMET p3 words 1535183	
	word	sim to poverty	word	sim to poverty	word	sim to poverty
1	poverty	1	poverty	1	poverty	1
2	**debauchery**	0.5651	debasing	0.5461	degradation	0.5695
3	**wrongs**	0.5636	*misery*	0.5338	destitution	0.5530
4	**cupidity**	0.5542	cravings	0.5214	miseries	0.5468
5	breasts	0.5442	violating	0.5152	dregs	0.5398
6	wealth	0.5413	indigence	0.5092	alleviate	0.5265
7	**oppression**	0.5365	*punishments*	0.5033	compensations	0.5220
8	**sickness**	0.5335	debase	0.4981	*squalid*	0.5176
9	riches	0.5302	hardens	0.4974	misery	0.5104
10	unrelenting	0.5268	*untaught*	0.4946	penury	0.5019
11	joys	0.5214	degradation	0.4936	*squalor*	0.4984
12	**griefs**	0.5176	immoderate	0.4760	commiseration	0.4903
13	**hardship**	0.5168	unassisted	0.4756	privations	0.4876
14	baseness	0.5152	automaton	0.4745	brotherhood	0.4855
15	privation	0.5132	luxury	0.4723	sufferings	0.4851
16	barbarous	0.5130	extravagance	0.4713	lice	0.4811
17	destitute	0.5102	tutors	0.4689	toil	0.4800
18	**heartless**	0.5081	profligacy	0.4685	*intoxication*	0.4794
19	sordid	0.5050	*wretchedness*	0.4675	*thriftless*	0.4794
20	purest	0.5030	destitution	0.4667	hovels	0.4791

8.3.1 Think like a Republican

After we explored the associations of Dickens, we can turn to a more recent topic from political science. We are using the political speeches from CORPS-II (Section 1.9.9) and the presidential speeches (Section 1.9.11) to explore associations in political speeches by US politicians – the title of this subsection is a deliberate slight provocation and should be taken with a grain of salt.

We use two variants of two corpora. They are all available from the book's companion website. First, the Republicans (reponly) versus the Democrats (demonly) in Box 8.1 and second just the CORPS-II corpus and then a version which also includes Obama and Trump from the presidential speeches, a natural extension to CORPS-II. The input files for the extended versions refer to 'plusObama' or 'plusTrump', the semantic spaces and the variable in R have number 2 in them.

The code shown in Box 8.1[3] first loads the necessary libraries, then there is a block reloading the precompiled semantics spaces (available from the book's companion website) with the function *read.binary.vectors*. If you have enough computing power, you can also compute them yourself, see the commands using first the pre-processing function *prep_words2vec*.

Box 8.1 Code for loading or training the semantic spaces of Republicans and Democrats, with the *wordVectors* library, using large observation windows of ten and twenty words

```
library(Rtsne)
library(tsne)
library(ggplot2)
library(ggrepel)
library(wordVectors)

setwd("/Data/CORPS_II_RELEASE202/") ## adapt

## to re-load the calculated distributional spaces:
training_rep <- read.binary.vectors("SEL_perparty_v2_reponly.
      bin", nrows = Inf, cols = "All",rowname_list = NULL,
      rowname_regexp = NULL)
training_dem <- read.binary.vectors("SEL_perparty_v2_demonly.
      bin", nrows = Inf, cols = "All",rowname_list = NULL,
      rowname_regexp = NULL)

training_rep2 <- read.binary.vectors("SEL_perparty_v2_reponly2
      _out.txt.bin", nrows = Inf, cols = "All",rowname_list =
      NULL, rowname_regexp = NULL)
```

```
training_dem2 <- read.binary.vectors("SEL_perparty_v2_demonly2
    _out.txt.bin", nrows = Inf, cols = "All",rowname_list =
    NULL, rowname_regexp = NULL)

## ALTERNATIVE: train fresh from scratch: takes time!
prep_word2vec("SEL_perparty_v2_reponly.csv","SEL_perparty_v2
    _reponly_out.txt", lowercase=T)
prep_word2vec("SEL_perparty_v2_demonly.csv","SEL_perparty_v2
    _demonly_out.txt", lowercase=T)

prep_word2vec("SEL_perparty_v2_reponly_plusTrump.csv","SEL_
    perparty_v2_reponly_plusTrump_out.txt", lowercase=T)
prep_word2vec("SEL_perparty_v2_demonly_plusObama.csv","SEL_
    perparty_v2_demonly_plusObama_out.txt", lowercase=T)

### the training takes about 15 minutes (depending on your
    machine)
training_rep   <-   train_word2vec("SEL_perparty_v2_reponly_out
    .txt",output="SEL_perparty_v2_reponly_out.txt.bin",
    threads=4,vectors=200, window=10)
training_rep2 <- train_word2vec("SEL_perparty_v2_reponly_plusT
    rump_out.txt",output="SEL_perparty_v2_reponly2_out.txt.
    bin", threads=4,vectors=200, window=20)

closest_to(training_rep2,"immigration",30)
closest_to(training_rep2,"education",30)
closest_to(training_rep2,"freedom",30)
closest_to(training_rep2,"security",30)

### the training takes about 15 minutes (depending on your
    machine)
training_dem   <-   train_word2vec("SEL_perparty_v2_demonly_out
    .txt",output="SEL_perparty_v2_demonly_out.txt.bin",
    threads=4,vectors=200, window=10)
training_dem2 <- train_word2vec("SEL_perparty_v2_demonly_plusO
    bama_out.txt",output="SEL_perparty_v2_demonly2_out.txt.
    bin", threads=4,vectors=200, window=20)

closest_to(training_dem2,"immigration",30)
closest_to(training_dem2,"education",30)
closest_to(training_dem2,"freedom",30)
closest_to(training_dem2,"security",30)
```

With the function *closest_to* we can look at the nearest 'synonyms' or associations. We will use the term *synonym* here, which is inappropriate in a strict linguistic sense but appropriate as a technical term. To the right of the synonym, we can see its cosine similarity measure. Trained on the Democrats data, Table

Table 8.3 Synonyms of *Immigration* by Democrats (Left) and Republicans (Right)

> closest_to(training_dem2,"immigration",20)		> closest_to(training_rep2,"immigration",20)	
words imilarity to "immigration"		words imilarity to "immigration"	
1 immigration	1.0000000	1 immigration	1.0000000
2 fixing	0.5094118	2 reforming	0.7106817
3 borders	0.4902691	3 rebuilding	0.6407948
4 travel	0.4761715	4 dependence	0.6248787
5 immigrants	0.4574298	5 ending	0.5814193
6 undocumented	0.4568851	6 seriously	0.5697441
7 patchwork	0.4467963	7 coast	0.5242774
8 illegal	0.4395705	8 oil	0.5128031
9 broken	0.4378398	9 lawful	0.5112010
10 reform	0.4313633	10 keeping	0.5039928
11 crossings	0.4020195	11 outdated	0.4721135
12 comprehensive	0.4002898	12 gulf	0.4517478
13 border	0.3999060	13 safe	0.4438083
14 laws	0.3877088	14 foreign	0.4436695
15 easy	0.3843706	15 system	0.4340864
16 weve	0.3728148	16 rational	0.4211338
17 legal	0.3703380	17 enforcing	0.4200670
18 wrangling	0.3672420	18 borders	0.4166743
19 contentious	0.3633224	19 terrorism	0.4133484
20 fixes	0.3631680	20 aliens	0.4111462

8.3 shows that the word *borders* is a 49 percent synonym of *immigration*. The top Republican synonym *reforming* (71per cent) indicates the top priority that Republicans see in this topic.

For Republicans, *terrorism* and *aliens* appear in the top twenty, while Democrats use *travel* as euphemism, as in the following quote.

(19) To this day, America reaps incredible economic rewards because we remain a magnet for the best and brightest from across the globe. Folks *travel* here in the hopes of being a part of a culture of entrepreneurship and ingenuity, and by doing so they strengthen and enrich that culture. (Barack Obama, 1.7.2010)

We typically need to check the contexts to understand the word meaning. *Fixing* and *broken*, for instance, mirror quotes from Obama, while *ending* reflects Trump's speeches.

(20) That's why I'm pleased that there's bipartisan progress being made in an area that I know was close to his big heart – and that's *fixing* our *broken* immigration system. (Barack Obama, 18.3.2010)

(21) Now is the time for the Congress to show the world that America is committed to ending illegal immigration and putting the ruthless coyotes, cartels, drug dealers, and human traffickers out of business. (Donald Trump, from Karl Fogel's collection)

In the comparison of *freedom*, displayed in Table 8.4, the differences are small. A noticeable one is that democracy is a very strong association for Democrats (71 per cent) and considerably less for Republicans (58 per cent).

Associations of *religion* show strong differences, as we can see in Table 8.5: Democrats stress the right to freedom of religion and *sexual orientation* in one breath, and cherish *diversity* of *faiths, color, race, gender* and *ethnicity, regardless* of your *background*, while Republicans focus more on questions of *Christianity, worship* and *morality*. A good example of *prohibition*, showing the focus on traditional values and defending them on religious grounds, can be seen in the following.

(22) [. . .] the Bible, the inspired word of God. How ironic that even as America returns to its spiritual roots, our courts lag behind. They talk of our constitutional guarantee of religious *liberty* as if it meant *freedom*

Table 8.4 Synonyms of *Freedom* by Democrats (Left) and Republicans (Right)

	words imilarity to "freedom"			words imilarity to "freedom"	
1	freedom	1.0000000	1	freedom	1.0000000
2	democracy	0.7138029	2	peace	0.6913726
3	liberty	0.6470759	3	liberty	0.6679294
4	peace	0.6451573	4	democracy	0.5814536
5	ideals	0.5748947	5	cause	0.5531942
6	decency	0.5713733	6	free	0.5510884
7	equality	0.5677964	7	oppressed	0.5437299
8	prosperity	0.5652354	8	desire	0.5329525
9	dignity	0.5375290	9	throughout	0.5319551
10	juarez	0.5295310	10	defender	0.5316469
11	blessings	0.5285796	11	peaceful	0.5280956
12	beacon	0.5274474	12	peoples	0.5239777
13	advance	0.5217184	13	equality	0.5107186
14	encompass	0.5170916	14	hope	0.5049826
15	meaning	0.5046124	15	freedoms	0.5045756
16	indivisible	0.4983751	16	ideologies	0.5009692
17	strength	0.4959644	17	gift	0.5005423
18	anzio	0.4958442	18	hopes	0.4989640
19	birthright	0.4922379	19	spreads	0.4985716
20	nonviolence	0.4897596	20	world	0.4957233

`>closest_to(training_dem2, "freedom",20)` `>closest_to(training_rep2, "freedom",20)`

Table 8.5 Synonyms of *Religion* by Democrats (Left) and Republicans (Right)

> closest_to(training_dem2, "religion",20)			> closest_to(training_rep2, "religion",20)		
	word	similarity to "religion"		word	similarity to "religion"
1	religion	1.0000000	1	religion	1.0000000
2	ethnicity	0.7601372	2	religious	0.6847940
3	orientation	0.7101337	3	establishment	0.5488528
4	nationality	0.6807539	4	prohibiting	0.5375669
5	sexual	0.6714368	5	prohibition	0.5262416
6	gender	0.6678770	6	hmm	0.5111007
7	creed	0.6624419	7	denies	0.5097695
8	origin	0.6404919	8	creed	0.5074782
9	religious	0.6325804	9	tolerance	0.5054434
10	regardless	0.5830404	10	coercive	0.5054082
11	race	0.5639662	11	expression	0.5043848
12	color	0.5495128	12	beliefs	0.5034880
13	divisiveness	0.5348945	13	conscience	0.4946168
14	identities	0.5274019	14	christianity	0.4759880
15	cherish	0.5268597	15	pluralism	0.4687681
16	background	0.5163899	16	persecution	0.4684340
17	faith	0.5133050	17	rejects	0.4677896
18	diversity	0.5073170	18	worship	0.4675985
19	beliefs	0.5059677	19	intolerance	0.4673140
20	faiths	0.5056326	20	morality	0.4669159

from *religion, freedom* from – actually a *prohibition* on – all values rooted in *religion*. (Ronald Reagan, 1.2.1988)

We expected to see a strong difference in the associations to *global warming*. As we are just using monograms and not multiword units, we consider synonyms of warming in Table 8.6. While Democrats show the expected pattern, the associations of the Republicans do not seem to make sense. Checking the data reveals that there are 102 occurrences of *warming* in the democratic subcorpus, 81 of them are global warming. In contrast, the Republican data has only 7 occurrences and not a single one of *global warming*. Republicans state that they are *warming* up the crowd at campaign events and so on. The expression *global warming* simply does not exist in the Republican vocabulary and is probably systematically avoided.

Both Democrats and Republicans reject *socialist* governments and use the term almost as a swearword (Table 8.7), which sometimes surprises Europeans. While socialists are just *nutheads* for Democrats to which one should still try to talk, *socialist* is a synonym to ruthless dictators in the style of *Maduro* for Republicans.

Table 8.6 Synonyms of *Warming* by Democrats (Left) and Republicans (Right)

```
> closest_to(training_dem2,        > closest_to(training_rep2,
"warming",20)                       "warming",20)
   word similarity to "warming"        word similarity to "warming"
1          warming    1.0000000      1       warming    1.0000000
2          climate    0.7169318      2      evenings    0.5409156
3            gases    0.6142394      3          earl    0.5407320
4           global    0.6079334      4           lew    0.5400177
5           planet    0.5963864      5     catherine    0.5229638
6       greenhouse    0.5684940      6         marty    0.5180960
7   concentrations    0.5438328      7         ellis    0.5085401
8           gasses    0.5315859      8            lt    0.5009591
9      temperature    0.5305148      9         brent    0.5006545
10          warmer    0.5254716      10         issa    0.4995587
11         melting    0.5229324      11        betsy    0.4966426
12         dioxide    0.5166621      12        donna    0.4961063
13         droughts    0.5164435     13        tucson    0.4882761
14          oceans    0.5117078      14        wagner    0.4863141
15     catastrophes    0.5100810     15        feeney    0.4813802
16           polar    0.5100733      16        kinder    0.4809877
17            nino    0.5079820      17      limousine    0.4775863
18           kyoto    0.5066915      18       joining    0.4772320
19     temperatures    0.5066043     19        laurie    0.4766866
20      degradation    0.4964444     20      beauprez    0.4695957
```

(23)   The problem is that this kind of vilification and over-the-top rhetoric closes the door to the possibility of compromise. It undermines democratic deliberation. It prevents learning – since, after all, why should we listen to a fascist, or a *socialist*, or a right-wing *nut*, or a left-wing *nut*? It makes it nearly impossible for people who have legitimate but bridgeable differences to sit down at the same table and hash things out. (Barack Obama, 1.5.2010)

Table 8.8 shows differences in the interpretation of *security*. While both parties acknowledge both *social* security and *homeland* security, the main reading for Republicans is that there are threats at the *national borders* and *ports*, while for Democrats the health system (*medicare*) is the main pillar of security, how far one should *privatize* it? *Homeland* security and threats from abroad (*Afghanistan*) are also topics for them but to a lesser degree.

We have now made a number of local comparisons and found interesting differences. Would it not be possible to draw a semantic map, in which the semantic distances between all words are displayed? Yes, this is possible. First, we need a good algorithm which reduces the several hundred dimensions of

Table 8.7 Synonyms of *Socialist* by Democrats (Left) and Republicans (Right)

> closest_to(training_dem2, "socialist",20)		> closest_to(training_rep2, "socialist",20)	
word	similarity to "socialist"	word	similarity to "socialist"
1 socialist	1.0000000	1 socialist	1.0000000
2 nut	0.6495911	2 maduro	0.6556187
3 mop	0.6175925	3 venezuela	0.5780385
4 wing	0.4895846	4 socialism	0.5165975
5 accuse	0.4633263	5 puppet	0.5053274
6 grab	0.4590358	6 discredited	0.4717423
7 expedient	0.4557561	7 dictatorship	0.4566038
8 philosophy	0.4321525	8 takeover	0.4515139
9 party	0.4302306	9 openly	0.4477428
10 sidelines	0.4198819	10 sanctions	0.4417365
11 misplaced	0.4189314	11 venezuelan	0.4158290
12 silly	0.4152363	12 disastrous	0.4154640
13 label	0.4132946	13 authoritarian	0.4106670
14 viewpoint	0.4125511	14 anguish	0.4074953
15 sipping	0.4079890	15 brink	0.4039257
16 tea	0.4058833	16 deprivation	0.4027264
17 impatient	0.4051704	17 imposed	0.3915274
18 whining	0.4025227	18 mob	0.3897872
19 payback	0.4021294	19 dictatorships	0.3878995
20 slurpee	0.4005871	20 imprisoned	0.3875092

a vector space to just two. One such algorithm is t-SNE (van der Maaten and Hinton 2008), which we consider to perform better than PCA, because it detects non-linear correlations and thus can detect more complex types of correlation and is less susceptible to outliers.

We can simply plot the semantic space, and the wordvectors library uses t-SNE as standard. The semantic map for the Republicans, the result of the function *plot(rep2)*, is shown in Figure 8.2.

The map is locally very accurate and tells us that *two* and *four* are similar, or *men* and *women* too, that *terrorists* are in *Afghanistan* and so on. But there is no global interpretation, as we saw it in the conceptual maps of Chapter 7: *men* and *women* are no opposites of *national security*; *economy* and *business* are even displayed almost perfectly at opposing ends.

The map generated from the Democrats looks quite similar (see Figure 8.3). Democrats are equally aware the *states* are *united* (sometimes), at least when it comes to knowing that *two* and *four* are similar numbers – probably in reference to mid-term elections and presidents' length of term. As notable differences, we see a strong cluster of *health reform*, a focus on *school*, *children* and *education*, and *security* does not appear together with *national*.

Table 8.8 Synonyms of *Security* by Democrats (Left) and Republicans (Right)

> closest_to(training_dem2, "security",20)			> closest_to(training_rep2, "security",20)		
	word	similarity to "security"		word	similarity to "security"
1	security	1.0000000	1	security	1.0000000
2	social	0.7124437	2	social	0.6113480
3	ironclad	0.5671356	3	national	0.5534661
4	trust	0.5582247	4	safety	0.5155122
5	medicare	0.5475585	5	guarding	0.4703398
6	strengthen	0.5379759	6	homeland	0.4666555
7	privatize	0.5227336	7	strengthen	0.4450332
8	stability	0.5171674	8	borders	0.4289743
9	2050	0.5127850	9	threats	0.4270522
10	homeland	0.5101149	10	our	0.4229622
11	drawing	0.5050767	11	reorganizing	0.4211227
12	2029	0.5037621	12	vulnerabilities	0.4158892
13	lockbox	0.4916664	13	intercept	0.4143451
14	prosperity	0.4808327	14	reorganization	0.4058321
15	retirees	0.4743800	15	solvent	0.4042063
16	fund	0.4691266	16	analyzing	0.4018277
17	afghanistan's	0.4662992	17	ports	0.4012822
18	2053	0.4638691	18	younger	0.3997563
19	save	0.4607307	19	strengthened	0.3985839
20	solvent	0.4573498	20	council	0.3985574

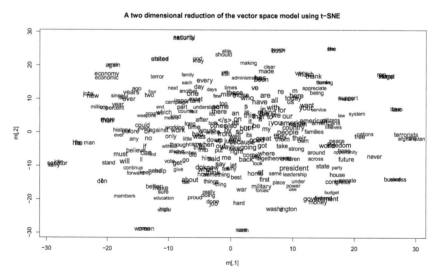

Figure 8.2 t-SNE map of the semantic space of Republican speeches.

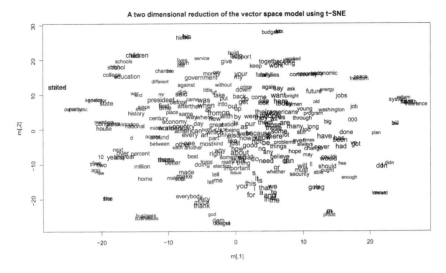

Figure 8.3 t-SNE map of the semantic space of Democratic speeches.

In addition to the simple obvious fact that common sense and everyday knowledge are similar for most people, one of the reasons why we may not see more differences is that we are looking at a low-resolution map. How far can we scale up to thousands of terms? In order to flexibly plot these parameters, we need to program things out in more detail. The code for 2,000 terms is given in Box 8.2.

Box 8.2 Code for semantic map with 2,000 terms

```
library(dplyr) # for mutate function

termsize=2000 ### how many terms in the map?

mytsne <- Rtsne(training_rep2[1:termsize,])
tsne_plot <- mytsne$Y %>% as.data.frame() %>%
  mutate(word = row.names(training_rep2)[1:termsize]) %>%
  ggplot(aes(x=V1,y=V2, label=word)) + geom_text(size=2)

plot(tsne_plot)

mytsne <- Rtsne(training_dem2[1:termsize,])
tsne_plot <- mytsne$Y %>% as.data.frame() %>%
  mutate(word = row.names(training_dem2)[1:termsize]) %>%
  ggplot(aes(x=V1,y=V2, label=word)) + geom_text(size=2)

plot(tsne_plot)
```

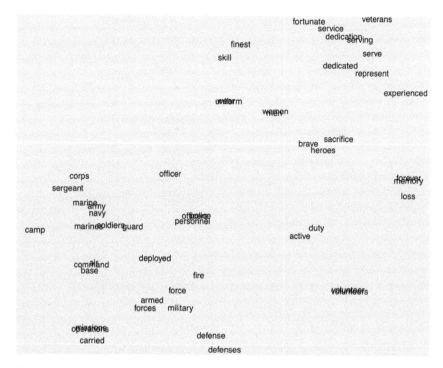

Figure 8.4 Excerpts from the Republican map from *military operations* to *veterans*.

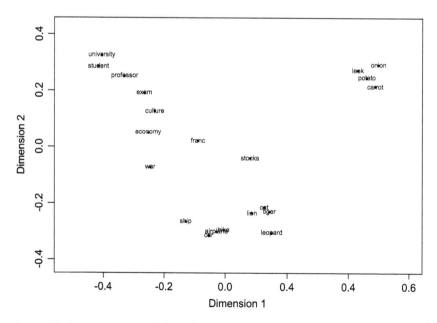

Figure 8.5 Semantic space of selected words, using the *LSAfun* library.

Figure 8.4 displays an excerpt from the Republican map with 2,000 terms from a semantic area to which Republicans pay due respect, *army* and *veterans*. This query shows us term relations in considerably more detail than the previous query shown in Figures 8.2 and 8.3, searching for the default 300 terms.

In this chapter, as well as in Chapter 7, we have trained and tested semantic maps. Their characteristics are different and their evaluations an important and challenging issue for future research. While KDE in Chapter 7 focused on the global distances, the maps shown here focus on local detail. Local detail is exactly the strength of the dimensionality reduction method of t-SNE that we use (e.g. Anowar 2021).

On the one hand, we can gain innumerable suggestions and inspiration from these maps; on the other hand, we are still faced with the existential task and dilemma of all literary scholars, namely to navigate in the vast space of interpretations, which inevitably entails placing some foci and underrepresenting others. While any interpretation runs the risk of misinterpretation, quantitative approaches like those presented here support us in making well-founded quantitatively based interpretations. Of course, these need to be juxtaposed with the traditional way of carrying out an interpretation, namely close reading.

Further Reading

As this is a young and quickly developing area of research, much information can also be found in blogs, such as *medium.com*, debugging forums such as *stackoverflow.c om* and new developing libraries in addition to research articles, and debates do not always come to the same conclusions.

Kozlowski et al. (2019): A study using word embedding to investigate associations of social class, wealth, gender and race and how much these associations correlate to survey findings. Pearson correlations between 0.27 and 0.90 are reported. Gender associations and clichés on musical styles correlate particularly strongly. A piece of research illustrating up to which point word embeddings can be used as mirrors of cognition and people's associations.

Günther et al. (2015): An easy-to-use library for pre-trained semantic spaces, allowing you compute similarities for general purposes. The article also features R code so you can directly start to experiment. We have used this library for predicting reading times (Schneider 2022c). Install the library and get a semantic space from

```
https://sites.google.com/site/fritzgntr/software-resources/
semantic_spaces
```

or from

```
www.lingexp.uni-tuebingen.de/z2/LSAspaces
```

Read the following descriptions to select a semantic space like EN_100k:

```
https://www.lingexp.uni-tuebingen.de/z2/LSAspaces/PLEASE
%20READ%20descriptions.txt
```

and you can execute experiments like the one in the following block:

```
library(LSAfun)
setwd("/Volumes/Macintosh_HD_1TB/Users/gschneid/Downloads")   #
adapt
load("EN_100k.rda")
Cosine("lion","tiger",tvectors=EN_100k)
Cosine("lion","wedding",tvectors=EN_100k)
words    =   c("lion","tiger","leopard","cat","potato","carrot"
,"leek","onion","student","university","professor","exam","e
conomy","stocks","franc","car","ship","airplane","bike","war
","culture")
plot_wordlist(words,method="MDS",dims=2, tvectors=EN_100k)
plot_wordlist(words,method="MDS",dims=3, tvectors=EN_100k)
```

The expected output of the second last line is given in Figure 8.5.

Ferreira (2023): A brief introduction to dimensionality reduction, giving a good overview of the most popular methods. It includes R code so you can experiment yourself. The Iris data set used is built-in in R, and there is no need to load the specific data set, but you need to adapt some variable names. In particular, the column *class* is called *Species*. The adapted code for PCA is, for example,

```
uiris = unique(iris)
colors = c("red","green","blue")
names(colors) = unique(uiris$Species)
#PCA
#princomp performs a principal components analysis on the given
numeric data matrix and returns the results as an object of
class princomp
pca = princomp(uiris[,1:4])$scores[,1:2]
plot(pca, t='n', main="PCA", "cex.main"=1, "cex.lab"=1)
points(pca, col=colors[uiris$Species], pch=19, cex=0.6)
legend("bottomright",legend=names(colors),col=colors,pch=19,bt
y="n")
```

Stoltz and Taylor (in progress): A R library for exploring and building text matrices and word embeddings. Under development, try at your own risk, but it looks promising at the time of writing this book.

BERT and GPT-x Models

As this book is drawing to a close, it is also witnessing the start of a new episode: large language models (LLM), like BERT, GPT-2, GPT-3 and GPT-4, are just creating the next revolution, or should we say explosion?

BERT models and GPT models (especially from 3.5 on) have made headlines and are likely to continue doing so. Particularly, ChatGPT[1] witnesses this revolution: for the first time, a general chatbot gives human-level answers to factual and informative questions. BERT stands for *bidirectional encoder representations from transformers*, and GPT stands for *generative pre-trained transformer*. Transformers are complex neural networks.

Can these methods also be used for digital humanities, content analysis, corpus linguistics? Yes, of course! On the one hand, we can profit from their stunning performance. But on the other hand, their complexity means that the methods are harder to understand and that we will work with existing, pre-trained models, which have fortunately been made available to the research community, for example on Hugging Face.[2] And working with LLMs also means that many things and old certainties are shifting.

First, while we set out to show how contested topics from society, history, politics can be analysed with DH and CL methods, we came to realize that text analytics and AI are also moving into the focus of disputes. After Ammaar Reshi asked GPT-3 to create an illustrated children's story and obtained both encouraging and hateful comments[3] up to an alleged death threat, it is clear that AI has lost its innocence when it is used to assess if people should be given a mortgage, but also in arts and humanities.

Second, all of a sudden, AI is achieving performance levels that are akin to human performance, and some old statistical certainties are challenged, such as:

1) If possible, calculate the models yourself, for reproducibility and control. This is simply no longer possible, but fortunately, many pre-trained models are made accessible to the public.

2) Domain adaptation is key: until the advent of ChatGPT it was clear that no generic system could reach the performance of a system that is trained with or adapted to a specific domain or task. For example, general chatbots, so-called chitchat chatbots, were entertaining but not very competent.

3) Supervised learning is better than unsupervised. But LLMs are largely unsupervised. They mainly learn to predict the next word using very large data sets and complex neural networks. The method is also called self-supervised.

4) Blackbox models always have a trust problem, as they cannot explain what they are doing. This also applies to LLMs; in fact, they are blacker than anything we have seen before, but their performance is so good that critics are often just overwhelmed.

5) Keep training and evaluation data separate in order not to overfit and do a fair comparison. As LLMs have seen the entire web and more, it is difficult or often impossible to find texts that the system has not seen yet. The base of seen texts and training instances is also constantly increasing, for example, with the thumbs-up or thumbs-down feedback that we give to ChatGPT.

9.1 Theoretical background

9.1.1 The revolution of LLMs

Let us start by explaining the above points. First, (1) *if possible, calculate the models yourself.*

When we trained our document classification model in Chapter 5, it used a couple of thousand word-based features. The relatively simple monogram model had 3,400 bag-of-words features, adding bigrams or lowering the frequency threshold would lead to around 10,000 features. This is considerably more than what is typically used in social science or linguistics, where a dozen to a hundred of often hand-coded and carefully selected features are used, for example in Bresnan et al. (2007), where the dative alternation is predicted with logistic regression. The dative alternation refers to the fact that two equivalent versions exist in English to express the dative:

(1) They gave a book to her.
(2) They gave her a book.

Factors influencing whether two objects or a prepositional phrase with *to* are used are, for instance, whether the benefactor (*her*) is a pronoun, how long the two objects are (there is a preference to put the one with fewer words first), the animacy of the benefactor and so on. Bresnan et al. (2007) correctly predict up to 95 percent of the binary decision which of the two variants to use, which surprised the research community.

Using a logarithmic perspective, the feature space in Bresnan et al. (2007) is 10^1 to 10^2. The feature spaces for document classification, also for distributional semantics with vector models (Chapter 8), are about 10^4, two to three orders of magnitude bigger than in 'classical' regression modelling of Bresnan et al. (2007). BERT models, and the first GPT model (GPT-1), have about $10^8 = 100$ million features (often the synonym *parameters* is used instead of *features*). *BERT base* has 110 millions, *BERT large* 345 millions and GPT-1 has 117 million parameters. This is four orders of magnitude more, a much bigger jump. If a logistic regression model takes a minute to train, a corresponding BERT or GPT-1 model would take approximately 10,000 minutes, which is seven days.

GPT-2 has 1.5 billion parameters ($1.5 \times 1,000$ millions $= 10^9$) and GPT-3 has 175 billion parameters ($1.75 \times 100,000$ millions $= 10^{11}$). All other things equal, if training time for a logarithmic model with 10^4 parameters is a minute, we would have to face training times between a month and ten years. These calculations are of course simplistic. On the one hand, with the help of graphics chips (GPU) the calculations can be sped up. Graphics chips, typically found on graphics card of fast computers and gaming consoles, have been designed to render three-dimensional objects fast to create realistic gaming worlds and manage to do matrix multiplications about two orders of magnitude faster than CPUs. On the other hand, transformers are much more complex than logistic regression – they are related, however, which brings us to a very brief explanation of neural networks.

Every neuron (or equivalently node) in a neural network is basically a binary logistic regression, say deciding between classes zero and one. The neuron 'fires' if the decision is one and not if the decision is zero. Between the input and the final output of the network, there are several layers, each with several nodes. In the simple feed-forward architecture, every node of a layer is connected to every node of the subsequent layer. In a neural network of 10 layers x 10 nodes, we have $100 = 10^2$ logistic regressions. The architecture of a transformer is more complex (Vaswani et al. 2017), in particular the arrangement of the connections. The number of layers varies, for GPT-1 there are 768, GPT-2 has 1,600 and GPT-3 12,288, and these numbers also affect the complexity of the calculations.

Such large models are typically also trained on billions of documents, attempts to scrape the entire web, complete Wikipedia dumps and so on. Also, the memory required to store these exceeds the capacities of any PC. To summarize, training these models ourselves is not feasible any longer, as the calculation times and memory demands are forbidding. Importantly, it would also be unecological: training a new GPT-3 model from scratch has been estimated to use 936 MWh.[4] This corresponds to the yearly electricity consumption of about 1,000 US households.[5]

Let us turn to point (2): *Domain adaptation is key.* Individually training is not only impossible, but it also makes less sense due to the problem of data availability and a shift in ambitions. Data availability has of course always been a problem. A good model needs large amounts of data, ideally annotated for the task to be solved, for example party affiliation in Chapter 5. Neural networks only start to excel document classification once they are given considerably more training data. The amount of training data is usually more decisive than the choice of algorithm. The real bottleneck is the availability of annotated training data for the task. In order to obtain a small further increase in performance, exponentially more data needs to be annotated, which is forbiddingly costly, or possibly simply more texts are not even available. But even then, if very large corpora are annotated, models achieving very good performance on the specific tasks sometimes perform much worse on only slightly different data, indicating overfitting and lack of robustness. The approach of transfer learning aims to profit from related tasks, making a method more robust, and ideally, due to the larger pool of training data, even better on the individual tasks.

LLMs are the upshot of this idea, which brings us to the closely related point (3) *supervised learning is better than unsupervised.* If large amounts of data are key, if data availability is the bottleneck and if we can profit from related tasks, let's find a meaningful task for which we have almost infinite amounts of correctly annotated data. One such task is the prediction of the next word, which is central in GPT and also in BERT – with the difference that BERT predicts words both from left to right and from right to left. This method is also called *self-supervised.* It is supervised because a class is predicted (the next word), but it is completely data-driven like unsupervised approaches, as no external manual annotation is used. Self-supervised LLMs are basically models trained for the wrong task (unless you want to generate text automatically).

Many pre-trained BERT and GPT-2 models are available on Hugging Face. They have excellent world knowledge but no task-specific knowledge. We can use these models, though, for any task as so-called *zero-shot model.* Task-specific knowledge can be added to them with further training instances. Such fine-tuned models are available for many tasks, such as sentiment detection, natural language inference and question answering. Many fine-tuned models can also be downloaded from Hugging Face. Users may then use these to further adapt them to their domain or slightly different task. Often, few training instances suffice. The resulting model is also called *few-shot model*. The argumentation is that zero-shot models have so much general world knowledge that only a few examples of the specific tasks suffice for the model to adapt it.

The transformers and its billions of parameters in state-of-the-art transformers are so complex, which brings us to point (4) *blackbox models* that it is impossible to understand what happens, but we can (and need to) evaluate them. According to Occam's razor, systems with more parameters than necessary are to be dispreferred. Either LLMs completely flout Occam's razor (interpretation 1), or reality does not generalize, because a billion of parameters is hardly enough (interpretation 2).

Both interpretations are equally disconcerting. While we all know that 'reality is stranger than fiction', we either have a statistical model that is accurate because it simply overfits everything (interpretation 1), or we have a reality from which it is hard to abstract more general principles (interpretation 2). Or perhaps both. Abstraction to general, interpretable principles has always been the goal of science and also of AI.

9.1.2 Contextualized word models and masked language models

Word embeddings as we have used them in Chapter 8 treat the context window as bag-of-words much like in document classification (Chapter 5) and topic modelling (Chapter 6). LLMs create different embeddings for the same word depending on different contexts, so-called conceptualized word embeddings. The crucial difference which transformers offer is *self-attention* (Vaswani et al. 2017). The self-attention mechanism puts different attention (which we can also be interpreted as weight) to different word embeddings in the context and decides which are the most relevant.

The LLM is used to predict the next word. About every fifteenth word in the texts is masked, and the model parameters are weighted to make the best possible predictions. BERT predicts words from both left to right and right to left, and also from the following sentence.

These explanations are very short and would need a lot more space to describe the details. Kjell et al. (2021) give some further explanations, and ample material can be found on the web.[6] However, explanations are either superficial (as ours) or mathematical assuming detailed background knowledge of neural networks. But even then, these approaches are so complex that they have to stay blackbox models, several orders of magnitude more blackbox than what we have seen in previous chapters – and then the world has seen before 2023. On the one hand, this can arouse suspicion; on the other hand, evaluations confirm a good, sometimes stunning, performance. Still, as in previous approaches, transformers make mistakes, and our experiments in the hands-on section give us an indication of typical mistakes, particularly the question-answering experiment in Section 9.2.2. You will see that the longer the chain of derivations that are needed, the higher the risk of error. In other words: this method can also give us excellent pointers to passages and topics deserving close reading, but close reading of these passages, for verification, interpretation, inspiration, insight, enlightenment and literary enjoyment, is always crucial.

Nevertheless, LLMs are recognized as an important method for DH (Underwood 2019). LLMs are now the driving force in the field of artificial intelligence (AI) and will fundamentally affect our working modes and lives. The *Forbes* magazine,[7] for instance, predicts that 'we will start seeing a shift from using AI for static tasks like classification, which can only serve a small number of use cases, to entire linguistic processes being aided by machine learning models, which can serve a tremendous amount of use cases'. The article continues predicting that 'businesses like ecommerce marketplaces will start using LLMs to create product descriptions, optimize existing content, and augment many other tasks. Like with many automation tools, these will not completely replace humans, at least in the foreseeable future, but improve work efficiency.'

Further, it is important to notice that when comparing GPT-2 to GPT-3 or GPT-4, a quantum leap has happened. While GPT-2 still has reduced deep semantic capacity, ChatGPT (whose first published version is based on GPT-3.5) is much better and reaches human-level competence.

Finally, from a linguistic perspective, the commonly held view that texts written in natural language are simply seen as 'unstructured data' is inaccurate. Language expresses knowledge in all its nuances. While approaches relying on repetition of words (for example keyword extraction, document classification, topic modelling) or short context (for example distributional semantics) allows us to get an accurate overview known as distant reading (Moretti 2013), the deep-semantic approach of transformer models also brings automated close reading to the realm of possibilities, literally respecting text as data, as in the vision of Grimmer et al. (2022).

9.2 Hands-on

LLMs such as BERT, GPT-2, GPT-3 and GPT-4 are so large that we cannot train them ourselves, as we did for document classification in Chapter 5, topic modelling in Chapter 6 or distributional semantics in Chapter 8. Instead, we will use pre-trained models from Hugging Face and apply them on our computers.

These pre-trained models are typically loaded and applied in Python, but they can also be used in R. We are aware of two such libraries, *RBERT*[8] and *text*[9]; we will use the latter. We use the R library *text* by Kjell et al. (2021).

9.2.1 Installation of the *text* package and Python via *reticulate* and *conda*

The R library *text* installs Python under the hood via *conda*[10] and then uses it (or another existing Python installation) by means of *reticulate*.[11] The installation is simple and briefly described in the following.

The installation is described step by step on the website of text (www.r-text .org), and you just need to follow it. We will provide a summary of the code in Box 9.1.[12]

Box 9.1 Installation of the text package and Python via conda

```
install.packages("text") ### accept 'install from sources' ("Yes")

library(text)

# Install text required python packages in a conda environment (with
    defaults).
textrpp_install()

# Initialize the installed conda environment.
# save_profile = TRUE saves the settings so that you don't have to run
    textrpp_initialize() after restarting R.
textrpp_initialize(save_profile = TRUE)

# Example text
texts <- c("I feel great!")

# Defaults
embeddings <- textEmbed(texts)
embeddings
```

We recommend to install the CRAN version. You will likely have to install from sources (so you will need to answer 'Yes' when asked), which in turn requires that you have a development tool (*Xcode* on Mac or *Rtools* on Windows). You have probably already installed them in Section 8.3 when we needed them for the library *wordVectors*.

The Python installation happens by means of the command *textrpp_install()*. The installation will take several minutes. You do not need to know anything about Python, conda or reticulate for this step, nor do you need to install the reticulate library.

After successful installation, an easy way to test if all worked, and at the same time do a first experiment, is to test the task that GPT-2 (and largely BERT too) can do best: the prediction of the next word iteratively to generate a short text. Ever since we started using model statistics in Chapter 5, models have the advantage to make predictions. Now finally, instead of predicting classes, we predict language. Also, this experiment is suggested on the website of the text library, and you can see some examples in Box 9.2. The first one is convincing, and the second one reveals that knowledge of household instruments is still a bit limited.

Box 9.2 Some of our more and less successful text generation experiments

```
> generated_text2 <- textGeneration("After the battle of Hastings", model
    = "gpt2")
Setting `pad_token_id` to `eos_token_id`:50256 for open-end generation.
x completed: Duration: 15.243155 secs
> generated_text2
# A tibble: 1 × 1
  x_generated
  <chr>
1 After the battle of Hastings, there was a battle to the death for the
    throne. It was an extraordinary, and rather heroic episode, and,
    with it the victory of Hastings — which …
> generated_text3 <- textGeneration("The technical advantage of this new
    dishwasher", model = "gpt2")
Setting `pad_token_id` to `eos_token_id`:50256 for open-end generation.
x completed: Duration: 12.222720 secs
> generated_text3
# A tibble: 1 × 1
  x_generated
  <chr>
1 The technical advantage of this new dishwasher is that when you add flour
    and sodium the dishwasher stops boiling, which is easy compared to
    regular washing. The dishwasher is…
```

9.2.2 Finding specific information from patient interviews with question answering

Question answering (QA) is an important application of computational linguistics (see, e.g., Jurafsky and Martin 2009, Chapter 23 for methods). QA is typically used to find general world knowledge questions, but also experts need to find specific information fast in an ever-growing amount of data and further specializing fields. Many data sets and competitions for QA exist (see Zhang et al. (2023) for an overview on factual QA). To find specific answers, a two-step procedure is usually applied: first, a small set of suitable documents matching our question are found, for instance, with document classification or Google search, and then the specific passage answering our question is located in them. We will perform the second step in this hands-on: given a suitable document, we find the exact passage answering our question with a BERT model.

A data set specifically addressing the task of extracting research questions in scientific research articles is QASPER (Dasigi et al. 2021), which contains 5,049 gold-standard answers from 1,585 natural language processing papers. Although it has been specifically adapted to research texts, it can be used to find factual questions on formal language texts generally. This data set has been used to fine-tune a BERT model for the task of QA and is available on Hugging Face.[13] In other words, this is a few-shot model that has been adapted to the right task or almost the right task that we want to address. We will use it to answer questions from the medical domain. In the hands-on experiment shown in Box 9.3, we use an excerpt of a patient interview from the DIPEx database.[14] The patient was in the intensive care unit and reports on her experiences. Open interviews allow one to find information that surveys may miss because they do not always ask the right questions. But the free text interviews are hard to process automatically, and we need advanced natural language processing to turn the so-called unstructured information into a structured format, which we can then feed into a database or contrast to classical surveys.

While we cannot expect the stunning performance of ChatGPT (which has a model that is still several orders of magnitude larger), the BERT model reveals impressive powers of abstraction, as our experiment in Box 9.3 shows – and you can run it in your own living room. The text library offers textQA as function for QA, which needs three parameters: the context document, the question and the model (z-uo/bert-qasper is the QASPER model).

Box 9.3 QA with QASPER on a patient report from DIPEx

```
mtptext = "Ms Anna A. was very tired during her stay in the
    intensive care unit. She was particularly disturbed by the
    noise and the light, but she also received a lot of care
    from the nursing staff. So I remember the time that passed
    at first very slowly, an immense tiredness, the impression
    of not understanding what was happening to me. And then
    the noise, the light that was very strong. And at the
    beginning, too, when I was under morphine, well, that was
    unpleasant for me because I started having hallucinations
    and I couldn't stand that. And then the fact of lying in
    bed all the time and then (almost) not being able to move,
    that was difficult. I: Do you have a more specific, practical
    example where you felt that way? E: Yes, already the fact
    that I had to be washed, for example, completely, or, that's
    it, I couldn't get up. So I was in bed and the nurses had
    to wash me. That was a bit difficult; well, they did it very
    well, it was admirable and they really did everything to not
    make me feel indebted or whatever; well, very well, but for
    me it was difficult. And the other thing that was also difficult
    was the heat and the thirst. So I couldn't drink, I was
    thirsty, that was difficult. And the heat, I was always hot."

mtptext

## qasper model with DIPEx example
qa_examples <- textQA(question = "What disturbed the patient?",
                      model = "z-uo/bert-qasper",
                      context = mtptext); qa_examples
What disturbed the patient? completed: Duration: 9.256563 secs
# A tibble: 1 × 4
 score start     end answer
 <dbl> <int> <int> <chr>
1 0.653 108   127 noise and the light

qa_examples <- textQA(question = "What annoyed the patient?",
                      model = "z-uo/bert-qasper",
                      context = mtptext); qa_examples
What annoyed the patient? completed: Duration: 8.966461 secs
# A tibble: 1 × 4
 score start  end answer
 <dbl> <int> <int> <chr>
1 0.330  108   127 noise and the light

qa_examples <- textQA(question = "Who is the patient?",
                      model = "z-uo/bert-qasper",
                      context = mtptext); qa_examples
Who is the patient? completed: Duration: 9.024735 secs
```

```
# A tibble: 1 × 4
 score start  end answer
 <dbl> <int> <int> <chr>
1 0.708   0     10 Ms Anna A.

qa_examples <- textQA(question = "Did the patient sleep well?",
                      model = "z-uo/bert-qasper",
                      context = mtptext); qa_examples
Did the patient sleep well? completed: Duration: 9.075212 secs
# A tibble: 1 × 4
  score start  end answer
  <dbl> <int> <int> <chr>
1 0.0223   0     25 Ms Anna A. was very tired

## qasper model with DIPEx example
qa_examples <- textQA(question = "Was the patient thirsty?",
                      model = "z-uo/bert-qasper",
                      context = mtptext); qa_examples
Was the patient thirsty? completed: Duration: 9.450319 secs
# A tibble: 1 × 4
  score start  end answer
  <dbl> <int> <int> <chr>
1 0.0849 1147  1178 I couldn't drink, I was thirsty

qa_examples <- textQA(question = "Was the patient generally
     satisfied?",
                      model = "z-uo/bert-qasper",
                      context = mtptext); qa_examples
Was the patient generally satisfied? completed: Duration:
     8.822719 secs
# A tibble: 1 × 4
  score start  end answer
  <dbl> <int> <int> <chr>
1 0.0534 133   187 she also received a lot of care from the
     nursing staff

qa_examples <- textQA(question = "Did the hospital staff make
mistakes?",
                      model = "z-uo/bert-qasper",
                      context = mtptext); qa_examples
Did the hospital staff make mistakes? completed: Duration:
8.859901 secs
# A tibble: 1 × 4
 score start  end answer
 <dbl> <int> <int> <chr>
1 0.111  956 1023 they really did everything to not make me feel
     indebted or whatever
```

Verbatim passages are found easily (*What disturbed the patient?*) but also near-synonyms (*What annoyed the patient?*), although with a slightly lower score. Without explicit prompting, the system realizes that the text comes from a hospital situation and that the person anonymized to *Anna* must be a patient (*Who is the patient?*, but also all other questions rely on this inference). If knowledge is quite generic but not deep enough, this can also lead to errors: while the BERT model recognizes that to be tired and sleeping are closely related, the answer (*Did the patient sleep well?*) is not helpful. Observe, though, that it is delivered with a very low confidence score (0.022). Even more inference steps (e.g. latent information on what a patient in hospital needs to be satisfied) are involved for finding suitable passages for the last two questions *Was the patient generally satisfied?* and *Did the hospital staff make mistakes?*. The last question is also answered convincingly, even though it does not express explicitly that the staff did *not* make any mistakes.

You can experiment yourself to find out how deep the knowledge of BERT QASPER actually is by using texts of your own: summaries of plots of literary works, technical manuals, medical leaflets, description of medical symptoms or diseases, brief financial reports, party programs – the only limit is the capacity of your PC and your curiosity.

9.2.3 A picture of the US presidential campaigns

In the hands-on in the previous section, we only had to embed a single text (and a short question). In order to perform improved document classification, we would need to embed entire corpora. This is unfortunately often too taxing for many small PCs unless you have GPU support. We tried to embed the presidential speeches corpus (Section 1.9.11) and CORPS-II (Section 1.9.9) but typically ran into memory overflows which crashed the R session. There is the option of using extra small BERT models such as TinyBERT (Jiao et al. 2019, on Hugging Face as prajjwal1/bert-tiny[15]), but they come with a certain loss in performance and may still not get through. We are reaching the practical limits of today's PCs.

Kjell et al. (2021) give an example where they just use the keywords that patients selected themselves and then draw a map of harmony in life (HILS) versus satisfaction with life (SWLS). Obviously, the two are closely related (see the graph on https://www.r-text.org), but we can see that *anger* and *stressed* have lower HILS than SWLS, indicating that they affect harmony more than general satisfaction, while *anxious* and *harmonious* exhibit the opposite pattern.

We are basing our next hands-on experiment Kjell et al. (2021), in particular their website, and extract keywords from the presidential debates to plot keywords against the left–right political spectrum on the horizontal axis and the year of campaign on the vertical axis.

First, we recommend executing the example of Kjell et al. step by step from their website (https://www.r-text.org), as given in Box 9.4.[16]

Box 9.4 Kjell's original experiment, plotting HILS against SWLS words

```
### from https://www.r-text.org

library(text)
# Use data (DP_projections_HILS_SWLS_100) that have been pre-
        processed with the textProjectionData function; the
        preprocessed test-data included in the package is called:
        DP_projections_HILS_SWLS_100
plot_projection <- textProjectionPlot(
  word_data = DP_projections_HILS_SWLS_100,
  y_axes = TRUE, ## make a 2-dimensional plot instead of
    1-dimension
  title_top = "Supervised Bicentroid Projection of Harmony in
    life words",
  x_axes_label = "Low vs. High HILS score",
  y_axes_label = "Low vs. High SWLS score",
  position_jitter_hight = 0.5,
  position_jitter_width = 0.8
)
plot_projection$final_plot
```

The provided data, DP_projections_HILS_SWLS_100, are the word embeddings of the HILS and SWLS keywords, column 3 of Language_based_assessment_data_8. They can be re-created as shown on the website, and this piece of code can be used as blueprint to embed texts ourselves.

Box 9.5 Embed a text yourself

```
## from http://www.r-text.org/articles/text.html

# View example data including both text and numerical variables
Language_based_assessment_data_8

# Transform the text data to BERT word embeddings
word_embeddings <- textEmbed(
```

```
texts  =  Language_based_assessment_data_8[3],   ##  webpage
    example takes column [3]=harmonywords
model = "bert-base-uncased", ## BERT base model
layers = -2,
aggregation_from_tokens_to_texts = "mean",
aggregation_from_tokens_to_word_types = "mean",
keep_token_embeddings = FALSE)
```

Let us apply the same procedure to the presidential debates corpus (Section 1.9.11), a corpus that we have also used in Chapters 6 and 8. As embedding the entire corpus overtaxes most PCs, we use the top 200 keywords from each candidate in each campaign. The keyword extraction process is described in detail in Chapter 4. We add the candidate names to the keyword list, and the year and party (0=Democrat and 1=Republican) as metadata for the two dimensions to be plotted. We have assigned Bernie Sanders to the Democratic Party, which is contested, as he officially acted as independent candidate, but sometimes also as Democrat.

Box 9.6 Our adaptation and experiment: Keyword extraction of the presidential debates and BERT experiment

```
## take debates, get TFIDF

setwd("~/Documents/DebateProjectVrana/Corpora/Debates_Archive_
    untagged_texts/") # adapt!
library(readtext)
library(quanteda)

debates = readtext("*.txt", docvarsfrom = "filenames")

cdebates = corpus(debates)
dtm <- dfm(cdebates, tolower=T, remove = stopwords("english"))
dtm_tfidf = dfm_tfidf(dtm)
keystring=""

cands   =   c("Bush","Gore","McCain","Bush","Kerry","Clinton",
    "McCain","Obama","Romney","Obama","Romney","Clinton","S
    anders","Trump")

for (i in(1:length(cdebates))) {
  mytfidf=dfm_sort(dtm_tfidf[i,],decreasing=T,margin="features")
  mytfidf200 = as.data.frame(mytfidf)[1:200]
  print(i); print(mytfidf200)
  stringoftop200 = paste(colnames(mytfidf200), collapse=" ")
```

```
  keystring[i] = paste(cands[i], stringoftop200, sep=" ")
  }

print(mytfidf200)

word_embeddings3 <- textEmbed(
  texts = keystring,  ## from presidential debates
  model = "bert-base-uncased",
  layers = -1, ### default is minus 2
  aggregation_from_tokens_to_texts = "mean",
  aggregation_from_tokens_to_word_types = "mean",
  keep_token_embeddings = FALSE)

years=c(2000,2000,2000,2004,2004,2008,2008,2008,2008,2012,2
    012,2016,2016,2016)

party=c(1,0,1,1, 0,0,1,0, 1,0,1,0, 0,1)

projection_results <- textProjection(
  words = keystring,
  word_embeddings = word_embeddings3$texts,
  word_types_embeddings = word_embeddings3$word_types,
  x= party,
  y= years
)

projection_results$word_data

options(ggrepel.max.overlaps = 10000)

plot_projection <- textProjectionPlot(
  word_data = projection_results,
  min_freq_words_plot = 1,
  plot_n_word_extreme = 100,
  plot_n_word_frequency = 100,
  plot_n_words_middle = 20,
  y_axes = TRUE,
  p_alpha = 0.1,
  p_adjust_method = "fdr",
  x_axes_label = "Party",
  y_axes_label = "Year",
)

plot_projection$final_plot
```

Figure 9.1 shows us the results. We can see Bernie Sanders ranting against banks and big business at the top left and Donald Trump's style on the top right (*stupid, horribly*). *Climate* change is topic for the left in 2012 and *immigration* for the right. Further down in history, *AIDS, empowerment* and *racial* issues are found more on the left, while the *Bible, virtue, sacred* and *agricultural* are stronger

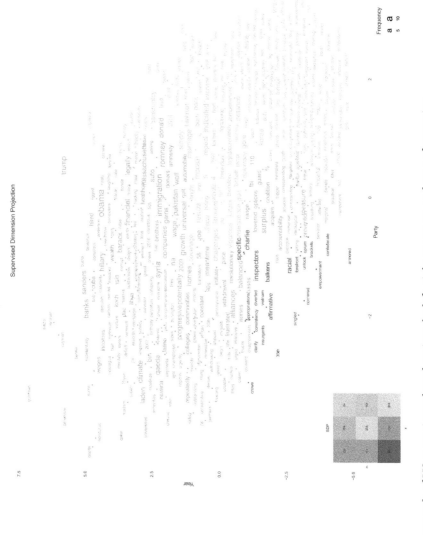

Figure 9.1 Keywords of US campaigns plotted against the left–right spectrum and year of campaign.

keywords for the right. Having said that, not all keywords seem very convincing. The bridge of interpretation that needs to be built from this experiment to tangible interpretations is still quite long. After generating conceptual maps with KDE (Chapter 7), word2vec word embeddings (Chapter 8) and now BERT models, the question as to which method is best suited for which purpose is still largely unanswered and opens up many research questions – perhaps you will help us to answer them?

Further Reading

Kjell et al. (2021): The article from the developers of the text library, which brings Hugging Face and BERT and GPT-2 to R. Their study on keywords relating to harmony in life (HILS) and satisfaction with life (SWLS) is exciting to read, and the perfect preparation for our hands-on experiment in Section 9.2.2.

Underwood (2019): Ted Underwood is well-known for his digital humanities research. In this blog, he summarizes an experiment, shows that BERT models can beat document classification in sentiment detection and discussed the background, applications and possible hesitations by colleagues from history and literature studies. He rightly points out that using BERT models is still hard, but the good news is that it has become easier in the three years since his post, and it will become easier still.

Jiao (2019): A BERT model that is particularly small but claims to achieve almost the same performance as the original BERT (BERT base). If you are looking for a challenge, this could be your next experiment.

Bhalla (2023): This book is not a book on ChatGPT, one cannot run ChatGPT on one's own computer and one needs a paying licence to connect to ChatGPT from one's own R programs. But if you have a paying licence, then that is an attractive possibility. Systematically, send all your questions to ChatGPT and then process the answers. Or you may want to send a long collection of documents to ChatGPT, one after the other, explicitly asking for a yes–no answer to your classification question (e.g. 'Does the above document contain hate speech? Please answer just with "yes" or "no"'). For many tasks, ChatGPT will beat document classification as we have seen it in Chapter 5. Deepanshu Bhalja shows simple code to access ChatGPT from R via an API.

Rodriguez (2023): Juan Cruz Rodriguez has wrapped code similar to the one from Bhalla (2023) into a simple R library called *chatgpt*, allowing you to access ChatGPT with one-liners. In particular, the library also adds help to programmers, using ChatGPT's extensive knowledge on programming languages, including R. This opens up an entirely new way for you to debug your R code and ask for finished code snippets for simple routines. Of course, in order to learn R you will need to interpret the code that ChatGPT delivers to you, and improve it where needed – ChatGPT is your coding partner. There is no doubt that this is the future of programming.

10

Conclusion

We have taken a long journey together through corpus linguistics, digital humanities, text analytics and content analysis. We have seen theoretical background and case studies from a variety of backgrounds: from linguistics, literature, history, political science and health. We started with simple, obvious approaches that are easy to implement, looked at their disadvantages and, by consequence, turned to more advanced, but also more difficult, approaches.

After setting the stage, motivating this book, outlining the differences and many commonalities of the research fields, and presenting the used corpora, we started with our first case studies in Chapter 2, looking at spikes of frequencies of words and part-of-speech tags, both with a linguistic and cultural history motivation. The approach we used was to count frequencies, and we have seen how this can be done easily with UNIX and with the *AntConc* concordance. In Chapter 2, you learnt how to count absolute frequencies and the basics of UNIX.

In Chapter 3, we started employing more statistical approaches: we moved on to using the statistics program R, and we looked at the differences between written and spoken registers, first from a stylistic viewpoint and then from a political one. The absolute frequencies seen there are easy to calculate but hard to put into perspective. Then, you learnt how to use R and how to create and interpret frequency lists.

In order to put differences into perspective, we then introduced the systematic comparison of relative frequencies with the help of O/E overuse metrics and by using the keyword measure TFIDF. After a hands-on experiment from popular culture (fairy tales) and US presidential debates, we presented a case study from historical sociolinguistics on overuse of part-of-speech tags comparing higher and lower classes. In Chapter 4, you learnt how to calculate relative frequencies and how to use R libraries, as from this point on, the approaches are too difficult to program every step ourselves.

In the next step, in Chapter 5, we showed how to overcome the restriction that overuse metrics consider individual features in isolation by using model statistics, which allow us to see the features in all their interactions and to make predictions. In supervised classification, we predict the periods of utterances for historical linguistics in the case study and parties of US politicians in our hands-on experiments. We put special emphasis on evaluation, which measures how much we can trust the model, and the interpretation of the features. In order to carry out these tasks, we got to know the powerful *quanteda* library in R and the fast, robust and user-friendly graphical tool *LightSide*. In Chapter 6, you learnt how to use supervised models to perform document classification in R and in *LightSide*.

Further, we addressed situations in which no known classes can be predicted, for instance, because they are unknown. To this end, we introduced unsupervised approaches, such as the famous topic models, first with two case studies, one from cultural history (court trials) and the other from literature (Charles Dickens). The hands-on experiments then allowed us to conduct a history experiment using *Mallet* and a political experiment in R, with the *stm* library. Next, you learnt how to use the popular unsupervised method of topic modelling and how to interpret its results.

Also topic models come with certain shortcomings, especially that the similarity between topics from topic modelling is unknown, and the view is one-dimensional. Thus, in Chapter 7, we present semantic maps of various types which give us a graded view in at least two dimensions. Our first approach, conceptual maps with kernel density estimation, is more exotic than topic models but has several advantages. This is illustrated by taking a journey through associations in religious studies and debated political topics (our case studies) and cultural history and US politics, if you followed our hands-on experiment. Next, you learnt another unsupervised method and explored semantic spaces.

Distributional semantics and word embeddings, introduced in Chapter 8, is another classic. It can be used for synonymy detection, but also for a fine-grained exploration of cognitive associations. This is exemplified in a case study from literature (Charles Dickens' visions) and in the hands-on section explores the associations of Republicans and Democrats in the United States. Then, you learnt how to use the word embedding package word2vec in R and how to use it for lexical research.

Using several methods leading to compatible results is one method to add trust to them and to aid our interpretation. Different methods often also bring new aspects to the foreground. We made the case for triangulation using, for example, topic modelling and the several ways of drawing semantic maps that we introduced. There are further ways to explore semantic landscapes and to draw maps, among other things, which led us to the last chapter. Building on the previous chapters, we then introduce the latest and most complex models, large language models (LLM) like BERT and GPT-2. GPT-3 and GPT-4 were introduced in Chapter 9. They offer new types of word embeddings, which have shown improved performance on many tasks at the cost of longer processing times. They are so complex that they are 'black-box' models, which places particularly high demands on the evaluation and interpretation. Our hands-on experiments with text generation, QA and semantic mapping may have shown you what is possible and what sometimes goes astray, as in all other methods presented in this book.

You now have a toolset, the necessary programming and interpretation skills, so you should be equipped to conduct experiments and interpretations on your own data sets and your own areas of interest – happy experimenting! Often students ask which method is best, that is, which one they should use. Fortunately, there is a clear answer: all of them! Or rather, at least as many as your project time allows and you manage to install on your computer. The more advanced, the more 'blackbox' a method is, the more you will have to argue why it makes sense to use it and why the method probably suggests the results that it does by showing that simpler methods lead to compatible, although more word-centred and local, results. But importantly: do not forget to build the bridge to the real text: distant reading approaches point to those documents and passages that are key to our research question; we need to do close reading, interpretation, argument building, building and testing of hypotheses and theories ourselves.

Notes

Acknowledgements

1   https://www.digitalreligions.uzh.ch/en.html

Chapter 1

1   http://www.culturomics.org.
2   https://books.google.com/ngrams.
3   http://www.tei-c.org/index.xml.
4   One reviewer pointed out that in their view, almost all of these methods and research topics could also be shared, so we can of these as prototypical. The comment, however, also illustrates how difficult it is to attempt to draw borderlines between disciplines. Most importantly, it underlines the versatility of the methods – any can be used in any of these disciplines – and the need for the interdisciplinary approach that we take here.
5   https://varieng.helsinki.fi/CoRD/corpora/CEEM/index.html.
6   https://eebo.chadwyck.com/about/about.htm.
7   OBC can be downloaded from CLARIN at http://fedora.clarin-d.uni-saarland.de/oldbailey/.
8   https://perswww.kuleuven.be/~u0044428/.
9   https://www.projects.alc.manchester.ac.uk/archer/.
10 https://ota.bodleian.ox.ac.uk/.
11 https://www.gutenberg.org.
12 https://www.english-corpora.org/coha/.
13 https://catalog.ldc.upenn.edu/LDC2008T19.

Chapter 2

1   https://ota.bodleian.ox.ac.uk/repository/xmlui/bitstream/handle/20.500.12024/1656/wooligh-1656.txt?sequence=5&isAllowed=y.
2   https://ota.bodleian.ox.ac.uk/repository/xmlui/bitstream/handle/20.500.12024/3041/3041.txt?sequence=8&isAllowed=y.

3　https://www.laurenceanthony.net/software/tagant/.
4　http://www.cis.uni-muenchen.de/~schmid/tools/TreeTagger/.

Chapter 3

1　https://ota.bodleian.ox.ac.uk/repository/xmlui/handle/20.500.12024/2553.
2　The full code can be found in the file "03_BNCBaby_spo_wri.R" on the companion website.
3　In Chapter 4, we will see that the *readtext* library also offers an option to read in entire folders.
4　https://www.linguistics.ucsb.edu/research/santa-barbara-corpus.
5　https://github.com/LeoVrana/PresidentialDebates.

Chapter 4

1　During the finishing phases of this book, the library *gutenbergr* was temporarily not available for recent versions of R. You can find the "2591.txt" and the adapted R code on the companion website of this book.
2　The full code can be found in the file "04_fairy_tales_TFIDF.R" on the companion website.
3　You can also use the folder "Debates_Archive_untagged_texts" on the companion website.
4　Box 4.5 corresponds to the file "04_US_debates_kewords.R" on the companion website.
5　Box 4.6 refers to "03_BNCBaby_spo_wri.R" on the companion website.

Chapter 5

1　As we are interested in both content and stylistic features, we have not used a stopword list. For authorship attribution, mainly stopword features are used.
2　Rank 147 may, prima facie, not seem salient, but given that we observe 13,715 features, this feature is within the top 2 per cent.
3　http://ankara.lti.cs.cmu.edu/side/.
4　The *LightSide* manual (Mayfiled et al. 2014: 4) also tells you how to increase the maximally allowed memory, which is often necessary for larger corpora.
5　https://muellerstefan.net/files/quanteda-cheatsheet.pdf.
6　The code can be found in file "05_doc_class_script.R" on the companion website.

Chapter 6

1   http://ucrel.lancs.ac.uk/wmatrix/.
2   http://mallet.cs.umass.edu/topics.php.
3   https://mimno.github.io/Mallet/index.
4   https://github.com/mimno/Mallet/releases.
5   The distribution can be found in the file "CLMET_distribution.zip" on the companion website.
6   The filenames are "CLMET3_1_1to3_forMallet100.Periodtextmarked3_ln.csv" for the input text and "CLMET3_1_1to3_forMallet100.Periodtextmarked3_ln.mallet" for the mallet format.

Chapter 7

1   http://dclure.org/logs/tuning-textplot/ The website is no longer accessible, but can still be found via web.archive.org, at https://web.archive.org/web/20210802034506/http://dclure.org/logs/tuning-textplot/.
2   https://www.gephi.org.
3   See file "SEL_perparty_v2.t500.skim5.bw2000.pdf" on the companion website.

Chapter 8

1   https://github.com/bmschmidt/wordVectors.
2   https://cran.r-project.org/bin/windows/Rtools/.
3   The code is available at "08_DistrSem.R" on the companion website, the filenames are as in the code.

Chapter 9

1   https://openai.com/blog/chatgpt/.
2   https://huggingface.co.
3   https://twitter.com/ammaar/status/1601284293363261441.
4   https://www.numenta.com/blog/2022/05/24/ai-is-harming-our-planet/.
5   https://www.eia.gov/tools/faqs/faq.php?id=97&t=3.
6   For example https://medium.com/analytics-vidhya/understanding-the-bert-model -a04e1c7933a9.

7　https://www.forbes.com/sites/garydrenik/2023/01/11/large-language-models-will
-define-artificial-intelligence/?sh=40b3f1b2b60f (11 January 2023).

8　https://www.rdocumentation.org/packages/RBERT/versions/0.1.11.

9　https://www.r-text.org.

10　https://www.conda.io.

11　https://rstudio.github.io/reticulate/.

12　The code can be found in file "09_BERT_usingmylocalConda.R" on the companion
website.

13　https://huggingface.co/z-uo/bert-qasper.

14　https://dipexinternational.org.

15　https://huggingface.co/prajjwal1/bert-tiny.

16　The script can be found in the file "09_BERT_experiment.R" on the companion
website.

References

Aarts, Bas. 2019. Syntactic Argumentation. In Bas Aarts, Jill Bowie, and Gergana Popova (eds), *The Oxford Handbook of English Grammar*, 21–39. Oxford: Oxford University Press.

Adolphs, Svenja. 2006. *Introducing Electronic Text Analysis: A Practical Guide for Language and Literary Studies*. London and New York: Routledge.

Ananiadou, Sophia, Douglas B. Kell, and Jun-ichi Tsujii. 2006. Text Mining and Its Potential Applications in Systems Biology. *Trends in Biotechnology*, 24(12), 571–9.

Anderwald, Liselotte. 2017. *Get, get*-constructions and the *get*-passive in 19th-century English: Corpus Analysis and Prescriptive Comments. In Sebastian Hoffmann, Andrea Sand, and Sabine Arndt-Lappe (eds), *Exploring Recent Diachrony: Corpus Studies of Lexicogrammar and Language Practices in Late Modern English, VARIENG Volume 18*. https://varieng.helsinki.fi/series/volumes/18/anderwald/.

Anowar, Farzana, Samira Sadaoui, and Bassant Selim. 2021. Conceptual and Empirical Comparison of Dimensionality Reduction Algorithms (PCA, KPCA, LDA, MDS, SVD, LLE, ISOMAP, LE, ICA, t-SNE). *Computer Science Review*, 40, 100378.

Anthony, Lawrence. 2004. AntConc: A Learner and Classroom Friendly, Multi-Platform Corpus Analysis Toolkit. *Proceedings of IWLeL 2004: An Interactive Workshop on Language e-Learning*, 7–13.

Arun, Rajkumar, Vommina Suresh, and C. E. Veni Madhavan. 2009. Stopword Graphs and Authorship Attribution in Text Corpora. In *Semantic Computing, 2009. ICSC '09. IEEE International Conference on Semantic Computing*, 192–6.

Aston, Guy and Lou Burnard. 1998. *The BNC Handbook: Exploring the British National Corpus with SARA*. Edinburgh Textbooks in Empirical Linguistics. Edinburgh: Edinburgh University Press.

Baker, Paul. 2010a. Research Methods in Linguistics. In Lia Litosseliti (ed.), *Research Methods in Linguistics*. London: Continuum.

Baker, Paul, 2010b. *Sociolinguistics and Corpus Linguistics*. Edinburgh: Edinburgh University Press.

Baroni, Marco, Georgiana Dinu, and Germán Kruszewski. 2014. Don't Count, Predict! A Systematic Comparison of Context-counting vs. Context-predicting Semantic Vectors. In *Proceedings of the 52nd Annual Meeting of the Association for Computational Linguistics*, 238–47.

Baroni, Marco and Alessandro Lenci. 2010. Distributional Memory: A General Framework for Corpus-based Semantics. *Computational Linguistics*, 36(4), 673–721.

Begley, Sharon. 2017. Trump Wasn't Always So Linguistically Challenged. What Could Explain the Change? *Statnews*, May 30. https://www.statnews.com/2017/05/23/donald-trump-speaking-style-interviews/ (accessed 1 November 2019).

Bender, Courtney and Omar McRoberts. 2012. Mapping a Field: Why and How to Study Spirituality. *SSRC Working Papers*, 1–27. https://tif.ssrc.org/wp-content/uploads/2010/05/Why-and-How-to-Study-Spirtuality.pdf.

Bhalla, Deepanshu. 2023. ChatGPT in R: Everything You Need to Know. *Listen Data Blog*. https://www.listendata.com/2023/05/chatgpt-in-r.html.

Biber, Douglas. 1988. *Variation across Speech and Writing*. Cambridge: Cambridge University Press.

Biber, Douglas, Edward Finegan, and Dwight Atkinson. 1994. ARCHER and Its Challenges: Compiling and Exploring a Representative Corpus of Historical English Registers. In Udo Fries, Peter Schneider, and Gunnel Tottie (eds), *Creating and Using English Language Corpora. Papers from the 14th International Conference on English Language Research on Computerized Corpora, Zurich 1993*, 1–13. Amsterdam: Rodopi.

Blei, David M. 2012. Probabilistic Topic Models. *Communications of the ACM*, 55(4), 77–84.

BNC Consortium. 2007. *British National Corpus, Baby Edition, Oxford Text Archive*. http://hdl.handle.net/20.500.12024/2553.

Bresnan, Joan, Anna Cueni, Tatiana Nikitina, and Harald Baayen. 2007. Predicting the Dative Alternation. In G. Boume and I. Kraemer, and J. Zwarts (eds), *Cognitive Foundations of Interpretation*, 69–94. Amsterdam: Royal Netherlands Academy of Science.

Burrows, John. 2002. 'Delta': A Measure of Stylistic Difference and a Guide to Likely Authorship. *Literary and Linguistic Computing*, 17(3), 267–87.

Buzan, Tony and Barry Buzan. 1993. *The Mind Map Book: How to Use the Radiant Thinking to Maximize Your Brain's Untapped Potential*. London: Penguin.

Bybee, Joan. 2007. *Frequency of Use and the Organization of Language*. Oxford: Oxford University Press.

Cam-Stei, Duncan. 2019. Word Embedding Explained, a Comparison and Code Tutorial. https://medium.com/@dcameronsteinke/tf-idf-vs-word-embedding-a-comparison-and-code-tutorial-5ba341379ab0.

Card, Dallas, Serina Chang, Chris Becker, Julia Mendelsohn, Rob Voigt, Leah Boustan, Ran Abramitzky, and Dan Jurafsky. 2022. Computational Analysis of 140 Years of US Political Speeches Reveals More Positive but Increasingly Polarized Framing of Immigration. *Proceedings of the National Academy of Sciences*, 119, 31. https://www.pnas.org/doi/full/10.1073/pnas.2120510119.

Culpepper, Jonathan and Merja Kytö. 2000. Gender Voices in the Spoken Interaction of the Past: A Pilot Study Based on Early Modern English Trial Proceedings. In D. Kastovsky and A. Mettinger (eds), *The History of English in a Social Context*, 129 ed., 53–89. Berlin: Mouton de Gruyter.

Culpeper, Jonathan and Merja Kyoto. 2010. *Early Modern English Dialogues: Spoken Interactionas Writing*. Cambridge: Cambridge University Press

Dasigi, Pradeep, Kyle Lo, Iz Beltagy, Arman Cohan, Noah A. Smith, and Matt Gardner. 2021. *A Dataset of Information-Seeking Questions and Answers Anchored in Research Papers. arXiv*. https://arxiv.org/abs/2105.03011.

Deerwester, Scott, Susan T. Dumais, George W. Furnas, Thomas K. Landauer, and Richard Harshman. 1990. Indexing by Latent Semantic Analysis. *Journal of the American Society of Information Science*, 41(6), 391–407.

De Smet, Hendrik. 2005. A Corpus of Late Modern English. *ICAME Journal*, 29, 69–82. https://icame.info/icame-journal-29/.

Diesner, Jana and Kathleen Carley. 2004. *Automap1.2 – Extract, Analyze, Represent, and Compare Mental Models from Texts*. Technical Report CMU-ISRI-04-100, Carnegie Mellon University, School of Computer Science, Institute for Software Research International, Pittsburgh, PA.

Dubinsky, Ellen and Thanh Nguyen. 2012–2023. *Introduction to Digital Humanities Resources*. http://webhost.bridgew.edu/edubinsky/DH/index.html.

Emblen J. D. 1992. Religion and Spirituality Defined According to Current Use in Nursing Literature. *Journal of Professional Nursing: Official Journal of the American Association of Colleges of Nursing*, 8(1), 41–7. https://doi.org/10.1016/8755-7223(92)90116-g.

Eve, Martin Paul. 2022. *The Digital Humanities and Literary Studies*. Oxford: Oxford University Press.

Evert, Stefan. 2006. How Random Is a Corpus? The Library Metaphor. *Zeitschrift für Anglistik und Amerikanistik*, 54(2), 177–90.

Evert, Stefan. 2009. Corpora and Collocations. *Corpus Linguistics. An International Handbook*, Article 58, 1212–48.

Ferreira, Pedro G. 2023. *Dimensionality Reduction*. Unpublished Document. http://www.pgferreira.net/personal_website/UL_Tutorial/UnsupervisedLearning.html (accessed July 15, 2023).

Firoozeh, N., A. Nazarenkoc, F. Alizon, and B. Daille 2020. Keyword Extraction: Issues and Methods. *Natural Language Engineering*, 26(3), 259–91. doi:10.1017/S1351324919000457.

Firth, John Rupert. 1957. A Synopsis of Linguistic Theory 1930–1955. In J. R. Firth et al. *Studies in Linguistic Analysis*. Special volume of the Philological Society, 1–32. Oxford: Blackwell.

Fitzmaurice, Suan, Justyna A. Robinson, Marc Alexander, Iona C. Hine, Seth Mehl, and Fraser Dallachy. 2017. Linguistic {DNA}: Investigating Conceptual Change in Early Modern English Discourse. *Studia Neophilologica*, 89(2), 1–18.

Fowler, J. W. (1981). *Stages of Faith: The Psychology of Human Development and the Quest for Meaning*. San Francisco: Harper & Row.

Gavin, Michael. 2022. *Literary Mathematics: Quantitative Theory for Textual Studies*. Stanford Text Technologies Series. Stanford: Stanford University Press.

Ghanem, Salma. 1997. Filling the Tapestry: The Second Level of Agenda Setting. In Maxwell McCombs, Donald L. Shaw, and David Weaver (eds), *Communication and Democracy: Exploring the Intellectual Frontiers in Agenda-Setting Theory*, 3–14. Mahwah, NJ: Lawrence Erlbaum.

Goldberg, Adele E. 1995. *Constructions: A Construction Grammar Approach to Argument Structure*. Chicago: University of Chicago Press.

Goldberg, Adele. 2003. Constructions: A New Theoretical Approach to Language. *Trends in Cognitive Science*, 7(5), 219–24.

Goldberg, Adele. 2006. *Constructions at Work: The Nature of Generalization in Language*. Oxford: Oxford University Press.

Gries, Stefan. 2006. Exploring Variability within and between Corpora: Some Methodological Considerations. *Corpora*, 1(2), 109–51.

Gries, Stefan. 2010. Methodological Skills in Corpus Linguistics: A Polemic and Some Pointers towards Quantitative Methods. In Tonay Harris and Maria Morena Jaen (eds), *Corpus Linguistics in Language Teaching*, 121–46. Frankfurt a. M.: Peter Lang. https://stgries.info/research/2010_STG_MethSkillsCorpLing_CorpLingLgTeaching .pdf (accessed July 15, 2023).

Grimmer, Justin, Margaret E. Roberts, and Brandon M. Stewart. 2022. *Text as Data: A New Framework for Machine Learning and the Social Sciences*. Princeton: Princeton University Press.

Grimmer, Justin and Brandon Stewart. 2013. Text as Data: The Promise and Pitfalls of Automatic Content Analysis Methods for Political Texts. *Political Analysis*, 21(3), 267–97.

Guerini, Marco, Danilo Giampiccolo, Giovanni Moretti, Rachele Sprugnoli, and Carlo Strapparava. 2013. The New Release of CORPS: A Corpus of Political Speeches Annotated with Audience Reactions. In Isabella Poggi, Francesca D'Errico, Laura Vincze, and Alessandro Vinciarelli (eds), *Multimodal Communication in Political Speech. Shaping Minds and Social Action*. Lecture Notes in Computer Science 7688, 86–98. Berlin: Springer.

Günther, Fritz, Carolin Dudschig, and Barbara Kaup. 2015. *Behavior Research Methods*, 47, 930–44. https://link.springer.com/article/10.3758/s13428-014-0529-0.

Harris, Zellig. 1968. *Mathematical Structures of Language*. New York: Wiley.

Harris, Zellig. 1970. Distributional Structure. *Papers in Structural and Transformational Linguistics*. Formal Linguistics Series, 775–94. Dordrecht: Springer. https://doi.org /10.1007/978-94-017-6059-1_36.

Hey Tony, Stewart Tansley, and Kristin Tolle. 2009. Jim Grey on eScience: A Transformed Scientific Method. In: Tony Hey, Stewart Tansley and Kristin Tolle (eds), *The Fourth Paradigm: Data-Intensive Scientific Discovery*, XVII–XXXI. Redmond: Microsoft Research. https://www.microsoft.com/en-us/research/uploads/ prod/2009/10/Fourth_Paradigm.pdf

Hilpert, Martin and Stefan Gries. 2016. Quantitative Approaches to Diachronic Corpus Linguistics. In Merja Kytö and Paivi Pahta (eds), *The Cambridge Handbook of English Historical Linguistics*, 36–53. Cambridge: Cambridge University Press.

Huber, Magnus. 2007. The Old Bailey Proceedings, 1674–1834. Evaluating and Annotating a Corpus of 18th- and 19th-century Spoken English. In Anneli Meurman-Solin and Arja Nurmi (eds), *Studies in VARIENG: Studies in Variation, Contacts and Change in English*, vol. 1. http://www.helsinki.fi/varieng/series/volumes /01/huber/ (accessed 1 January 2023).

Huber, Magnus, Magnus Nissel, and Karin Puga. 2016. *The Old Bailey Corpus 2.0, 1720–1913: Manual.* http://fedora.clarin-d.uni-saarland.de/oldbailey/documentation .html (accessed 1 January 2023).

Hundt, Marianne. 2001. What Corpora Can Tell Us about the Grammaticalisation of Voice in *get*-constructions. *Studies in Language*, 25, 49–88.

Hundt, Marianne, Gerold Schneider, and Elena Seoane. 2016. The Use of the *be*-passive in Academic Englishes: Local vs Global Usage in an International Language. *Corpora*, 11(1), 29–61. ISSN 1749-5032.

Jacobi, Carina, Wouter van Atteveldt, and Kasper Welbers. 2016. Quantitative Analysis of Large Amounts of Journalistic Texts Using Topic Modelling. *Digital Journalism*, 4(1), 89–106. https://www.tandfonline.com/doi/full/10.1080/21670811.2015 .1093271 (accessed 15 July 2023).

Jacomy, Mathieu, Tommaso Venturini, Sebastien Heymann, and Mathieu Bastian. 2014. ForceAtlas2, a Continuous Graph Layout Algorithm for Handy Network Visualization Designed for the Gephi Software. *PLOS ONE*, 9(6), e98679. https://doi .org/10.1371/journal.pone.0098679 (accessed 7 January 2023).

Jiao, Xiaoqi, Yichun Yin, Lifeng Shang, Xin Jiang, Xiao Chen, Linlin Li, Fang Wang, and Qun Liu. 2019. TinyBERT: Distilling BERT for Natural Language Understanding. arXiv. https://arxiv.org/abs/1909.10351 (accessed 15 July 2023).

Jockers, Matthew L. 2014. *Text Analysis with R for Students of Literature.* New York: Springer.

Jonsson, Ewa. *Conversational Writing: A Multidimensional Study of Synchronous and Supersynchronous Computer-Mediated Communication.* Frankfurt am Main: Peter Lang.

Jurafsky, Daniel and James H. Martin. 2009. *Speech and Language Processing: An Introduction to Natural Language Processing, Computational Linguistics, and Speech Recognition.* Upper Saddle River, NJ: Pearson Prentice Hall.

Kailash, Sudha. 2012. Charles Dickens as a Social Critic. *International Journal of Research in Economics & Social Sciences*, 2(8), 1–51.

Karlgren, Jussi and Magnus Sahlgren. 2001. From Words to Understanding. In Yoshinori Uesaka, Pentti Kanerva and Hideki Asoh (eds), *Foundations of Real-World Intelligence*, 294–308. California: CSLI Publications.

Kaufman, Micki. 2020. Everything on Paper Will Be Used Against Me. *Quantifying Kissinger.* http://blog.quantifyingkissinger.com (accessed 7 January 2023).

Kilimci, Zeynep H. and Selim Akyokus. 2018. Deep Learning- and Word Embedding-Based Heterogeneous Classifier Ensembles for Text Classification. *Complexity*, 2018, 7130146. https://www.hindawi.com/journals/complexity/2018 /7130146/.

Kim, S.-H., N. Lee, and P.E. King. 2020. Dimensions of Religion and Spirituality: A Longitudinal Topic Modeling Approach. *Journal for the Scientific Study of Religion*, 59, 62–83. https://doi.org/10.1111/jssr.12639.

Kitchin, Rob. 2014. Big Data, New Epistemologies and Paradigm Shifts. *Big Data & Society*, April–June, 1–12. doi:10.1177/2053951714528481.

Kjell, Oscar N. E., Salvatore Giorgi, and H. Andrew Schwartz. 2021. The Text-package: An R-package for Analyzing and Visualizing Human Language Using Natural Language Processing and Deep Learning. *PsyArXiv*. April 16. doi:10.31234/osf.io/293kt.

Kozlowski, Austin C., Matt Taddy, and James A. Evans. 2019. The Geometry of Culture: Analyzing the Meanings of Class through Word Embeddings. *American Sociological Review*, 84(5), 905–49.

Krippendorff, Klaus. 2004. *Content Analysis: An Introduction to Its Methodology*. 2nd ed. Thousand Oaks: SAGE Publications.

Krippendorff, Klaus. 2019. *Content Analysis: An Introduction to Its Methodology*. 4th ed. Thousand Oaks: SAGE Publications.

Ladle, Richard J., Ricardo A. Correia, Yuno Do, Gea-Jae Joo, Ana C. M. Malhado, Raphael Proulx, Jean-Michel Roberge, and Paul Jepson. 2016. Conservation Culturomics. *Frontiers in Ecology and the Environment*, 14(5), 269–75.

Lee, Chang-Hwan, Fernando Gutierrez, and Dejing Dou. 2011. Calculating Feature Weights in Naïve Bayes with Kullback-Leibler Measure. In *Proceedings of IEEE International Conference on Data Mining*, 1146–51. http://ix.cs.uoregon.edu/~dou/research/papers/icdm11_fw.pdf.

Leech, Geoffrey, Marianne Hundt, Christian Mair, and Nicholas Smith. 2009. *Change in Contemporary English. A Grammatical Study*. Cambridge: Cambridge University Press.

Lenci, Alessandro. 2008. Distributional Semantics in Linguistic and Cognitive Research. In Alessandro Lenci (ed.), *From Context to Meaning: Distributional Models of the Lexicon in Linguistics and Cognitive Science. Italian Journal of Linguistics*, 20(1), 1–31.

Levy, Roger and T. Florian Jaeger. 2007. Speakers Optimize Information Density Through Syntactic Reduction. In *Proceedings of the Twentieth Annual Conference on Neural Information Processing Systems*. Vancouver, Canada.

Lindquist, Hans. 2009. *Corpus Linguistics and the Description of English*. Edinburgh: Edinburgh University Press.

López-Couso, Maria José, Bas Aarts, and Belén Méndez-Naya. 2012. Late Modern English Syntax. In Alexander Bergs and Laurel J. Brinton (eds), *Historical Linguistics of English: An International Handbook*, vol. I. Handbooks of Linguistics and Communication Science [HSK] 34.1, 869–87. Mouton de Gruyter.

Los, Bettelou. 2005. *The Rise of the To-Infinitive*. Oxford: Oxford University Press.

Lu, Xiaofei. 2014. *Computational Methods for Corpus Annotation and Analysis*. Dordrecht: Springer.

Mahlberg, Michaela. 2013. *Corpus Stylistics and Dickens's Fiction*. New York and London: Routledge.

Mahlberg, Michaela 2015. Literary Style. In Douglas Biber and Randy Reppen (eds), *The Cambridge Handbook of Corpus Linguistics*, 346–61. Cambridge: Cambridge University Press.

Mair, Christian. 2006. The 19th Century as a Critical Period in the Formation of the Modern English System of Nonfinite Complement Clauses: The Case of Remember. In Merja Kytö and Erik Smitterberg (eds), *Nineteenth-Century English: Stability and Change*, 215–28. Cambridge: Cambridge University Press.

Malvern, David D., Brian J. Richards, Ngoni Chipere, and Pilar Durán. 2004. *Lexical Diversity and Language Development*. Houndmills: Palgrave MacMillan.

Mayfield, Elijah, David Adamson, and Carolyn P. Rosé. 2014. *LightSide: Researcher's Workbench User Manual*. https://ankara.lti.cs.cmu.edu/side/LightSide_Researchers _Manual.pdf (accessed July 15, 2023).

McClure, David. 2015. *Textplot*. https://github.com/davidmcclure/textplot (accessed 7 January 2023).

McEnery, Tony and Andrew Wilson. 2001. *Corpus Linguistics: An Introduction*. 2nd ed. Edinburgh: Edinburgh University Press.

Michel, Jean-Baptiste, Yuan Kui Shen, Aviva P. Aiden, Adrian Veres, Matthew K. Gray, Joseph P. Pickett, Dale Hoiberg, Dan Clancy, Peter Norvig, Jon Orwant, Steven Pinker, Martin A. Nowak, and Erez Lieberman Aiden. 2010. Quantitative Analysis of Culture Using Millions of Digitized Books. *Science*, 331(6014), 176–82.

Mikolov, Tomas, Kai Chen, Greg Corrado, and Jeffrey Dean. 2013. Efficient Estimation of Word Representations in Vector Space. https://arxiv.org/abs/1301.3781.

Miller, George A. and Walter G. Charles. 1991. Contextual Correlates of Semantic Similarity. *Language and Cognitive Processes*, 6, 1–28.

Mockford, Jack. 2014. 'They are Exactly as Banknotes are': Perceptions and Technologies of Bank Note Forgery During the Bank Restriction Period, 1797–1821. Doctoral Thesis, University of Hertfordshire.

Moretti, Franco. 2013. *Distant Reading*. London: Verso.

Moretti, Franco. 2000. Conjectures on World Literature. *New Left Review*, January/ February. https://newleftreview.org/issues/ii1/articles/franco-moretti-conjectures-on -world-literature.

Mosteller, Frederick and David Wallace. 1964. *Inference and Disputed Authorship: The Federalist*. Addison-Wesley Series in Behavioral Science; Quantitative Methods. Reading, MA, Palo Alto, and London: Addison-Wesley.

Munafò, Marcus R. and George Davey Smith. 2018. Robust Research Needs Many Lines of Evidence. *Nature*, 553, 399–401.

Neubert, Frank. 2016. *Die Diskursive Konstitution von Religion*. Berlin: Springer.

Newman, L.J. 2004. Faith, Spirituality, and Religion: A Model for Understanding the Differences. *College Student Affairs Journal*, 23(2), 102–10. https://eric.ed.gov/?id =EJ956981.

Oakes, Michael P. 2014. *Literary Detective Work on the Computer*. Amsterdam and Philadelphia, PA: Benjamins.

Ourednik; André (2022). *Maps and Spaces: Text2Landscape*. https://ourednik.info/maps /2022/02/04/text2landscape-visualize-a-text-in-multiple-spaces-with-r-network -visualization-word-embeddings-principal-component-analysis-and-self-organizing -maps/ (accessed 7 January 2023).

Paul Victor, C. and J. V. Treschuk. 2020. Critical Literature Review on the Definition Clarity of the Concept of Faith, Religion, and Spirituality. *Journal of Holistic Nursing*, 38(1), 107–13. https://journals.sagepub.com/doi/full/10.1177/0898010119895368

Peng-Keller, Simon. 2019. Genealogies of 'Spirituality': An Historical Analysis of a Travelling Term. *Journal for the Study of Spirituality*, 9(2), 86–98.

Peng-Keller, Simon, Fabian Winiger, and Raphael Rauch 2022. *The Spirit of Global Health—The World Health Organization and the 'Spiritual Dimension' of Health (1946–2021)*. Oxford: Oxford University Press.

Peters, Gerhard and John T. Wooley. 2023. Presidential Debates. http://www.presidency .ucsb.edu/debates.php (accessed 1 January 2023).

Popcak, R. and G. Popcak. 2014. Faith, Spirituality, Belief, Religion . . . What's the Difference? *Faith on the Couch Blogs*. https://www.patheos.com/blogs/ faithonthecouch/2014/05/faith-spirituality-belief-religion-whats-the-difference/.

Prensky, Marc. 2009 H. Sapiens Digital: From Digital Immigrants and Digital Natives to Digital Wisdom. *Innovate*, 5(3). http://www.innovateonline.info/index.php? view1/4article&id1/4705.

Quinn, Kevin, Burt L. Monroe, Michael Colaresi, Michael H. Crespin, and Dragomir R. Radev 2010. How to Analyze Political Attention with Minimal Assumptions and Costs. *American Journal of Political Science*, 54(1), 209–28.

Rayson, Paul. 2008. From Key Words to Key Semantic Domains. *International Journal of Corpus Linguistics*, 13(4), 519–49.

Röder, Michael, Andreas Both, and Alexander Hinneburg. 2015. Exploring the Space of Topic Coherence Measures. *Proceedings of WSDM'15*, February 2–6, Shanghai, China.

Ronan, Patricia and Gerold Schneider. 2020. A Man Who Was Just an Incredible Man, an Incredible Man: Age Factors and Coherence in Donald Trump's Spontaneous Speech. In Ulrike Schneider and Matthias Eitelmann (eds), *Linguistic Enquiries into Donald Trump's Language. From 'Fake News' to 'Tremendous Success'*, 62–84. London: Bloomsbury.

Roth, Randolph. 2001. Homicide in Early Modern England 1549–1800: The Need for a Quantitative Analysis. *Crime, History & Societies*, 5(2), 33–67. https://journals .openedition.org/chs/737 (accessed September 10, 2018).

Rouberol, Balthazar. 2020. *Text Processing in the Shell*. Unpublished manuscript. https:// blog.balthazar-rouberol.com/text-processing-in-the-shell.

Rüdiger, Matthias, David Antons, Amol M. Joshi, and Torsten-Oliver Salge. 2022. Topic Modeling Revisited: New Evidence on Algorithm Performance and Quality Metrics. *PLoS ONE*, 17(4), e0266325. https://doi.org/ 10.1371/journal.pone.0266325.

Sahlgren, Magnus. 2006. *The Word-Space Model: Using Distributional Analysis to Represent Syntagmatic and Paradigmatic Relations between Words in High-dimensional Vector Spaces*. Doctoral Thesis, University of Stockholm.

Schmidt, Benjamin N. 2012. Words Alone: Dismantling Topic Models in the Humanities. *Journal of Digital Humanities*, 2(1). https://journalofdigitalhumanities.org/2-1/words-alone-by-benjamin-m-schmidt/.

Schneider, Gerold. 2013. Describing Irish English with the ICE Ireland Corpus. In *Cahier de ILSL*, Université de Lausanne. https://www.unil.ch/clsl/files/live/sites/clsl/files/shared/CLSL%2038%20Ireland%20and%20its%20Contacts%20print.pdf.

Schneider, Gerold. 2018. Differences between Swiss High German and German High German Via Data-driven Methods. *Proceedings of SwissText 2018*, June 12–13, Winterthur. http://ceur-ws.org/Vol-2226/.

Schneider, Gerold. 2020. Changes in Society and Language: Charting Poverty. In Paula Rautionaho, Arja Nurmi, and Juhani Klemola (eds), *Corpora and the Changing Society: Studies in the Evolution of English*, 29–56. Amsterdam: Benjamins. https://benjamins.com/catalog/scl.96.

Schneider, Gerold. 2022a. Syntactic Changes in Verbal Clauses and Noun Phrases from 1500 Onwards. In Bettelou Los, Claire Cowie, and Patrick Honeybone (eds), *English Historical Linguistics: Change in Structure and Meaning. Current Issues in Linguistic Theory Series*, 163–200. Amsterdam: Benjamins.

Schneider, Gerold. 2022b. Comparing Data-driven to Corpus-based Approaches for Diachronic Variation: Document-classification and Overuse Metrics. In Julia Schlüter and Ole Schützler (eds), *Data and Methods in Corpus Linguistics: Comparative Approaches*, 291–322. Cambridge: Cambridge University Press.

Schneider, Gerold. 2022c. Systematically Detecting Patterns of Social, Historical and Linguistic Change: The Framing of Poverty in Times of Poverty. *Transactions of the Philological Society*, 120, 447–73. https://doi.org/10.1111/1467-968X.12252.

Schneider, Gerold. 2022d. Recent Changes in Spoken British English According to Spoken BNC2014. In Susanne Flach and Martin Hilpert (eds), *Broadening the Spectrum of Corpus Linguistics: New Approaches to Variability and Change*. [Studies in Corpus Linguistics], 173–95. Amsterdam: John Benjamins.

Schneider, Gerold and Max Lauber. 2019. *Introduction to Statistics for Linguists*. Pressbooks. https://dlf.uzh.ch/openbooks/statisticsforlinguists/.

Schneider, Gerold and Maud Reveilhac. 2022. Measuring Attitudes to Migration in the Media Automatically with Complementary Data Sources and Methods. In Patricia Ronan and Evelyn Ziegler (eds), *Language and Identity in Migration Contexts*, 207–52. Frankfurt am Main: Peter Lang.

Schoch, David. 2022. *Network Visualizations in R: Using Ggraph and Graphlayouts*. https://mr.schochastics.net/material/netVizR/ (accessed 15 July 2023).

Schreiber-Gregory, Deanna. 2018. Regulation Techniques for Multicollinearity: Lasso, Ridge, and Elastic Nets. *Proceedings of Western Users of SAS Software Conferences*

2018, September 5–7, Sacramento, CA. https://www.lexjansen.com/wuss/2018/131
_Final_Paper_PDF.pdf.

Schreibman, Susan, Ray Siemens, and John Unsworth (eds.). 2004. *A Companion to Digital Humanities*. Malden, MA, Oxford and Carlton: Blackwell. http://www.digitalhumanities.org/companion/.

Schulte im Walde, Sabine and Alissa Melinger. 2008. An In-Depth Look into the Co-Occurrence Distribution of Semantic Associates. *Italian Journal of Linguistics. Special Issue on From Context to Meaning: Distributional Models of the Lexicon in Linguistics and Cognitive Science*, 20(1), 89–128.

Schwartz, H. Andrew and Lyle H. Ungar. 2015. Data-Driven Content Analysis of Social Media: A Systematic Overview of Automated Methods. *The ANNALS of the American Academy of Political and Social Science*, 659(1), 78–94.

Sclafani, Jennifer. 2018. *Talking Donald Trump. A Sociolinguistic Study of Style, Metadiscourse, and Political Identity*. London: Routledge.

Shannon, Claude E. 1951. Prediction and Entropy of Printed English. *The Bell System Technical Journal*, 30, 50–64.

Sinclair, John. 1991. *Corpus, Concordance, Collocation*. Oxford: Oxford University Press.

Sinclair, John and Ronald Carter. 2004. *Trust the Text: Language, Corpus and Discourse*. London: Routledge.

Smith, Nathaniel J. and Roger Levy. 2013. The Effect of Word Predictability on Reading Time is Logarithmic. *Cognition*, 128(3), 302–19.

Stoltz, Dustin and Marshall A. Taylor. In progress. *Text2Map*. https://cultural cartography.gitlab.io/text2map/.

Taavitsainen, Irma and Turo Hiltunen. 2019. *Late Modern English Medical Texts: Writing Medicine in the Eighteenth Century*. Amsterdam: Benjamins.

Taavitsainen, Irma and Andreas Jucker. 2015. Twenty Years of Historical Pragmatics: Origins, Developments and Changing Thought Styles. *Journal of Historical Pragmatics*, 16(1), 1–24.

Taavitsainen, Irma and Pävi Pahta. 2010. *Early Modern English Medical Texts*: *Corpus Description and Studies*. Amsterdam: Benjamins.

Tajfel, Henri and John C. Turner. 1986. The Social Identity Theory of Intergroup Behavior. In S. Worchel and W.G. Austin (eds), *Psychology of Intergroup Relation*, 7–24, Chicago: Hall Publishers.

Tausczik, Yla R. and James W. Pennebaker. 2010. The Psychological Meaning of Words: LIWC and Computerized Text Analysis Methods. *Journal of Language and Social Psychology*, 29(1), 24–54.

Tognini-Bonelli, Elena. 2001. *Corpus Linguistics at Work*. Amsterdam: Benjamins.

Turney, Peter D. and Patrick Pantel. 2010. From Frequency to Meaning: Vector Space Models of Semantics. *Journal of Artificial Intelligence Research*, 37, 141–88.

Tyrkkö, Jukka. 2016. Looking for Rhetorical Thresholds: Pronoun Frequencies in Political Speeches. *Varieng 17*. http://www.helsinki.fi/varieng/series/volumes/17/tyrkko/.

Underwood, Ted. 2019. Do Humanists Need BERT? Stone and the Sjhell Blog. July 15. https://tedunderwood.com/2019/07/15/do-humanists-need-bert/.

Van Atteveldt, Wouter. 2008. *Semantic Network Analysis: Techniques for Extracting, Representing, and Querying Media Content.* Doctoral dissertation. Charleston, SC: BookSurge.

Van der Maaten, Laurens and Geoffrey Hinton. 2008. Visualizing Data Using t-SNE. *Journal of Machine Learning Research*, 9(11), 2579–605. https://www.jmlr.org/papers /volume9/vandermaaten08a/vandermaaten08a.pdf.

Vaswani, Ashish, Noam Shazeer, Niki Parmar, Jakob Uszkoreit, Llion Jones, Aidan N. Gomez, Lukasz Kaiser, and Illia Polosukhin. 2017. *Attention Is All You Need.* arXiv. https://arxiv.org/abs/1706.03762

Vrana, Leo and Gerold Schneider. 2017. Saying Whatever It Takes: Creating and Analyzing Corpora From US Presidential Debate Transcripts. *Extended Abstracts of Corpus Linguistics Conference*, July 24–28, Birmingham.

Welbers, Kasper, Wouter van Atteveldt, and Kenneth Benoit. 2017. Text Analysis in R. *Communication Methods and Measures*, 11(4), 245–65. https://www.researchgate.net /publication/320820767_Text_Analysis_in_R.

Wilkinson, Mark, Michel Dumontier, IJsbrand Jan Aalbersberg, Gabrielle Appleton, Myles Axton, Arie Baak, Niklas Blomberg, Jan-Willem Boiten, Luiz Bonino da Silva Santos, Philip E. Bourne, Jildau Bouwman, Anthony J. Brookes, Tim Clark, Mercè Crosas, Ingrid Dillo, Olivier Dumon, Scott Edmunds, Chris T. Evelo, Richard Finkers, Alejandra Gonzalez-Beltran, Alasdair J.G. Gray, Paul Groth, Carole Goble, Jeffrey S. Grethe, Jaap Heringa, Peter A.C. 't Hoen, Rob Hooft, Tobias Kuhn, Ruben Kok, Joost Kok, Scott J. Lusher, Maryann E. Martone, Albert Mons, Abel L. Packer, Bengt Persson, Philippe Rocca-Serra, Marco Roos, Rene van Schaik, Susanna-Assunta Sansone, Erik Schultes, Thierry Sengstag, Ted Slater, George Strawn, Morris A. Swertz, Mark Thompson, Johan van der Lei, Erik van Mulligen, Jan Velterop, Andra Waagmeester, Peter Wittenburg, Katherine Wolstencroft, Jun Zhao, and Barend Mons. 2016. The FAIR Guiding Principles for Scientific Data Management and Stewardship. *Nature Scientific Data*, 3, 160018. https://doi.org/10.1038/sdata .2016.18.

Wittgenstein, Ludwig. 1953. *Philosophical Investigations. Philosophische Untersuchungen.* Translated by G. E. M. Anscombe. Oxford: Blackwell.

Yang, Ji Seung, Carly Rosvold, and Nan Bernstein Ratner. 2022. Measurement of Lexical Diversity in Children's Spoken Language: Computational and Conceptual Considerations. *Frontiers in Psychology*, 13, 905789. https://www.ncbi.nlm.nih.gov/ pmc/articles/PMC9257278/.

Yang, Li-gong, Jian Zhu, and Tang Shi-ping. 2013. Keywords Extraction Based on Text Classification. *Advanced Materials Research*, 765–767, 1604–9.

Zhang, Lingxi, Jing Zhang, Xirui Ke, Haoyang Li, Xinmei Huang, Zhonghui Shao, Shulin Cao, and Xin Lv. 2023. A Survey on Complex Factual Question

Answering. *AI Open*, 4, 1–12. https://www.sciencedirect.com/science/article/pii/
   S2666651022000249.

Zipf, George Kingsley. 1965. *The Psycho-Biology of Language: An Introduction to
   Dynamic Philology*. Cambridge, MA: MIT Press.

Zucchini, Walter. 2003. *Applied Smoothing Techniques – Part 1: Kernel Density
   Estimation*. http://staff.ustc.edu.cn/~zwp/teach/Math-Stat/kernel.pdf (accessed 7
   January 2023).

Index

www.ingramcontent.com/pod-product-compliance
Ingram Content Group UK Ltd.
Pitfield, Milton Keynes, MK11 3LW, UK
UKHW021429050225
4464UKWH00003B/74